AUXILIARY SAIL VESSEL OPERATIONS

AUXILIARY SAIL VESSEL OPERATIONS

FOR THE ASPIRING PROFESSIONAL SAILOR

G. Andy Chase

Drawings by
Eric A. Chase

For Aaron—
Congratulations on your graduation from
Deerfield! Here's hoping you get in some
great sailing—   Best wishes
                                    Andy Chase

CORNELL MARITIME PRESS
CENTREVILLE, MARYLAND

Library of Congress Cataloging-in-Publication Data

Chase, G. Andy.
    Auxiliary sail vessel operations : for the aspiring professional sailor / G. Andy Chase ; drawings by Eric A. Chase. — 1st ed.
      p.   cm.
    Includes bibliographical references and index.
    ISBN 0-87033-493-X (hardcover)
    1. Sailing.   I. Title.
    VK543.C47   1997
    623.88—dc21   97-4133

Manufactured in the United States of America

First edition

CONTENTS

FOREWORD

"Assume you are aboard an 80-foot schooner running downwind into an anchorage area with limited maneuvering room." Thus begins one of the discussions in this book's chapter on advanced maneuvers under sail. If you can easily picture this operating assumption and it quickens your heart, you're in the right place. If it gives you pause at the same time that it excites your imagination, all the better. If the intricacies of professionally operating and managing sailing vessels and yachts in both traditional and modern configurations inspires your curiosity and fascination, this is surely a book for you. *Auxiliary Sail Vessel Operations* is a treatise designed to provide the aspiring professional seaman—man or woman—with a thorough introduction to the art and science of what is broadly referred to as seamanship aboard sailing vessels and yachts. It is a book that examines not only the fundamentals of such subjects as vessel maneuvers under power and sail, but the principles of yacht and vessel management for safety, efficiency, and economy—the critical and defining criteria for the professional.

But this book is far more. It is at once a study of hydrodynamic and aerodynamic theory, basic and advanced sailing maneuvers, planning and managing for crew and vessel safety, meteorology for sailors, heavy-weather sailing and hurricane maneuvers, emergencies at sea, and the various aspects of vessel administration as related to rules and regulations. Refined from years of study and practical application, the book is about cultivating and developing the critical attributes of the professional sailor. But while it is designed for the aspiring professional, it should also be required reading for recreational sailors, whose experience might be much enhanced by an understanding of the elements with which the professional works.

Initially created as a course curriculum for classes in sail vessel operations at the Maine Maritime Academy (MMA) in Castine, Maine, this work has been developed over the years to provide a firm foundation for men and women who are working toward earning U.S. Coast Guard licenses to operate auxiliary-powered sailing yachts and vessels. It has served as both a classroom text and a manual of basic principles on board MMA's 80-foot auxiliary-powered gaff schooner *Bowdoin,* of which the author, Andy Chase, was captain for several years. As in any text or manual, there may be elements with which the reader and student is intimately familiar, and others with which he or she may have no experience. This is just as it should be. The value and importance of a book like this is its ability to engage the reader in matters of both theory and practice in such a way as to encourage an ever deeper understanding of the subjects it covers. And that is its objective. Albeit thorough, this book is an introduction. It does not pretend to be exhaustive. Designed to accompany the sailor as a study guide and a point of reference, it acquaints the reader with the myriad constant and critical elements of professional yacht and vessel management. And while it is scrupulously committed to advancing the science of sailing yachts and vessels, the book also serves to encourage the art—to call attention to the critical role that varied experience plays in the development of the professional sailor. It is the kind of book that, properly utilized, can richly inform instinct and intuition at sea. The arts of seamanship that so often elude description are built wholly on this instinct and intuition.

Andy Chase writes with the firm voice of an instructor experienced not only in the field of maritime education (he is associate professor of nautical science at MMA), but in the field of professional sailing and merchant vessels (he holds a 1,600-ton ocean master's license for auxiliary sail, and an unlimited license for power-driven vessels). Moreover, though he understands the critical need for a firm foundation in this field, and is a demanding teacher with rigorous standards, he also knows from experience that even the greenest hand, carefully encouraged and properly informed, has the potential to become the finest seaman. I have had the pleasure of studying with him, and I have witnessed his gifts as an educator. He brings to his work an enthusiasm and commitment that is inspiring both in the classroom and at sea. It results, perhaps, from his own love of learning. When he writes that he has learned from everyone with whom he has sailed, you can believe him; his curiosity is broad and unceasing. He is a careful listener and a sharp-eyed observer. But he is more than an avid student, and more than a schooner master; he is a master of context and connection. When he writes of the physics of meteorological forces, he does so not only with a fascination with the forces themselves, but from the standpoint of their effects on a vessel and her crew—and he knows well the power of these effects. His understandings are far from merely theoretical. They are rooted in the high regard he holds for the maritime traditions whose elegant evolutions have grown from the wisdom and experience of professional sailors for centuries. And he understands his role and responsibility in nurturing those traditions in the future.

The call of the sea is powerfully romantic, and the maritime field has attracted some of its best and brightest with this romance. But this is a field far more complex and scientific than romantic. The demands of coastal passage making, ocean voyaging, and managing vessel and crew require nothing but the highest levels of knowledge, experience, action, and accountability. The skill and experience required to manage these elements properly can only be acquired over time. This book, with its focus on the many moving parts that contribute to the whole, is an indispensable instrument to the acquisition of that experience.

Jon Wilson, Editor-in-Chief
WoodenBoat Magazine

ACKNOWLEDGMENTS

This book began as a curriculum for a course of the same name at the Maine Maritime Academy, in Castine, Maine. From that beginning, over a three-year period, the material was gradually worked into its present form with the help of numerous people. Chief among these were my students, who provided me with an extremely valuable source of feedback and inspiration. To them I owe a great debt, for their enthusiasm, patience, and good humor. As I prepared the first draft, my father, E. Dixwell Chase, took on the task of preliminary editing for me. His patience and thoroughness were extraordinary, and I wish to thank him especially for that effort. As the final draft was nearing completion, Jon Wilson, founding editor of *WoodenBoat* magazine, and, more recently, of *Hope* magazine, made me the remarkable offer of reading and commenting on the manuscript. Given his commitments to his own work and his time constraints of getting out the first few issues of a new magazine, I was truly astonished, and flattered, to find that he not only read the work, but did a very comprehensive editing job on the entire manuscript. His comments, criticism, and suggestions have made this text substantially better than it could otherwise have been. My brother, Eric Chase, invested a great deal of time that should rightly have been invested in his architecture practice in drawing the illustrations, with little hope of significant remuneration. His drawings have leant a measure of clarity and style to the text that the reader will undoubtedly appreciate. My good friend, John McPhee, also took time out of his work to give me a crash course in writing style. I only hope I did justice to his efforts. Finally, I would like to thank my wife, Lauren Sahl, for her encouragement and assistance throughout the entire project. As a scientist and a scholar, she provided continuous and very valuable input. I never would have pursued such an unlikely project without such a positive and supportive environment in which to work.

INTRODUCTION

There are a sufficient number of books on the market for anyone who desires to learn to sail, build or maintain a boat, select a boat for their own purpose, or just dream about going to sea. What has been lacking is a text that is written specifically for the sailor who is working his or her way up from the recreational level of sailing to the professional. This book fills that gap.

There are a large number of commercial sailing vessels at sea at the present time. (As of 1997, the U.S. Coast Guard had 506 active, inspected sailing vessels in their files.) These vessels, whether in the charter business, the sail training business, the passenger business, or even the cargo business, all need professional sailors. There are many more uninspected vessels whose owners, though not required by regulation, choose to hire professional, licensed crew. In many cases it is the insurance companies that provide the impetus to hire licensed crew, providing breaks in rates for vessels so manned.

Obtaining a license to operate an inspected, auxiliary sail vessel (a sailing vessel with an auxiliary engine) involves acquiring a substantial amount of sea time aboard sailing vessels of suitable size, and then passing a comprehensive exam on all aspects of seamanship. Since it is impossible for an examiner to determine unequivocally that a person is fully competent to handle any situation encountered at sea, the sea time requirement is very important to the process. The assumption is made that a person spending a year or two at sea will have seen and experienced enough different situations to be prepared to handle any possible future situation. But there is a problem with such an assumption. The quality of that sea time cannot be controlled. Present standards require that the time be served on the class of waters for which the license is being issued, namely ocean, near coastal, or inland; and aboard vessels of approximately the same size as that for which the license is being written. These criteria do not guarantee that a candidate has ever seen rough weather. They do not guarantee that the candidate has ever actually handled the vessel or attempted to recover a man overboard from the water while under sail. A candidate may have received "training" on Marconi-rigged sloops yet be licensed to sail a gaff-rigged, square-topsail schooner. In fact, the candidate may never have received any real training at all. Not every skipper or mate is a good teacher and, without such a teacher, the aspiring sailor will have great difficulty learning and practicing skills during time at sea.

This book provides a text for aspiring auxiliary sail license candidates who wish to improve the quality of their sea time. It assumes a basic level of understanding of sailing, such as that of a recreational sailor. It does not presume to contain all that a professional sailor needs to know. There are substantial categories of information that have been completely avoided, such as engineering and navigation, since they are thoroughly covered in other books. This book focuses on the skills and knowledge that are unique to a sailing vessel, especially in commercial operation. It provides a text that a recreational sailor will find useful in preparation for putting to sea as a deckhand aboard a commercial sailing vessel. It provides enough information to make him or her a capable deckhand. Once aboard, the sailor should use this book as a basis for continued study. The first lesson learned will probably be that virtually everything is done differently from one vessel to another. Therefore, the reader should not so much try to memorize how a certain evolution is presented here, but why it is done that way. The more the reader understands how something works, the easier it will be to figure out how to adapt that method to a new vessel or set of conditions.

Finally, I do not pretend to have invented any of this. In that sense, this is not an original work, but my own compilation and interpretation of what others have taught me over the years. Insofar as I have presented it accurately, I give the lion's share of the credit for this work to my teachers. If I have made any errors or omissions, I take full responsibility. My teachers have been many—too many to recognize them all here. Every master, mate, engineer, cook, deckhand, and friend I have sailed with has taught me something. But I would be very remiss not to single out three who have had an extraordinary impact on my learning the art of seamanship and sailing. In their order of appearance in my life, I wish especially to thank my father, E. Dixwell Chase; my oldest brother, Captain Carl Chase; and Captain Jim Sharp, all of whom taught and inspired me for many years, in many ways.

AUXILIARY SAIL VESSEL OPERATIONS

CHAPTER ONE

RIGS: TYPES AND APPLICATIONS

Sailing rigs developed not by calculation and design but by accident, experiment, and evolution—a long process. The design work in sail and rig development came at the end of thousands of years, after most of the trial-and-error work had been done.

It is true that the modern, high-aspect-ratio Marconi (also known as Bermuda or jib-headed) sailing rigs are more efficient than the traditional rigs for sailing to windward, but evolution does not work with a single goal in mind. Evolution adapts a species to a particular set of parameters or conditions. Sailors in every seaport had different sets of problems to deal with and, as a result, they often led evolution along a slightly different track. Most sailors took for granted that sailing to windward simply could not be accomplished, so they developed their sailing routes accordingly. Some did not have that luxury, so they had to drive evolution to windward. In the end they learned to provide some means of auxiliary power to get where their evolving designs could not get them.

In the eyes of the Western sailor, the highest form of sailing ships to evolve were the big ocean barques of the late nineteenth and early twentieth centuries. The best known of these today are the famous German ships of the Laeisz Line, known as the "P-Line" ships. All had names starting with P, such as *Preussen, Pamir, Padua, Potosi, and Peking*. These were big, four- and five-masted barques (with the exception of *Preussen,* which was a ship), built of steel, rigged with steel wire and chain, and manned by a crew of about forty—no bigger than the merchant ships' crews of the 1970s. They were fast (they could sail at speeds of over 16 knots), and they were built to withstand the fiercest gales. They had evolved for the long ocean voyages from Europe to the ports of Australia, the Far East, and the Pacific, by way of Cape Horn and the Cape of Good Hope, areas renowned for severe weather.

These big barques, however, were only exceptional in their own routes, and in their own time. They could not work well to windward and they were very deep, requiring them to stay well offshore. The perfection in their design had taken long to develop, and they were thus rendered obsolete at about the time they reached their zenith, as the steam engine took over in the early twentieth century. Elsewhere in the world other designs, less widely known, met their owners' needs equally well (and in some cases, better). The Chinese junk, the Arab dhow, the proa of the South Pacific, the Dutch boier, the famous clipper ship, the down-easter schooner, the Gloucester fishing schooner, the Nantucket whaleboat, even the little sixteen-foot Bequia boat all were products of different paths of evolution of the sailing vessel. Along each coastline, in every ocean and sea, for each different type of cargo and for every different challenge, a different type of vessel and sailing rig evolved. Each had its strengths, and each had its compromises.

Compromise is still at the heart of it all. To this day, with all our computers, wind tunnels, and tank tests, sailing vessel design remains a balance of compromises. There is no one sailing rig that is simply best. There will only be a rig that best suits a particular set of conditions. Viewed the other way around, as from the perspective of the sailor hired to man a given vessel, there must be an understanding of the compromises inherent in the particular rig you will be sailing. Sailing *Preussen* must have been an extraordinary thrill, as long as the ship was well offshore. Beating her up through the narrow Straits of Dover in a northeasterly gale, however, must have been something of a nightmare. Her master would need to be very well aware of the limitations (compromises) of her rig in order to make such a passage safely. It is for this reason that different rigs and their limitations must be studied so that at the critical moment one can make the decision to choose another route or another time rather than attempt a passage of which a particular rig is not capable.

For starters, this book discusses rigs in the broadest of terms, looking at general differences between the general rig classes. It then takes a closer look at the individual rig types, their sails, and how they work together. It is beyond the scope of this book to get into the more exotic rigs, such as junks, lateens, flettner rotors, and such. The text will stick to square, gaff, and Marconi rigs.

SQUARE RIGS

The square rig developed from the earliest sails, which were probably simple hides hung from a crosspiece on a crude mast. They were effective enough to catch some wind and sail dead before it, but some early sailor found it was also possible to sail across the wind, to some degree. It was only a matter of time before sailors found that if they trimmed the sail so it remained full of wind, they could keep turning toward the wind and sail somewhat into it. The square rig never made it much beyond that stage. Even the most modern square-rigged vessels, designed after the aerodynamics of sails became well understood, cannot sail much closer than a modest close reach. With that limitation accepted, however, square-riggers can sail very well indeed on all other points of sailing, as evidenced by the extraordinary performance of the big barques mentioned above. In fact, they even have some distinct advantages over more modern rigs. They are better suited for the long, primarily downwind, tradewind ocean passages. They carry their sails in the optimum configuration for downwind sailing, without long, overhanging, swinging booms that are always in danger of jibing, and without resorting to spinnakers that require constant attention.

One of the main disadvantages of square-rigged vessels in modern times is that they require a large crew of highly trained seamen. They require a willingness to work high aloft on swaying, jerking, slippery yards in the dark of night, with a gale of wind trying to tear you from your handholds. It is dangerous work even with present-day safety devices (such as harnesses), and it is not always easy to assemble a crew to sail such a vessel. Most present-day crews are made up largely of volunteers (or low-paid, virtual volunteers), many of whom can participate for only a short time, making it difficult to keep a full crew long enough to get them trained and working smoothly as a team. Handling such a vessel is tricky and can be dangerous, and with such a novice crew it would be foolish to attempt some of the maneuvers that once were performed as a matter of course.

On a positive note, however, the square-rigger is a most effective tool for sail training. The crew must learn a great deal of seamanship and teamwork just to get the ship under way. Virtually all trainees who make a trip on board such a vessel come away with skills that they never even knew they were there to learn. What they learn has perhaps more to do with developing self-confidence and mutual confidence, learning to believe in one's ability to do something difficult, and learning to rely on others to do their part, so that the entire evolution can be accomplished safely and efficiently.

Another disadvantage of the square rig involves the complexities and time involved in executing the basic sailing maneuvers of tacking, wearing, and jibing. These will be discussed in more detail in subsequent chapters. The maneuvers are not simple or quick and can require considerable sea room to accomplish. This can become a serious problem if the ship is allowed to get into a position where such room is not available. The master of such a vessel must plan far ahead to avoid such hazardous situations.

In close-quarters maneuvering, with occasional assistance from an anchor, docklines, or a tug, a skillfully handled square-rigger is very maneuverable. By virtue of the number of sails, well distributed along the length of the vessel, each of which is individually controllable, the balance of forces can be minutely controlled, allowing extraordinary maneuvers to be carried out under sail. The subject of balance is taken up in a later chapter, but the ability to control this balance certainly ranks as one of the square-rigger's chief advantages over other rigs.

GAFF RIGS

The gaff rig was a logical next step as sailors realized that fore-and-aft sails enabled them to sail closer to the wind, although they did not yet understand why. Rotating a shortened yard 90 degrees, securing the forward end to the mast, and suspending a sail from it allowed them to have a large sail stretched out in a fore-and-aft manner that could now be trimmed in almost amidships or parallel to the centerline of the ship. With this arrangement they could sail to within about 55 or 60 degrees of the wind—a remarkable improvement from the 70 or 80 degrees for the square rig. What they did not understand yet was that when close-hauled it was the leading edge of this sail that was doing most of the work, while the rest was doing little more than adding drag. Off the wind, however, say, at 150 to 180 degrees, the whole sail was at work, and this is why the gaff rig is still effective for a route that involves a good deal of reaching and running, with a limited amount of windward work.

While the relative windward ability of the gaff rig was probably the major reason for its popularity, the reduction in complexity of the rig and the resultant reduction in crew size was also a major advantage. Whereas to handle the sails typically carried on a single square-rigged mast during a tack might have required as many as ten seamen, a gaff-rigged schooner of two or three masts could be tacked with three. It would not be uncommon for a coastwise two-masted schooner of a hundred tons to sail with a crew of six, and maybe as few as four. It would have been impossible to sail even a small barque (of similar size) with fewer than a dozen men.

The chief disadvantage of the gaff rig is the gaff itself. It is a large, heavy, unwieldy spar suspended 50 to 75 feet in the air, with lateral control provided primarily by the wind-filled sail. When becalmed, with a long ocean swell, this lateral control is lost, the gaff swings with each roll, and there is potential for damage to the spars and rigging. The big down-easters (schooners with three to seven masts) were famous for "rolling their sticks out" in a calm, meaning that the forces from these swinging gaffs could actually bring the mast down. There could also be too much wind, and handling a gaff in a blow at sea is still a very dangerous operation requiring great care. A maneuver like jibing, which was never much of a problem in a square-rigged ship, suddenly, with the gaff rig, became a very delicate operation requiring a considerable degree of skill and experience.

As for balance, the gaff rig compares favorably to the square rig for going to windward, when sails can be trimmed in very close, but for maneuvering, with a smaller number of larger sails to work with, there is less flexibility for fine work. Although the gaff sail can be controlled with fewer people than a square sail, some degree of control is lost as a result of having fewer options and fewer hands available to exercise them.

The risks involved with jibing a gaff sail make downwind sailing delicate work. During the actual moment of jibing, the whole sail is caught aback and, with nothing to stop it, it comes swinging over the deck to the opposite side, gaining momentum all the way. When it finally fetches up against the sheet on the new tack, it may, if the jibe has not been executed properly, do considerable damage, breaking rigging, spars, and/or the mast itself. This hazard can make prolonged downwind sailing (such as trade wind sailing) exhausting and nerve-racking, whereas on a square-rigger it is the most pleasant of all passages.

MARCONI RIGS

In the last decade of the nineteenth century the Marconi or Bermuda rig evolved from the gaff rig. Presumably someone finally got tired of the gaff and its hazards and simply dispensed with it, resorting to a triangular sail, pointed at the top. It must have come as some surprise to find that windward performance, rather than suffering, actually improved. As the capabilities of this rig continued to improve and impress sailors, the understanding of aerodynamics also improved and started to be applied to the work of a sail. The evolution of the Marconi rig was greatly expedited by scientific research and led to the understanding of the sail as a wing operating in a fluid, leading to higher-aspect ratios (taller masts, shorter booms) in mainsails; larger, overlapping jibs; and the "slot" between the two. Each of these is dealt with in later chapters. Great strides came quickly, as the science of aerodynamics became better understood.

As the efficiency of the "jib-headed" (Marconi) sail increased, it became in some ways easier and in some ways harder to handle. Since the boom became shorter, it was less of a hazard. Masts grew taller, requiring advances in rigging techniques to hold them up. Since a taller sail with a shorter foot could develop more power than earlier low-aspect-ratio sails, the sail area decreased, so the crew had an easier time handling a smaller area of sailcloth. But (make no mistake) the smaller sail in no way reduced the forces that sailors were dealing with when under way. Quite the contrary, the more efficient sails were delivering power that was all out of proportion to their size. Much of the traditional hardware and rigging was no longer sufficient to handle the loads, and gear technology had to develop as fast as sail design to cope with the new stresses.

For sailing downwind, total exposed sail area is what is most important, and this is what the Marconi rig lacks. The spinnaker is an answer to this problem, but while spinnakers are fine for racing, they can be a burden for cruising or long ocean passage-making, as they require much attention and do have potential for trouble. Therefore some Marconi-rigged vessels that embark on long downwind passages resort to more traditional sail technology and rig a yard from which they set a passage sail or sails. These are nothing more than a simplified form of square sail, acknowledging the fact that when off the wind, the square rig is still unsurpassed.

Given all the different qualities and compromises of the various rigs, it is no wonder that numerous combinations were developed, with considerable success. The vast majority of square-rigged vessels employed a combination of fore-and-aft and square-rigged sails. The more windward work a sailor anticipated, the more fore-and-aft sails he would employ, especially if manpower was a consideration. The more long-distance, trade winds work the sailor anticipated, the more square sails he would set, as long as he could afford the increased crew size. Marconi sails were also combined with gaff rigs in many different combinations, such as the schooner yacht with the Marconi main and a gaff foresail.

Unfortunately, for the master of a vessel, owners often buy what they can afford or what pleases their aesthetic sense rather than what makes the most practical sense, so the master must be well aware of the limitations of the rig and sail the vessel accordingly, allowing greater margins for safety when the rig does not suit the route.

VARIATIONS OF RIG TYPES

Sloops and Cutters

The simplest rig configuration is the sloop, carrying a mainsail and a jib (fig. 1-1a). The mainsail was once considered the principal driving sail, though in modern vessels the genoa jib often provides the greater power. To be more precise, it is really the combination of the two that does the work when properly trimmed, as the airflow developed between them complements the work done by each. This will be discussed more in depth in a later section on sail theory. The jib on modern rigs is not only the principal driving sail, but is also very important for balance and maneuvering.

In cutters the mainmast is stepped farther aft (traditional cutters carry the mast almost amidships, whereas more modern ones look more and more like sloops), giving a bigger foretriangle (the area defined by the mast, the headstay, and the deck), and thereby allowing room for more headsails (fig. 1-1b). The jib is set out on the end of the bowsprit, hanked on to a stay there called the headstay or jibstay; the second headsail is hanked onto the (shorter) forestay (whose lower end would be secured to the stem), and therefore called the fore staysail. On cutters with no bowsprit, the jib is flown from the stem, and the forestay, with fore staysail attached, touches down somewhere in the middle of the foredeck. The fore staysail, since it is cut with no overlap of the mast, may have a small boom or club and a single sheet. This makes it very handy for tight maneuvering, since once you strike (douse) the jib you no longer have jib sheets to trim at every tack, and the entire sail plan becomes self-tending.

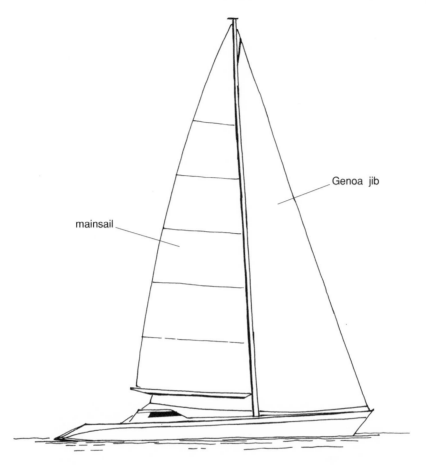

Fig. 1-1a. *A Marconi-rigged sloop.*

Schooners

With the addition of a second mast, the number of options dramatically increases. On two-masted schooners the mainsail is the largest, and aftermost, sail. The mainmast is logically the taller mast. That distinction will normally suffice to distinguish a schooner rig from others, but within the schooner family there are a number of variations.

On the traditional and most common two-masted, gaff-rigged schooner (fig. 1-2), there is a very large mainsail set on a mainmast that may be nearly amidships. The main boom on these vessels can be an extraordinary spar. The main boom on the Gloucester fishing schooner *Adventure* is 74 feet long. It is not unusual for the mainsail to have more sail area than the entire remainder of the rig. These schooners evolved to become remarkable sailors, being fast, powerful in a sea and to windward, and sturdy. But those huge mainsails take

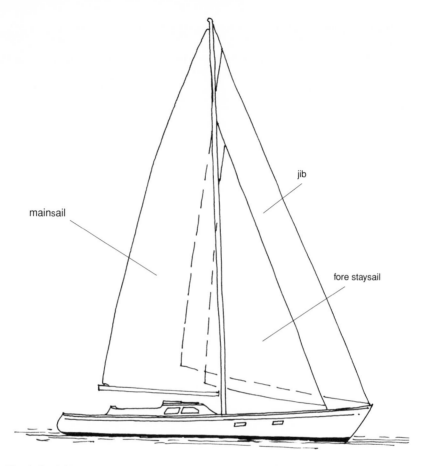

Fig. 1-1b. *A Marconi-rigged cutter. Note that the headsails occupy a proportionally larger percentage of the total sail plan than on a sloop.*

charge of every evolution, as will be seen in the discussion on balance, and an accidental jibe with this rig can be catastrophic.

Moving forward from the mainmast, there is a foresail which is considerably smaller than the main. The foremast on which it hoists is likewise shorter and, because the mainsail has used up nearly half of the vessel, the foreboom is short by comparison. Next forward will generally be a fore staysail (the fishermen called this the jumbo), set on the forestay, which may lead to the center of the foredeck or the stem head, depending on whether there is a bowsprit and how long the bowsprit is. If the bowsprit is fitted with a jibboom, which is an additional spar fitted to the bowsprit much as a bayonet is fitted to a rifle, then the forestay and the fore staysail may be led to the end of the bowsprit instead of to the deck. The peril here is that if the bowsprit breaks (a vulnerable spar in a collision or plunging in heavy seas), the most important support for the whole rig is lost.

Moving aloft to the light-weather sails (fig. 1-3), there are often gaff topsails set above both the mainsail and foresails. They are hoisted on the topmasts, which are fitted bayonet-like to the top of the lower mast. These small sails do more work than it would appear. Wind aloft is normally stronger and from farther aft than the wind near the deck (see chapter 3 on sail theory), so the topsails will have not only more, but more favorable, air. For this reason, all vessels try to get more light-air sails, higher up, leading to considerable additional rigging and canvas aloft, and may require sending one or more hands aloft to set or furl the sails.

Between the two masts schooners may set a fisherman staysail. This sail is a quadrilateral sail stretching from main topmast head to foremast head, to an approximately horizontal foot a third or more of the way down the foremast. It is set "flying," meaning that it is not hanked on to anything, but hoisted from the deck by a halyard at each upper corner, with a tack and sheet to hold down the forward and after lower corners, respectively. This sail is quite a handful when the breeze picks up, and additional hands may be required to deal with it.

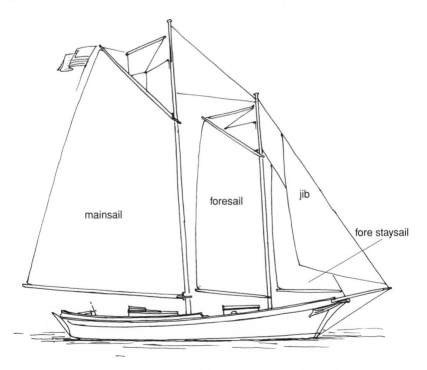

Fig. 1-2. *A gaff-rigged, two-masted schooner under "four lowers" (the four working sails set).*

Forward of the foremast, light air jibs may include a jib topsail (set above the jib on the fore topmast stay) and a variety of combinations of extra or oversize jibs such as outer jibs and balloon jibs.

Variations on the two-masted, gaff-rigged schooner are many. The Marconi mainsail is common, dispensing with the cumbersome main gaff and allowing for a taller, more efficient sail with a shorter main boom. The staysail schooner (fig. 1-4) takes that concept one step further, utilizing the Marconi mainsail with its own main staysail. This gives the mainmast the configuration of a sloop rig, but with a foremast in front. Forward of and above the main staysail there might be a fisherman staysail, or a wishbone trysail. The latter is a sail that looks like an inverted jib, with its clew stretched out between two bowed spars in the configuration of the now-familiar windsurfer sail. The wishbone gaff hangs in the same location and manner of the traditional fore gaff, and the triangular shape of the sail is such that it fills the space left above the main staysail. Forward of the foremast on a staysail schooner, the rig is the same as would be found on any other schooner. The advantage of the staysail rig is that the gaffs are eliminated, the sails are of more efficient shapes for sailing to

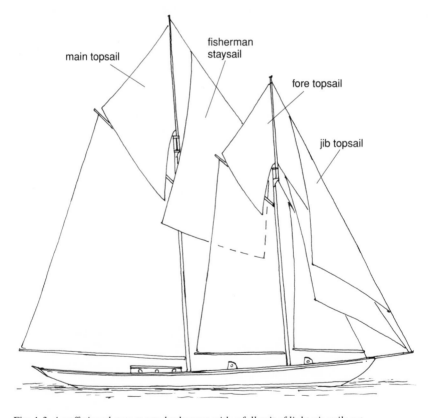

Fig. 1-3. *A gaff-rigged, two-masted schooner with a full suit of light-air sails set.*

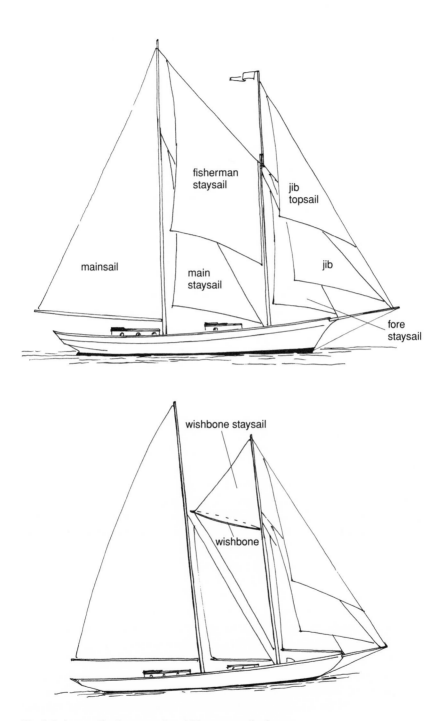

fisherman
staysail

jib
topsail

mainsail

main
staysail

jib

fore
staysail

wishbone staysail

wishbone

Fig. 1-4. *A staysail schooner and a wishbone staysail schooner.*

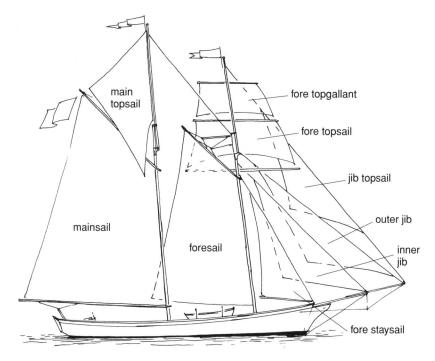

Fig. 1-5. *A square-topsail schooner.*

windward, and they are each smaller and more likely to be self-tending, requiring no adjustment when tacking.

Another variation combines the advantages of a squaresail for off-the-wind work with the better windward abilities of the gaff rig. Known as a square-topsail schooner (fig.1-5), this vessel (with two or more masts) will carry a gaff-rigged mainsail, main topsail, foresail, and headsails, and, in addition, a squaresail set between two yards high on the foremast. The fore topsail is then a square sail, set from a fore-topsail yard which hoists on the fore topmast. Below that there is a lower yard, which is fixed on the foremast, just below the butt of the fore topmast. This lower yard, on other square-riggers, would carry a course (another square sail), but in this case is normally there to provide a sheeting point for the topsail clews (lower corners). There may be a raffee (a triangular sail with one corner at the top of the topmast and the lower corners at the ends of the topmast yard), or a topgallant, set above the topsail. This combination makes a very powerful rig for a traditional vessel.

When schooners have three or more masts, it is common for all the masts to be of the same height (fig. 1-6). The foremast (and sail) will be the foremost, followed by the main. Aft of the main comes the mizzen, followed by the spanker. The sails are normally all the same size, though the last one aft may be somewhat larger, having the longest boom. Each may have a topmast and

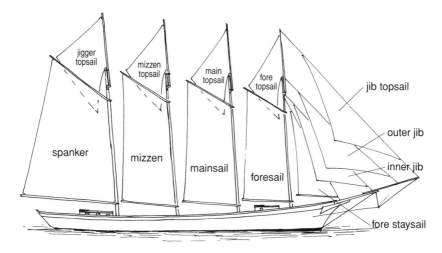

Fig. 1-6. *A four-masted, gaff-rigged schooner. Note that although the aftermost mast is rightfully called the jigger mast, and the topsail set there the jigger topsail, the gaff sail set there is called the spanker.*

topsail, named for the mast on which it sets. The headsails are named the same as those on a two-master.

Ketches and Yawls

If two masts are arranged with the taller mast forward, the vessel is either a ketch or a yawl. The sail set on the after mast is the mizzen. There are both gaff-rigged and Marconi-rigged ketches and yawls. The technical difference between a ketch and a yawl is that on a ketch the mizzenmast is stepped (mounted) forward of the rudderpost, while on a yawl the mizzen is stepped aft of it. What this really means is that on a ketch the mizzen, stepped farther forward, is a large sail with a tall mast and does a significant share of the work (fig. 1-7a). On a yawl the mizzen, being so far aft, is almost an afterthought whose purpose is primarily one of balance. The mizzen on most yawls is really quite small, looking like little more than an oversized flag. It is sometimes called a jigger, which somehow sounds fitting (see figure 1-7b).

It is not unusual to set a mizzen staysail on ketches and yawls (fig. 1-8a). This is a three-sided sail with the head at the masthead of the mizzen and the tack secured to a fitting on deck abaft the mainmast. These, like spinnakers, are reaching and running sails which are used to make up for the Marconi rig's deficiencies off the wind. On some of the more modern racing ketches the two masts are stepped far enough apart to allow for a mizzen stay to be permanently rigged, and mizzen staysails are carried as a matter of course, both on and off the wind.

Spinnakers are the Marconi rig's answer to the loss of sail area for downwind work (fig. 1-8b). They are set flying (only the corners are attached—no

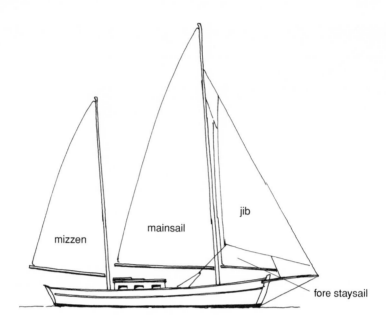

Fig. 1-7a. *A Marconi-rigged ketch.*

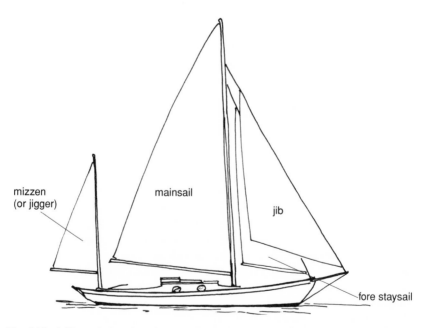

Fig. 1-7b. *A Marconi-rigged yawl. Note the small size of the mizzen, sometimes called the jigger.*

Fig. 1-8a. *Mizzen staysail.*

Fig. 1-8b. *Spinnaker.*

edge is secured to either a stay or a spar) from the foredeck, from a single halyard at or near the masthead and tended by a sheet and a tack, or guy, from the two lower corners. The windward corner is also supported by a spinnaker pole, extending out from a point part way up the mainmast and suspended by its own set of rigging. Spinnakers come in a virtually endless variety of shapes and sizes (not to mention colors), each one cut for a specific off-wind sailing angle from reaching to running. They can be fairly tricky to set, douse, and jibe, and even to keep full once set. They require a well-drilled crew and close attention, since much of their tremendous power is being delivered right to the top of the mast, where it has the maximum leverage to drag the vessel over. They are set on most of the modern rigs mentioned above, and even on some of the traditional ones.

Square Rig

A typical "modern" (circa 1926) four-masted barque is *Kruzhenstern* (ex-*Padua*) (see figure 1-9). Starting with the foremast, the largest and lowermost squaresail is called the foresail, or sometimes just the fore. (While the lowermost squares on all the masts are collectively called the courses, they are individually referred to by their own names.) Above the foresail, the foremast will end and a fore topmast will be fitted, bayonet-like, as with the topmast of a gaff-rigged schooner. There are two square sails set from this, the lower and upper fore topsails. Above them is another mast, this one called the fore topgallant (pronounced t'gallant) mast. On this mast are set two more squaresails, the lower and upper fore topgallant sails. Above this is another mast, the fore royal mast, with just one square sail, the fore royal. Some vessels, generally earlier ones, combined their "split" topsails and topgallants into single sails by the same names, while some carried split royals and even skysails above them.

For each mast the same logic applies, only the prefix changes. Fore topgallant becomes the main topgallant, or mizzen topgallant, depending on which mast it is on. The fourth mast, farthest aft, is called the jigger. On a barque, the jigger mast carries a gaff-rigged sail, which is called the spanker.

Numerous staysails are set forward and in between the masts. Again there is a logical pattern. Each is a staysail, and each carries the name of the stay it is set on, which in turn is named for the mast it is supporting. Thus, the fore-topmast staysail, the mizzen-royal staysail, and the main-topgallant staysail are set on the fore-topmast stay, the mizzen-royal stay, and the fore-topmast stay, respectively. Forward of the fore-topmast staysail are the inner, outer, and flying jibs.

It is important to note that there is a virtually endless number of variations among square rigs, and each has its own details in nomenclature. There will almost certainly be some differences on each vessel encountered.

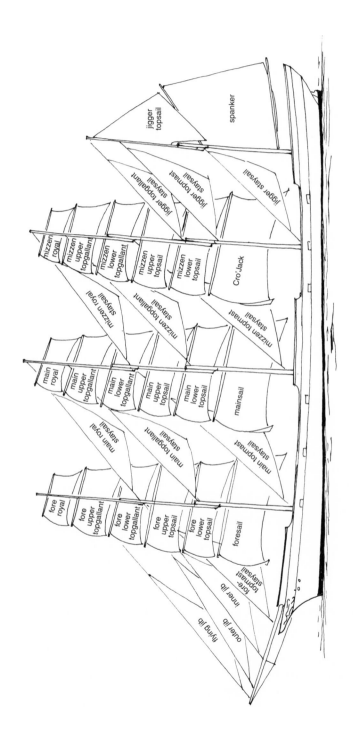

Fig. 1-9. *The sails of a four-masted barque.*

Further reading (see bibliography for details): Herreshoff, *The Common Sense of Yacht Design*, chap. 2; de Kerchove, *International Maritime Dictionary;* Schult, *The Sailing Dictionary;* Underhill, *Sailing Ship Rigs and Rigging.*

CHAPTER TWO

INTRODUCTION TO SQUARE RIG

A square-rigged vessel is certainly the most complicated-looking ship when viewed from alongside the dock. To the uninitiated, it would appear to be a hopelessly confusing rig to learn. It is, however, only a number of simple parts all built upon one another. The most complicated square-rigged ship will only be a combination of many similar parts tied together.

All square-rigged ships are, of course, not identical, but they are very similar. A hundred years ago, ships would often sail with crews signed on only a day earlier, most of whom might never have sailed on that particular ship. At best it would be dark within twelve hours, and the crew would have to be able to find every line in the dark and know just what its function would be. For this reason the layout of the major parts of the running rigging was more or less standardized throughout the sailing ship fleets of the world. Most crews, especially in the later days of commercial sail, were an international mix, so a chief mate could not even rely on being able to explain to a new hand where to find a given line. An able seaman had to know enough about the layout of standard vessels to be able to learn quickly the idiosyncrasies of a particular ship.

The process of sailing a square-rigger is more complicated indeed than that of a fore-and-after, and it is beyond the scope of this book to cover the sailing maneuvers of such vessels. There are books on the subject to which the reader is referred in the bibliography; the purpose here is to provide enough of an introduction to the rig so that a sailor can report aboard and begin the process of learning without feeling intimidated. Once the parts of the rig are learned, the sailor should bring to bear all the concepts of sail maneuvering that will be covered in later chapters on the subject. The principles of balance, especially, will simplify the otherwise confusing pattern of sail- and shiphandling under a square rig.

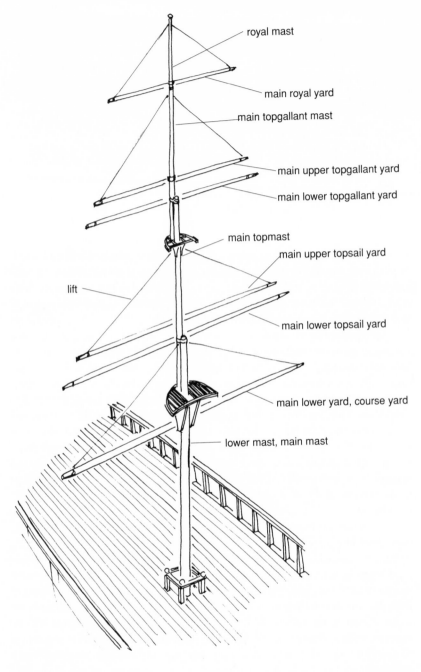

royal mast

main royal yard

main topgallant mast

main upper topgallant yard

main lower topgallant yard

main topmast

main upper topsail yard

lift

main lower topsail yard

main lower yard, course yard

lower mast, main mast

Fig 2-1. *Mast and yard arrangement, typical square-rigged mast (mainmast illustrated, others are similar).*

THE SQUARE SAIL AND ITS GEAR

A square sail is not square at all, but vaguely rectangular. It actually derives its name from being set approximately "square" to the vessel's hull, or athwartships. It is set (hangs) from a yard, which in turn is hung from a mast. The sail derives its individual name from the mast on which its yard is hung. Therefore, the fore upper topsail is the upper of the two sails set from the fore topmast, which is the mast just above the foremast.

The yard itself is hung from the mast by its own rigging, and its gear varies depending on whether it is a fixed or hoisting yard (see figure 2-1). On a given mast such as a fore topmast, there will be either one or two square sails set. It often comes as a surprise to the uninitiated that the yards from which many of these sails are set are hoisted on their masts. In the older-style ships, there would be a single large sail that filled the whole space defined by the fore topmast, and its yard would be raised from the base to the top of the fore topmast when setting the sail (fig. 2-2b). In later years most of these large sails were divided horizontally into two smaller sails, making them easier to handle. In this case the fore upper topsail yard would be raised and lowered, while the fore lower topsail yard would remain stationary or fixed (fig. 2-2a). There were two advantages to having yards that were hoisted and lowered on their masts. The first was to facilitate striking the sail in a hurry—for instance, in the event of a squall. With a hoisting yard, striking a sail to spill its wind is accomplished by slacking its halyard after casting off the sheets of the next sail above. This is a simple process requiring one crew member and only a few moments. With a fixed yard, however, the sail must be clewed up—a process requiring both more manpower and time. The second reason was to lower the weight of the yard and gear when that particular sail was not set. Lowering the center of gravity thus would improve the vessel's stability and reduce the strain on the whole rig as the vessel rolled.

In order to raise a yard, the halyard is hauled (fig. 2-3). The word halyard is derived from "haul the yard." One can imagine this is a great weight to lift, including not only the weight of the yard, but also of the sail and all the attached rigging. Aboard the USCG barque *Eagle,* for instance, the upper topsail yards are 63 feet long and weigh over 1½ tons, not including the rigging and the sails. It is therefore not uncommon to employ the assistance of a winch or capstan to accomplish this task, although it can be done with manpower alone. Once the yard is up, its weight is supported by the halyard, and its angle controlled (rotated) by braces, which lead aft from both ends of the yard to the deck or the mast next aft. When the yard is lowered it will settle into its lifts, which are wire ropes leading diagonally down and out from the top of the mast to the ends of the yard. Thus, when lowered, the weight of the yard is supported in three places—the halyard and the two lifts. The lifts may be adjustable or fixed-length. A fixed yard (one that does not get hoisted) is supported in the center by a piece of hardware called a crane and by the clewlines and sheets of the sail next above it. The course yards, however, do have their own fixed lifts. On top

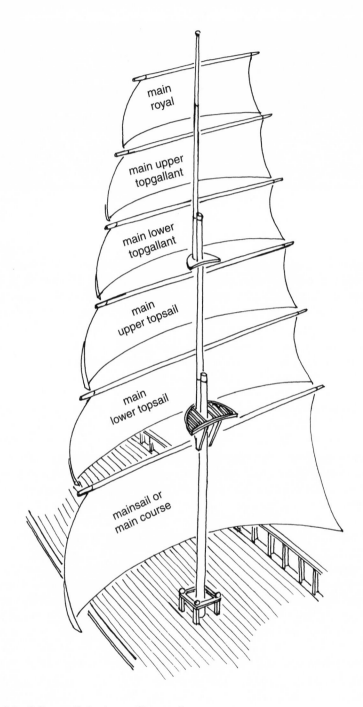

Fig. 2-2a. *Split topsails (mainmast illustrated).*

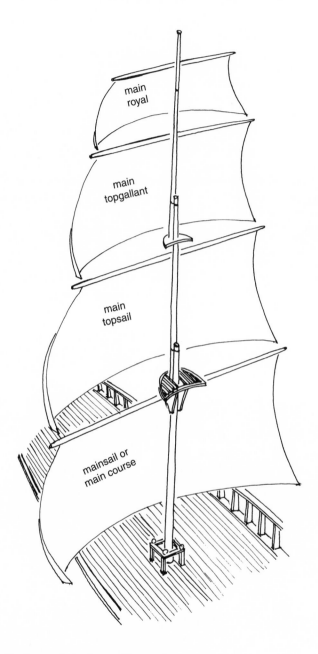

Fig. 2-2b. *Single topsails (mainmast illustrated).*

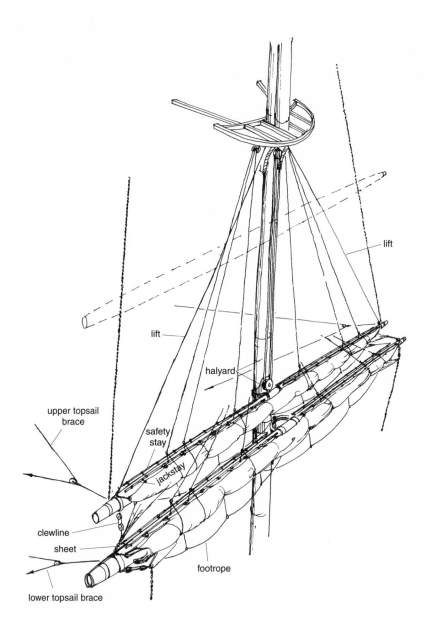

lift

lift

halyard

upper topsail
brace

safety
stay

jackstay

clewline

sheet

lower topsail brace

footrope

Fig. 2-3. *Squaresails, yards, and their rigging.*

of the forward, upper surface of the yard is an iron rod called the jackstay, to which the sail itself is secured. There is often another similar rod on the aft, upper face of the yard which is there solely as a handhold for the crew, to which the clip of a crewmember's safety harness can be attached. This is called the safety stay. Hanging below the yard are the footropes, on which the crew can stand while working with the sail.

The sail itself, as mentioned above, is vaguely rectangular. The top edge is called the head, the two sides are the leeches, and the bottom is the foot. The two lower corners are the clews (see figure 2-4a).

The clews are controlled by the sheets, which lead down to the next yard below. From the lowest sails (the courses), the sheets lead aft and down to the deck, while another line, called the tack, leads to the deck forward. Opposing the sheets (and on the courses, the tacks) are the clewlines, which haul the clews up to the yard when striking sail. Also used in striking sail are the bunt-lines—whose function it is to gather the sail at intermediate points up to the yard—and leechlines, which haul the midpoint of the long leech up to, and inward along, the yard (see figure 2-4b). In some cases one line will do double duty as a leech-buntline, as illustrated in figure 2-6. Explaining the process of setting and striking sail will help to clarify the functions of each line.

SETTING A SQUARE SAIL

A square sail, when properly furled, is secured neatly and tightly to its yard by gaskets, which are essentially the same as sail stops on smaller vessels. The only difference is that these gaskets remain tied in their positions on the yards when not in use rather than being brought down and put away. The first step in setting sail is to send hands aloft to cast off, or loosen, the gaskets.

When the crew gets the order to "lay aloft and loose the fore upper topsail," they will climb the ratlines, or ladders, tied to the shrouds. When they get up to the yard they will "lay out" along it, with their feet on the footropes, while holding on to the safety stay and/or the jackstay. The footropes are lengths of wire stretched loosely along the underside of the yard for the crew to stand on. Since they are secured in just a few places, they are free to sag and swing a certain amount. Therefore, when a crew member is about to step onto a footrope he must call out "laying on," thereby warning others on the yard that the footrope may move suddenly as he steps onto it. He should likewise call out "laying off" when stepping off the footrope, for the same reason. Once the hands are out on the yard they untie and cast off the gaskets, keeping a hold on the furled sail until all are ready, when the order is given to "let fall." The sail will then fall from the yard and will now be "in its gear," held loosely by its buntlines, clewlines, and, perhaps, leechlines (fig. 2-5). Now the hands can lay in to the mast, and all but two can lay to the deck. One or two may remain, one on each side, to "overhaul the gear," hauling extra slack through the various lines so they do not chafe the sail.

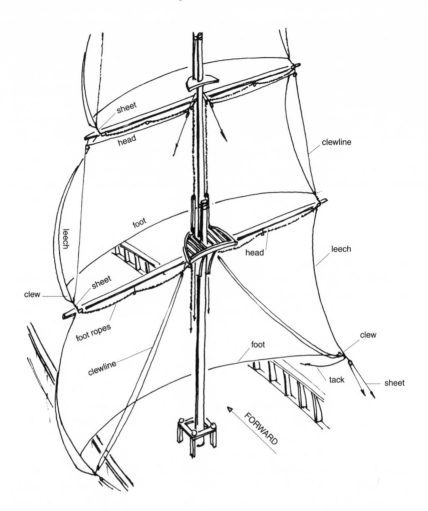

Fig. 2-4a. *Aft side view of a square-rigged mast, showing running rigging and parts of the sails.*

Now the sail can be set. The procedure is different for a hoisting yard than for a fixed yard. With a hoisting yard, such as the fore upper topsail, remember that the clewlines oppose the sheets. The first step is to sheet down the clews, so the clewlines must be slacked off and the sheets hauled home. This hauls the clews tight to the yard below, in this case to the lower topsail yard. Now the order can be given to "slack away on the clewlines and buntlines, haul away on the fore upper topsail halyard, slack away the braces." Note that the braces, leading from aft and below, will restrict the hoisting of the yard if not slacked. Once the yard is hoisted the sail is fully set. Buntlines and clewlines should now be overhauled by the hands aloft so they do not bind the sail (fig. 2-6).

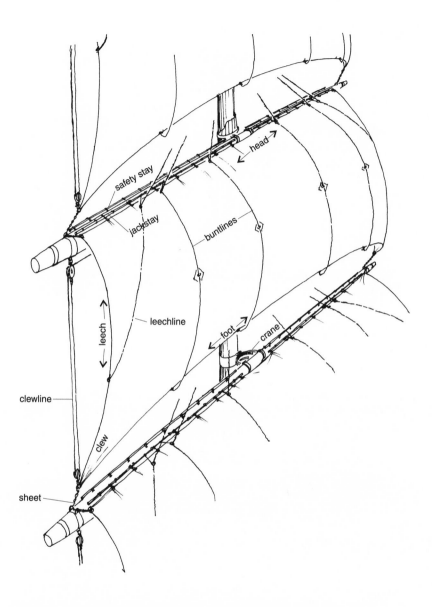

Fig. 2-4b. *Forward side view of a square sail and its running rigging.*

For a fixed yard, such as the fore lower topsail, the procedure again starts with the sail in its gear. With no hoisting to be done, the clewlines and buntlines are cast off and the sheets are sheeted home. Note that on the bigger sails there may be leechlines to slack, along with the clewlines and buntlines.

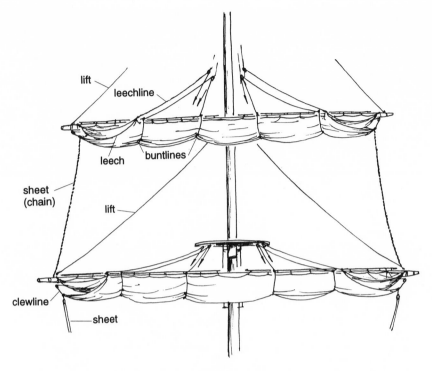

Fig. 2-5. *Square sails "in their gear." Note leechlines have hauled the midpoint of the leeches in along the spar to prevent leaving a large bundle of canvas at the ends. The sail has not yet been furled, or has just been unfurled and is ready to be set.*

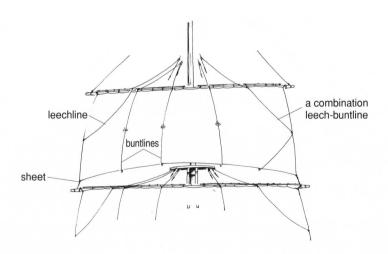

Fig. 2-6. *A square sail fully set. Note the extra slack in the clewlines and buntlines, so they don't tug on the sails and distort their shape, or chafe on the canvas.*

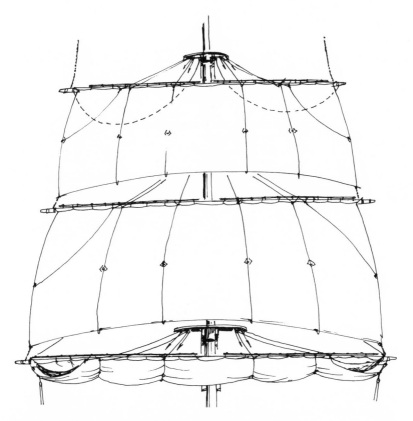

Fig. 2-7a. *Striking a square sail. Sails set, preparatory to striking.*

STRIKING A SQUARE SAIL

First, it must be noted that on board some vessels, the command to "strike" a sail means to dump it as quickly as possible—in an emergency. In this case, most of the preparatory steps are skipped, and some damage to the sail or rig is possible. The command to stow a sail under normal circumstances then would likely be: "Take in the . . . ." In this text, to "strike" a sail will mean to take in the sail under normal circumstances. This is one example of the many variations in both terminology and practice aboard different vessels. Striking is essentially the reverse of the setting sequence, but there are a few important points to note. Starting with the sail fully set (fig. 2-7a), the first step for a hoisting yard will be to lower the yard. This will let the sail belly out and dump most of its wind. But the sail on a hoisting yard may have enough wind in it so that the pressure of the yard against the mast will prevent the yard from sliding down of its own weight. Therefore, it must be hauled down. You must think through the running rigging you are now familiar with and remember which lines you have available to haul the yard

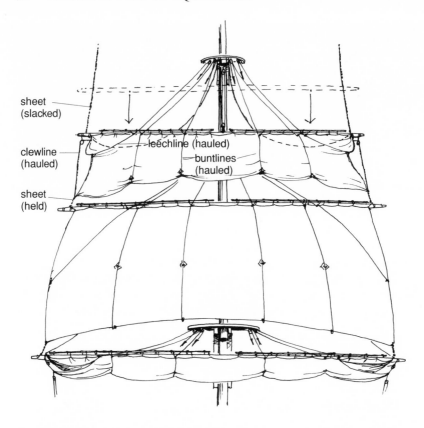

sheet
(slacked)

clewline
(hauled)

leechline (hauled)

buntlines
(hauled)

sheet
(held)

Fig. 2-7b. *Striking a square sail. "Clew down." Starting to strike the upper topsail. The clewlines are hauled, sheets held fast, and slack is taken up on the buntlines and leechlines. Note the sheet for the sail next above must be slacked to allow the yard to be lowered.*

down. These will be the clewlines, which dead-end at the clews (remember, they oppose the sheets) and lead up to the yardarm, then into the mast and down to the deck. By hauling the clewlines you will haul the yard down, as long as the sheets remain fast. Therefore, the first command is to "clew down" (fig. 2-7b). (Interestingly, the next command will be to "clew up.") When you clew down, you haul the yard down until it rests in its lifts. Consider again the gear you have learned about, and remember that the sheets for the sail next above must be slacked away to allow the yard to come down. Since the braces will go slack as you lower the yard, you will tighten the lee brace as it goes slack to hold the yard securely. Once the yard is down, the sail will be partially gathered in its gear, but not fully, so you must now clew up. The order is given and the sheets are cast off, the clewlines and buntlines are hauled, and the sail fully gathered up in its gear (fig. 2-7c). For a fixed yard, since it is not lowered, only the clewing up procedure is followed.

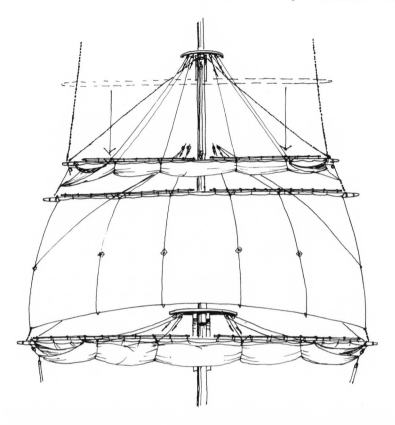

Fig. 2-7c. *Striking a square sail. "In its gear." The sail is ready for furling. Hands are now sent aloft to furl.*

Once the sail is in its gear, hands are ordered "aloft to stow the fore upper topsail." They lay out on the yard, and the person nearest the mast coordinates the furling effort. In unison, they gather up folds of the sail, dropping them successively into the belly thus formed. When all have the last fold in their hand, they roll the whole sail up onto the top of the yard and secure the sail, between the safety stay and the jackstay, with the gaskets. There should be one smooth skin of sail on top, so that it will shed water and not present any opening that the wind could lift.

Further reading (see bibliography for details): de Kerchove, *International Maritime Dictionary;* U.S. Coast Guard, *Eagle Seamanship;* Underhill, *Sailing Ship Rigs and Rigging;* Harland, *Seamanship in the Age of Sail;* Willoughby, *Square Rig Seamanship.*

CHAPTER THREE

SAIL THEORY

TRUE, RELATIVE, AND APPARENT WIND

A vessel at a mooring is at rest and is under the influence of the true wind (assuming there is no current). Every other vessel in the anchorage is feeling the same wind, and the direction and force of this wind can be observed by the small wave crests on the water surface—the whitecaps. A telltale flying from the masthead or a flag on the pier will confirm this observation of wind strength and direction.

Relative wind is the wind that is felt as a result of the motion of the vessel, without influence from the true wind. It is the wind you would feel on a dead calm day if you were motoring in any direction. As long as you are moving forward, the relative wind will be from dead ahead, no matter which way you turn. Therefore, the relative wind direction is always from dead ahead—or from the reciprocal of your course—at a speed which is equal to your boat's speed. On a dead calm day, a telltale at your masthead will indicate the relative wind, while a flag on a pier will hang limp.

Apparent wind is the combination of true and relative wind. The result of the combination is a wind that always blows from closer to dead ahead than the true wind. If you are moving across or into the true wind, the force of the apparent wind will always be greater than the force of the true wind. If the true wind is behind you, the apparent wind will be less strong. This is the wind you will feel and, more important, it is the wind the sails will "feel" blowing across them. The telltale at your masthead will indicate the apparent wind, but the wave crests and the flag on the pier will show the true wind. If the vessel proceeds on a beam reach, with the true wind coming from 90 degrees on one side, as she gathers headway the telltale at her masthead will begin to indicate a slightly stronger wind coming from a little forward of abeam.

The principle of true, relative, and apparent wind can be illustrated and, more importantly, measured by vectors (see figure 3-1). A vector, as used in this example, is a line with an arrow at its head, whose length indicates, to some

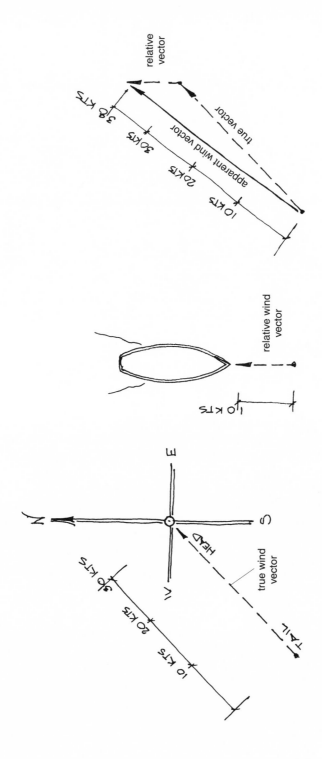

Fig. 3-1a. *Vector diagram of true, relative, and apparent wind.*

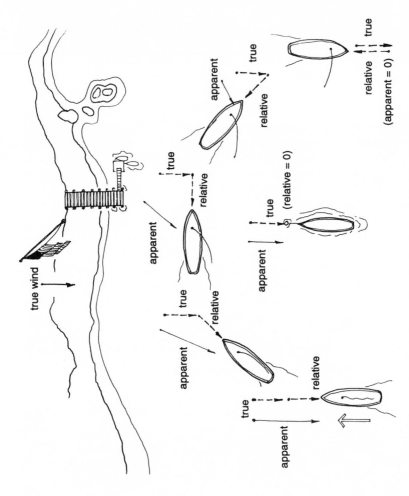

Fig. 3-1b. *The concept of true, relative, and apparent wind is demonstrated by a boat sailing through an anchorage.*

convenient scale, the speed of the wind and whose direction indicates the direction the wind is blowing. Each of the types of wind discussed can be represented with vectors. It is the nature—and advantage—of vectors that they can be added together to solve for an unknown quantity, called the resultant. If the true wind speed and direction, and the relative wind speed and direction, are known (by virtue of knowing the vessel's course and speed), a vector solution for the apparent wind can be produced. To do so, choose a scale to indicate speed, and draw a vector of a length that will represent the speed of the true wind. The direction of the vector must represent the direction of the true wind. Next, starting from the arrowhead end of that vector, draw another that represents the speed and direction of the relative wind. Its direction will be the reciprocal of the vessel's course, since the relative wind is always from dead ahead. The resultant vector is now drawn, originating where the first (true wind) vector started and ending where the second (relative wind) vector ended. The resultant always has its tail at the tail of the first vector and its head at the head of the last vector. Thus, the apparent wind vector is the resultant formed by summing the true and relative wind vectors.

There is one particular example of this relationship that is both visible and very useful when under way. Because of the friction between the moving air (wind) and the surface (water), the strength of the wind is reduced near the surface. Conversely, the strength of the wind increases with distance aloft. Returning to the vector solutions, the increase in true wind speed has an effect on the apparent wind direction as well. Since the true wind is blowing harder aloft, the apparent wind will be from an angle farther aft than the surface wind. The sails aloft will have not only a stronger apparent wind, but also a more favorable one. This happens to be fortunate for those who sail on low-tech sailing vessels whose sails tend to sag off to leeward aloft. This also explains why sailors go to such great lengths (and expense), to carry sails as high as possible—topsails, flying jibs, topgallants, fisherman staysails, etc. In light airs, high sails may be the only ones doing any work at all. This phenomenon is visible on board a tall square-rigger, where the sails will be trimmed in a fanlike pattern, the lower ones being trimmed tightly, the higher ones progressively less so.

Remarkably, some highly efficient sailing vessels can sail at speeds faster than the true wind. Iceboats are the most notable example, capable of speeds over 100 miles per hour in true winds of only 25 knots. For an example, assume that an iceboat starts on a beam reach in a 20-knot true wind. As the boat accelerates to 20 knots, the apparent wind draws ahead and increases in strength.

The vector solution now indicates an apparent wind of 28 knots from about 4 points (45 degrees) forward of abeam, closehauled (see figure 3-2A). Sheeting in to match this new wind angle, the boat now has the benefit of a 28-knot wind, and she speeds up to 40 knots. The apparent wind now increases to a strong gale of 45 knots, 27 degrees on the bow (see figure 3-2B). But with the

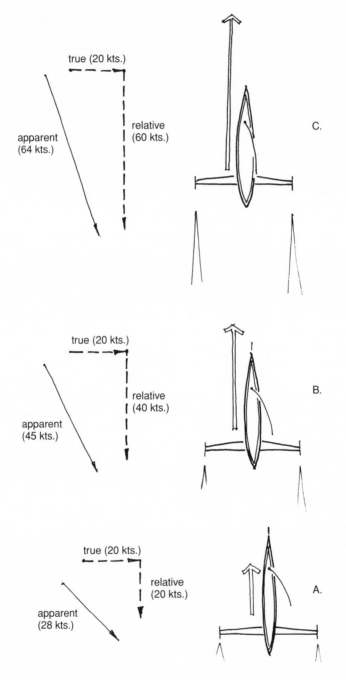

true (20 kts.)

relative
(60 kts.)

apparent
(64 kts.)

C.

true (20 kts.)

relative
(40 kts.)

apparent
(45 kts.)

B.

true (20 kts.)

relative
(20 kts.)

apparent
(28 kts.)

A.

Fig. 3-2. *Iceboats, and some very efficient water-sailing boats, are capable of sailing faster than the true wind, utilizing the principle of the apparent wind.*

increase of wind speed, the boat is capable of approximately 60 knots. The increased boat speed turns the apparent wind into a hurricane at 64 knots, now only 18.5 degrees on the bow (see figure 3-2C). Depending on the efficiency of the craft (and iceboats are terrifyingly efficient), it can go on and on. In fact, a Skeeter class iceboat has been clocked at 146 miles per hour. Two things become apparent from this example: iceboats and their rigs must be built to survive sailing in hurricane-force winds, and their sails must be designed extremely flat, to function at such close sailing angles.

Iceboats have the luxury of a nearly frictionless ride. The rest of us have to plow through the water; but, even so, great speeds are possible. The world sailing speed record on the water was initially set by the yacht *Crossbow* at 26.3 knots in 19 knots of true wind in 1975, and later beaten by herself at 36 knots. A new record was set in 1993 by the winged trimaran *Yellow Pages Endeavor* at 46.25 knots. Now you can buy—off the shelf—a "Trifoiler" trimaran/hydrofoil that is capable of speeds in excess of 50 knots!

These examples are given to set firmly the concept of apparent wind, because without it it is difficult to grasp what the sails themselves are working with. Remember, you can *see* the true wind (on the water), but you *feel* the apparent wind. More importantly, it is to the *apparent* wind that you trim the sails.

AERODYNAMIC LIFT

Aerodynamic lift is the force that a sail harnesses from the kinetic energy of a moving airstream. The word "lift" is used loosely here, since we are actually describing a horizontal force, but since this force is compared to the force developed by an airplane wing, it is standard practice to use the word in both cases. The "lift" is transferred from the sails to the hull of a boat by way of the mast and its support system—the standing rigging, the running rigging, the step, the partners—and the vessel moves through the water in a direction that is guided by the keel (or centerboard) and the rudder.

A sail is often compared to a wing, which is a reasonably accurate comparison. A sail is a wing standing vertically in the airstream. Many of us have a general understanding of the principles of lift developed by a wing. The same principles hold true for a sail. An airplane wing is developing a force which lifts the airplane into the air. The sail is providing a force which pulls a boat forward. In both cases the force is directed at 90 degrees to the wing (sail). (More accurately, it is at 90 degrees to the surface of the wing which, being a curved surface, complicates things. This will be explored in more detail shortly.)

In neither case is this the direction in which the craft actually wants to go, so other means are employed to control the direction of final travel. On an airplane, engines provide forward thrust to move the craft forward, while the wing primarily holds the craft up. On a vessel under sail, there is no such added force, but a keel of some kind, and a rudder, are employed to prevent the craft from sliding too much to leeward (where most of the aerodynamic lift is directed) and gain as much forward movement as can be gleaned from the total force available.

One of the most popular theories of aerodynamic lift asserts that the air moving over the curved upper wing surface has farther to travel than the air following the lower, straight surface, and therefore the air moving over the top must move faster than the air on the bottom, in order to "catch up." This develops a low-pressure area above the wing, as described by the Bernoulli theory, which will be explained in a moment. This theory works well for a wing with measurable thickness, but a sail has no significant thickness, so the distance the air must travel on the concave and convex sides is the same. Furthermore, this theory cannot fully explain how symmetrical wings work, or how a plane can fly upside down.

Other theories have come into and out of fashion, as aerodynamicists learn more about the science of fluid flow. Another popular theory now in some dispute is the slot theory, in which the airflow speeds up between a jib and a mainsail, enhancing the efficiency of the main. This has been argued against convincingly, after demonstrating that the airflow there in fact seems to be slower than was predicted. There is unquestionably some relationship between two or more adjacent sails, and it seems to be more a case of redirecting the airflow than speeding it up. Remember that each sail is sailing only on apparent wind, and the airflow from each sail will change the apparent wind angle for the sail next in line.

The field of aerodynamics continues to develop, and it is probable that a theory considered satisfactory now will continue to evolve as well. This brief treatment of a complex subject draws extensively from three books: *The Theory and Practice of Sail* and *The Aero-Hydrodynamics of Sailing* by C. A. Marchaj, and *Sail Power* by Wallace Ross.

To begin, two underlying principles must be examined—Venturi's Theorem and Bernoulli's Theorem. G. B. Venturi showed that a fluid (air is a fluid) passing through a tube increases its velocity as the tube is restricted. This can be visualized by understanding that air (at low velocities such as we are dealing with) is considered incompressible. (Although air can be compressed, as in a scuba tank, it requires great force and a sealed container. Compression would not occur in an open airstream, except at very high speeds.) Therefore, a given amount of air passing through a tube and encountering a restriction must move faster in order to get all of the air particles through the smaller opening within the same period of time as the air passing outside the tube.

Daniel Bernoulli found that within a given fluid stream, an area of increased velocity develops a corresponding decrease in pressure and, conversely, a decrease in velocity develops an increase in pressure, when compared to the surrounding unaffected fluid stream.

With these principles in mind, one can view a sail in an airstream and understand how its lift force develops. The air approaching the sail divides as it meets the leading edge. That which goes over the convex surface finds itself being restricted by the confines of the sail on the one hand and the undisturbed airstream on the other. Since restricted flow means increased velocity (per Venturi), the air speeds up. And since increased velocity means decreased pressure (per Bernoulli), the pressure drops. This holds until the air reaches the point of maximum depth of curve, or the belly of the sail. When the restriction eases, the velocity drops, and the pressure rises until it again matches the surrounding airstream at the trailing edge (see figure 3-3).

Meanwhile, that portion of the air which has flowed toward the concave side of the sail finds itself in a widening path. Being the opposite example of the Venturi effect, the air here slows down, with a corresponding increase in pressure, per Bernoulli. Again it reaches a maximum at the belly of the sail, where it begins to come back together and the pressure drops gradually until, at the trailing edge, it again matches the velocity of the air that moved over the convex side of the sail.

Thus it can be seen that high pressure is developed on the concave side, pushing the sail, and low pressure is developed on the convex side, pulling the sail. These two forces complement each other to develop a total force that propels the vessel.

A second aspect of the present theory describes a general circulation developed around an airfoil in an airstream. The circulation tries to flow aft along the convex side (in agreement with, and enhancing, the flow of the airstream), and

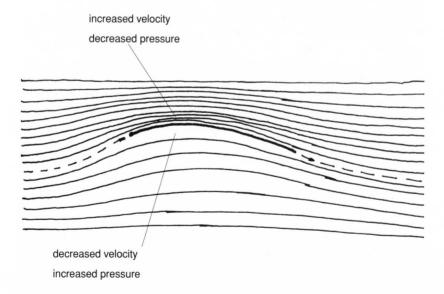

increased velocity

decreased pressure

decreased velocity

increased pressure

Fig. 3-3. *Airflow over a sail.*

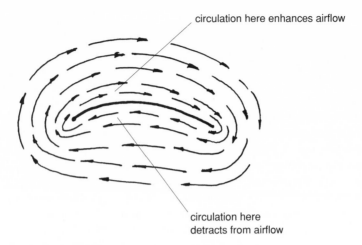

circulation here enhances airflow

circulation here
detracts from airflow

Fig. 3-4. *Circulation theory.*

forward along the concave side (counter to, and diminishing, the flow there). This combination works to the advantage of the Bernoulli and Venturi theories, adding to their effects (see figure 3-4).

What is even more satisfying is that the process described sets a chain reaction in motion that amplifies this force (see figure 3-5). Once the process is begun and there develops a pressure rise on the concave side and a pressure drop on the convex side, more air flow is encouraged toward the convex side. Air that is free to flow will always flow away from high pressure and toward low. Therefore, as the air is approaching the leading edge, some of the air which by rights is headed for the concave side is shunted to the convex side by its attraction to the low pressure there and the repulsion from the high pressure on the concave side. This causes yet more air to force its way into the narrowing Venturi slot there, creating a still faster flow, and still lower pressure. This goes on to a point where it reaches a maximum—when the attraction to the low-pressure side no longer overcomes the tendency for the air to flow straight along the high-pressure side.

Finally (for now), there is considerable evidence to support the deflection theory, which relies on Isaac Newton's statement that "for every action there is an equal and opposite reaction." Here it is the deflection of the airstream by the angled wing or sail that produces the opposite reaction of forcing the plane upwards, or the sailboat to windward. This is perhaps the simplest idea to grasp intuitively, and is easy to feel by holding your hand out the window of a fast-moving car, tilting your hand between the vertical and horizontal. What you are doing is changing the "angle of attack" of your hand, a concept that will be examined more closely later.

Initial flow.

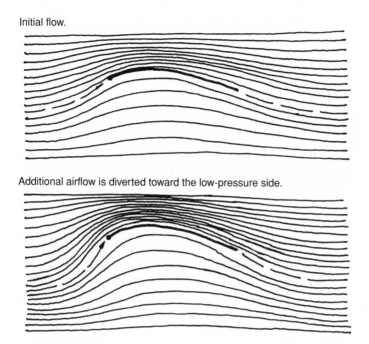

Additional airflow is diverted toward the low-pressure side.

Fig. 3-5. *Diversion theory.*

There are many theories, any of which might be more or less right or wrong. The result is an undeniable force, which is propelling the vessel. Our business now is to try to visualize this force to take advantage of it.

TOTAL AERODYNAMIC FORCE

The force that is developed by this whole process is actually made up of the combination of an infinite number of smaller force components acting on all the parts of the sail. It is impossible to deal with all of these individually, so it is convenient to average them all together into what is called a total aerodynamic force (TAF) (fig. 3-6).

The individual forces each act in a direction that is normal (perpendicular) to the curve of the sail, and their strength varies with their relationship to the deepest part of the curve. At the deepest part of the curve the forces are strongest. There are those on the concave side, pushing on the sail, and those on the convex side, pulling on the sail, but since the net result of all of them is to propel the boat in the same direction, they are all part of the same force. Combining them, we find that the average of all of these forces results in a vector that is approximately perpendicular to the chord of the sail—an

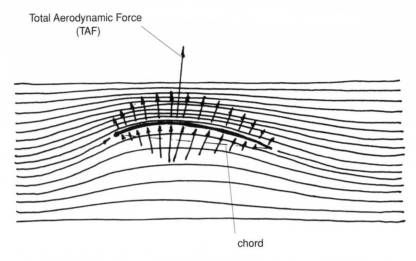

Total Aerodynamic Force
(TAF)

chord

Fig. 3-6. *The total aerodynamic force (TAF) is a theoretical sum of all the force components acting along the surface of the sail. Note that the TAF is perpendicular to the chord.*

imaginary line connecting the leech and the luff—and pointing toward the convex side. This is the direction in which the boat is being propelled by the wind.

Two observations about the total aerodynamic force are:

- It is proportional to the surface area of the sail—if you reduce sail area by half, the force is reduced by half.

- It is proportional to the square of the wind speed—if the wind speed is doubled, the aerodynamic force is quadrupled.

The critical factors that make the whole process work are the curve of the sail (sail shape) and the angle at which the leading edge is presented to the oncoming air stream (angle of attack, or angle of incidence).

Sail shape is designed and built into the sail by the sailmaker, but the sailor has some control over it by the use of various trimming lines, such as the sheet, halyard, downhaul, outhaul, cunningham, leechline, luff tensioner, and vang. Angle of attack is wholly controlled by the sailor by trimming the sheet, shifting the traveller, and/or adjusting the heading of the vessel.

The desired shape is a maximum curve, to a point. With too little curve in a sail, there will be too little deflection of the airstream and you will develop less than optimum aerodynamic lift. But too much curve is detrimental. A fluid will adhere to a curved surface as it flows by, following the curve in what is called laminar flow, but only to a limited degree. When the curve becomes too great for the flow to adhere, it will break away, leaving a vacuum between the airflow and the curved surface. The vacuum then draws some of the air in, in

A.

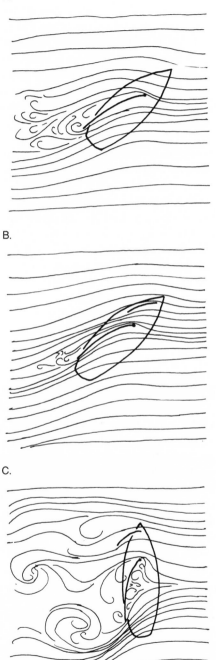

B.

Fig. 3-7. *Airflow over a sail or sails.*
In A, the mainsail is slightly over-
trimmed. The airflow breaks into tur-
bulent flow about halfway along the
sail. Note that a telltale, or flag, at the
leech of the mainsail would be curled
back along the leeward side of the
sail. In B, a jib is added, but the main-
sail is still trimmed exactly as it was
in A. Note that the airflow coming off
the jib has helped keep the flow over
the mainsail laminar for almost its en-
tire length. The telltale at the leech
would now be flying more or less
straight aft. In C, the jib is filling well,
with good flow, but the main has been
overtrimmed and there is turbulence
all around it. Note that in all cases the
airstream is even deflected to wind-
ward of the boat. This can be
visualized on board by holding up a
long stick with a long piece (several
feet) of light yarn or cassette tape
attached to the end.

C.

strong eddies called turbulence. The energy used up in these turbulent eddies is wasted energy which detracts from the power of the sail. This turbulence (and its effect on other sails) is demonstrated in figure 3-7.

When adjusting the angle of attack, power is again dependent on maintaining the laminar flow over the sail. In this case, if you overtrim the sail, giving too abrupt an angle of attack, the airflow cannot adhere to the sail and will break into turbulent flow. With too shallow an angle of attack there will be too little deflection of the airstream, giving less than optimum aerodynamic lift. (In the extreme case of undertrimming, the sail will simply luff, with no deflection taking place at all.)

The loss of power of a sail when the airflow goes into turbulent flow is very noticeable—the boat will lose substantial drive—though the sail shape will probably not change since the vacuum toward the convex side will continue to pull the sail into its shape. Too shallow an angle of attack will also be evidenced by a loss of power initially, and finally by a luff. It is important to realize that in either case—too much or too little angle—the sail will lose performance before it loses its shape. The sailor must be keenly aware of the apparent wind direction over the sail to maintain optimum performance. Lightweight telltales in strategic locations give good indications of wind flow, as illustrated in figure 3-8. These diagrams show the optimum sail shapes and attack angles, how they affect the performance of the sail, and how the telltales indicate that performance.

It also becomes apparent now why very tall, narrow (high-aspect-ratio) sails have become popular. In fact, any wing will perform best with a high aspect ratio. Aspect ratio is the ratio of the length of the leading edge of the wing (luff of the sail) to the width of the wing (foot of the sail). The place where the pressure change is greatest, and therefore where the maximum force is developed, is in the deepest part of the belly of the sail. From that point on, the power of the sail drops off toward the leech. At some point, given a wide enough sail, the airflow on the two sides of the sail becomes parallel to the surrounding airstream, and there is no longer any deflection or pressure change between the two sides. The leech becomes, in effect, a mere flag, providing no lift, but producing considerable drag. Worse, with an over-tight leech, a windward curl will develop which breaks the airstream, causing a severe drag. Better to get rid of as much of the leech as possible, leaving just the leading edge, the belly, and as little leech as is necessary to finish the sail. Battens were developed to prevent the leech curling, to a great degree.

DRIVE AND FORCE TRANSFER

Once the sail has developed its aerodynamic force, that force must be transmitted to the hull. Since the direction of the aerodynamic force is not the direction we care to go, the force must be redirected. We cannot actually redirect it, but we can at least burn up that which we do not want and make use of that component we desire.

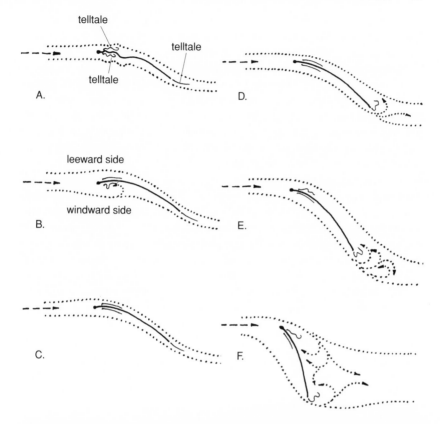

Fig. 3-8. *Use of telltales to monitor aerodynamic flow. In A, the luff telltales are both luffing, as is the luff of the sail. The air, however, is flowing smoothly off the leech, and the leech telltale is flying smoothly. In B, the leeward telltale at the luff is flying smoothly, indicating laminar flow there, but the windward telltale is luffing, indicating that the sail is still under-trimmed (or the boat is pointing too high), even though the sail itself is not luffing. This is called "pinching." In C, there is good laminar flow all along the sail, and all telltales are flying smoothly. In D, the sail is slightly overtrimmed, as evidenced by the leech telltale curling around to leeward. This could also be caused by an overtight leech. Note that the sail shape still appears fine. In E, the sail is overtrimmed more, and the leeward telltale at the luff also begins to flutter, indicating that the turbulence has spread forward. In F, the whole sail has stalled, and the windward side telltale is probably being flattened against the sail, rather than flying.*

We should first look at the aerodynamic push and pull that is going on with the sail and how that force finds its way to the hull. The sail is being pulled toward its convex side, so much so that it bellies out, straining in that direction, pulling against its lashings. The cloth of the sail, pulling first against its own stitching, then through the seizings on the mast hoops, track slides, or foot lashings, exerts its pull against the mast and boom. The force, then, is transferred first from the sail to the mast and boom.

The mast strains under the force of the sail, leaning hard against its support system—the shrouds, stays, mast step, and partners. The boom strains against the gooseneck or jaws, transferring some of its load to the mast, and against the main sheet, where it transfers the rest of its load to the traveller and its fastenings.

The shrouds and stays strain against the chainplates, which pull on their fastenings driven through the hull and frames. The partners bear against the deck beams; the mast step against the floors. The traveller, through-bolted to the deck beams as well, transfers the load to the deck. Through the frames and the hull skin, finally down to the keel itself, the various loads meet and encompass the whole vessel, to drive her along.

At every step along the way, the forces necessary to push or pull the vessel must be borne by the particular, individual parts that make up the vessel's structure and rig. It is effective to look at each item and view it as a part of a towing bridle which is dragging your vessel through the water. The main sheet is a towrope. The mast is a towing bitt. The shrouds are parts of a bridle. Each has a great deal of work to do, and if any one is weak or doing less than its share, the others are overburdened. If one fails—breaks, cracks, or slips suddenly—the others must suddenly absorb the shock load of that part's failure. The parts must achieve a perfect balance, or fail.

DIRECTIONAL TRANSFER

How does the aerodynamic force become directed so that the vessel goes forward instead of sideways?

The hull and keel or centerboard prevents the vessel from side-slipping—effectively limiting motion in any direction other than ahead (or astern!). It, like the sails, is in a wing-and-fluid relationship. This time it is a hydrodynamic force instead of an aerodynamic force, the main difference being that water is 795 times more dense than air, but the principles are the same.

A few observations about the total hydrodynamic force are:

- It is proportional to the area of the keel. If you double the keel area, you will double the hydrodynamic force.

- It is proportional to the square of the boat's speed. If you double the boat's speed, you quadruple the force.
- Notice the similarity of these observations to those concerning aerodynamic force.

Again we are dealing with shape, angle of attack, and laminar and turbulent flow.

Since the keel must perform equally well on either tack, with either side to windward, the shape must be symmetrical. This works well enough, though if a changeable shape could be developed for this purpose, the hull might perform better.

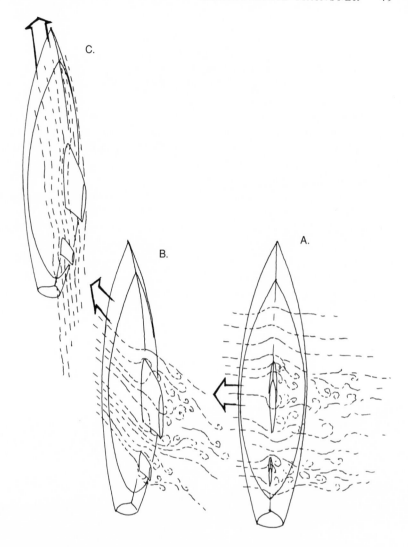

Fig. 3-9. *Hydrodynamic flow over the keel. The vessel is shown getting under way. In A, she is sliding sideways, with pure turbulent flow over the keel. In B, she begins to gain headway, and the flow begins to adhere to the keel, providing some hydrodynamic lift. In C, she is under way, the flow is mainly laminar, and the keel is keeping the boat on her track line, resisting any set to leeward.*

The angle of attack, which will now be called the angle of leeway, must again be regulated to maintain the laminar flow that allows the hydrodynamic force to be maximized. This is accomplished by getting the boat moving forward. Much like the apparent wind issue, the angle of leeway will be a result of the boat moving forward and its being pushed sideways by the aerodynamic

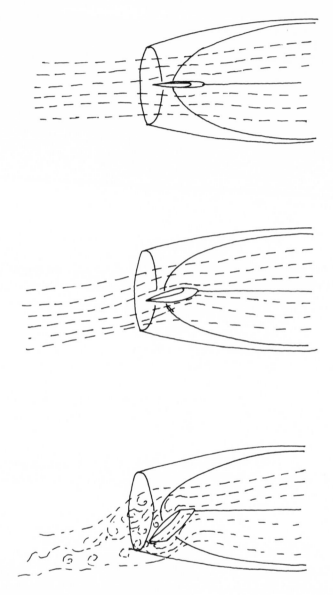

Fig. 3-10. *Hydrodynamic flow over the rudder.*

force. The boat must move forward fast enough so that the angle of leeway becomes shallow enough to let the flowing water adhere to the curve of the keel. If the aerodynamic force is slight, the boat needs only a little forward way, but when the aerodynamic force is great, it needs to be moving ahead faster.

Initially, when a boat is dead in the water and her sails first begin to fill, she will only slide sideways. The flow over the keel is perpendicular to the vessel, the total aerodynamic force is directed just forward of abeam, to leeward, and the hydrodynamic flow over the keel is purely turbulent. The keel provides almost no benefit at this point since all you are getting now is drag, and all you are making is leeway. But within moments, once the vessel gains some headway, the angle of leeway begins to move ahead, and the flow will turn from turbulent to laminar. There is no mistaking when this happens. The vessel heels a bit more and you will feel the keel get a grip on the water as the hydrodynamic force begins to provide lift. The total combination of all the forces is now driving the vessel forward (see figure 3-9).

Since the hydrodynamic lift is centered low at the approximate center of the keel, while the aerodynamic lift is high at the approximate center of the sail area, these forces form a couple that causes that heeling moment. The aerodynamic lift of the sail is pulling and pushing the boat in a direction that is perpendicular to the chord of the sail. This direction will be somewhat forward of abeam and to leeward. The hydrodynamic force on the keel below is resisting the drive to leeward but allowing the forward component to act. The vessel then moves ahead. Since it is necessary to have some forward motion to get the process started, you may have to head well off initially until the vessel begins to move ahead. Once it does you will then be able to sheet in gradually and head up until you are on the desired course. To try to head up before there is enough forward motion will result in more leeway and no headway, as the flow over the keel is purely turbulent.

The rudder works in much the same way as the keel. It is a wing in a fluid, working with laminar and turbulent flow, lift and drag. It is also moving through the fluid, but here the angle of attack is adjustable by the helmsperson. By varying the angle of attack, lift is developed to one side or the other, and since this lift is well aft of the center of lateral resistance (the geometric center of the underwater profile of the hull), it provides a lateral moment which turns the vessel.

It is important to think in terms of maximum efficiency of the wing. Maximum efficiency is achieved with maximum angle of attack without losing laminar flow. Once the angle of attack goes beyond that which can support laminar flow, the flow becomes turbulent, the lift falls away and is replaced by almost pure drag, and the rudder loses its efficiency (see figure 3-10). On most vessels there is a rudder stop that prevents the rudder from going beyond about 35 degrees to either side. At this angle it may lose some efficiency if speed is high and turbulent flow develops, but it is not likely to stall completely. What does happen if we oversteer is that there is more drag than lift, which does more to slow down than to turn the vessel. This can be annoying if in a race, or it can cause a serious problem in a vessel that is difficult to tack, and that is in a position where it cannot afford to miss a tack.

Keeping the single concept of lift and drag firmly in mind and acting upon it ensures that best use is made of the sails, keel or centerboard, and rudder.

Further reading (see bibliography for details): Chase, *Introduction to Nautical Science,* chap. 3; Marchaj, *Sailing Theory and Practice,* part 2; Glénans Sea Center, *The New Glénans Sailing Manual,* chap. 3; Ross, *Sail Power,* chaps. 1 and 2.

CHAPTER FOUR

TRIM AND BALANCE

Sail trim for high performance is a subject for serious racers and researchers, and as such goes beyond the scope of this book. What we are going to concern ourselves with is the basics of sail trim to get good performance from our sails, to make reasonable progress to windward, and to be able to identify problems with sails or rig that inhibit our ability to get where we want to go. Later, we will concern ourselves with balance—the concept that enables the sailor to handle and maneuver a vessel with confidence.

As discussed, the sail acts as a wing to develop aerodynamic lift from a moving airstream. In order to optimize that transfer of energy, sail shape must be optimized. Early sailors managed to get by with little or no understanding of these concepts, but by keen observation and experimentation were able to get fairly good results. That is still possible today, especially since naval architects and sailmakers have done much of the theoretical work for us. The difference between the weekender and the professional should lie in the depth of knowledge of the principles involved, and that extra knowledge can add up considerably to the advantage of the owner. Over the course of an ocean passage of ten to twenty days, the ability to gain an extra knot, and/or an extra few degrees of angle to windward, can easily shave several days off the trip. In some cases this can mean the difference between making the run in favorable conditions or being caught in adverse or severe conditions. This is one of the reasons owners hire professional captains.

To gain the extra few degrees to windward or the extra knot of boat speed, the sailor must pay close attention to each of the various factors that are providing aerodynamic lift. Sail shape, angle of attack, interaction between sails, balance, and correct choice of sails are all equally important factors.

SAIL SHAPE

The sailmaker builds a sail with certain parameters in mind. These include the range of wind speed expected; whether the sail will be for racing, casual cruising, limited passage making, extreme passage making, extensive windward work, or primarily off-wind work; and desired lifespan. The sailor then must be able to take this sail, identify its design limitations, and use it to best advantage. It is easy to ruin a sail by trying to make it do something it was never intended to do, or by using it under conditions it was not designed to handle. Delivery skippers should keep their hands off the racing wardrobe, and conversely the owner of a racing yacht should provide a good set of passage-making sails for the delivery crew to use.

A sail designed for a wind speed range of from 20 to 30 knots will probably be too stiff to develop sufficient draft (depth and location of belly) in less than 10 knots of wind. This is because sail cloth stretches, and the sail is designed to stretch into shape under a specified amount of wind. The boat will still sail, but performance will be substantially reduced. The sail will not suffer; however, since sunlight is detrimental to a sail at any time, if you have a suitable light-weather sail, the heavy-duty one should be spared the exposure. On the other hand, a light air sail left up as winds increase from 20 to 25 knots may suffer irreparable damage in one afternoon, at a cost to the owner that may exceed your wages for the trip.

If the sail does not have a label that gives some specifics about its design parameters, then look at indications like cloth weight, amount of tabling (reinforcing) at the corners, reef points or lack thereof, roping (boltrope is line sewn to the edge of a sail for reinforcement) or lack thereof, heft of clew, tack and head fittings, and overall size of the sail. There will be more discussion on these items individually in the chapter on sails, spars, and rigging. Until you have enough experience to evaluate these indicators yourself, you will have to rely on the advice of the owner, the sailmaker, or the skipper you are relieving to identify properly the different sails and their limitations.

The right sail chosen for the weather must be hoisted properly to get it set without wrinkles and without distorting the designed shape (see figure 4-1). Adjust the halyard so the head is where it is intended to be. Many modern vessels will have some sort of mark, such as a piece of tape on the halyard or at the masthead, to identify this point. Then adjust the downhaul (if there is one) so there are no wrinkles along the luff. If the luff is too loose, small, horizontal wrinkles will appear, while if it is too tight, long, vertical wrinkles will show up (see figure 4-1). On most large, gaff-rigged vessels there is no downhaul—the weight of the boom is all there is to tension the luff. Next, adjust outhaul tension so there are no wrinkles along the foot. (On a larger, traditional vessel, this will be done only once or twice a season.) Here, small, vertical wrinkles will show a loose foot, and long, horizontal ones indicate an overtight foot. Sheet tension will control the leech—too tight and it may curl to windward, too loose and it will fall off to leeward. The sheet will also control the amount by which the upper part of the leech will sag off to leeward, called twist. With a gaff sail, the tension on the peak halyard is important as well. Too much tension here will pull a long diagonal wrinkle between the peak and the tack, while too little tension will allow the peak to sag way off to leeward, and sometimes will leave large humps and hollows vertically along the foot. These first adjustments will get the sail set initially. Further adjustments will need to be made once under way (and periodically thereafter as conditions change), to establish and maintain the proper amount and location of draft, or belly.

Getting the draft located correctly is a matter of adjusting the tension of the various sides of the sail while the vessel is under way. Tensioning the luff (tightening the downhaul or the cunningham) will move the draft forward; less tension here will move it aft. The downhaul does this by pulling the forward end of the boom down, the cunningham by pulling on the sail itself, through a grommet set in the luff tabling just above the boom (see figure 4-2).

More wind velocity will move the draft aft; within limits this is corrected by tightening the luff. The deepest part of the belly should be about 30 to 40 percent of the way aft from the luff to the leech for a genoa or regular jib, and almost halfway aft for a main. The ideal draft for the main will move forward with a smaller genoa or jib with less overlap. This results because the main is "feeling" the apparent wind coming off the windward side of the jib, and the longer the jib overlap, the farther ahead this wind will be (see figure 4-3).

The outhaul controls tension of the foot. A slack foot introduces more belly into the sail, especially in the lower part of the sail. This is desirable for light winds, when the airflow can remain attached (laminar) over a deeper curve than in stronger winds. (If the sail is flatter aloft this is good, since the wind will be stronger aloft.) Conversely, in stronger winds, in order to maintain laminar flow, one should tension the outhaul, flattening the sail.

You may not have the sail and spar marks available to measure these factors, as a racing vessel would have, but you should develop an eye for a "sweet" curve in your sails. Try to imagine the streamlines of air flowing over your sails. You must give them smooth curves to flow over, constricting them just enough to develop maximum lift, without bending them so much that they stall or break into turbulent flow. Remember that all the sails should complement each other—the sail behind operating in the wind from the sail ahead. This will cause each successive sail aft to be trimmed a little tighter than the one ahead, since its apparent wind is from a little farther forward.

BALANCE

Picture a wind vane. There is an arrow with a small head and large feathers at the tail. When the wind blows it will point into the wind. Why? Because the head is small, presenting little wind resistance, catching little wind, and the tail feathers are large, presenting a great deal of wind resistance, catching a great deal of wind. The wind pressure is then greater at the tail than the head and overcomes the wind pressure at the head, blowing the tail downwind. This causes the head to point upwind. If the tail broke off, the vane would spin around and point downwind.

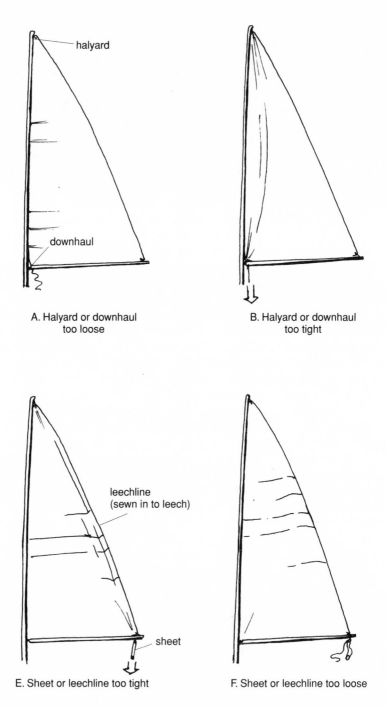

A. Halyard or downhaul
too loose

B. Halyard or downhaul
too tight

E. Sheet or leechline too tight

F. Sheet or leechline too loose

Fig. 4-1. *Tension on halyard, downhaul, outhaul, sheet, leechline, and peak halyard.*

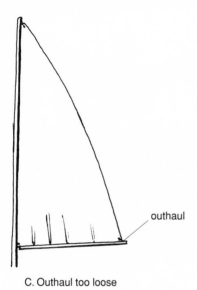

outhaul

C. Outhaul too loose

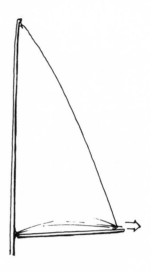

D. Outhaul too tight

Peak halyard

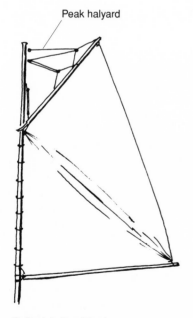

G. Peak halyard too loose

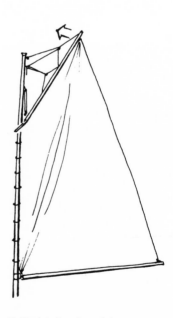

H. Peak halyard too tight

Fig. 4-1. *(continued)*

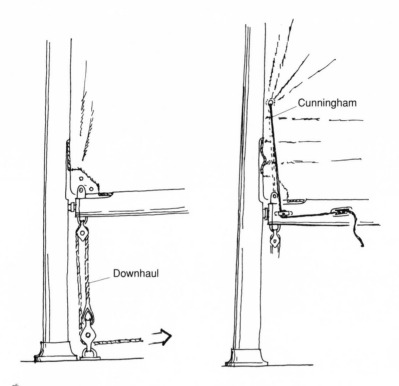

Fig. 4-2. *Downhaul and cunningham.*

This simple concept must dominate every maneuver you attempt in a sail vessel, and you will do well to utilize it in powerboats as well. You must always identify where the greatest amount of wind resistance—or sail force—is, and what effect it is having on your vessel.

Picture your vessel sailing comfortably on a beam reach. She is a ketch, with jib, main, and mizzen set and drawing well. She is well balanced—you need very little attention to the helm to maintain your course. Suddenly, without warning, the mizzen blows out and disintegrates. Before you can react, the vessel's head falls off to leeward. Why? Intuitively, you may know why, but let us look at the principles involved.

Center of Lateral Resistance and Center of Effort

The center of lateral resistance (CLR) is the pivot point of the wind vane. It is a complicated point to describe accurately, as it moves around in obedience to various hydrodynamic principles, but it is sufficient to say that it is the longitudinal, geometric center of the vessel's underwater area. The simplest way to find this is also the best way to describe it. Take a profile drawing of your vessel and with scissors cut out the underwater shape of the boat (see figure 4-4A).

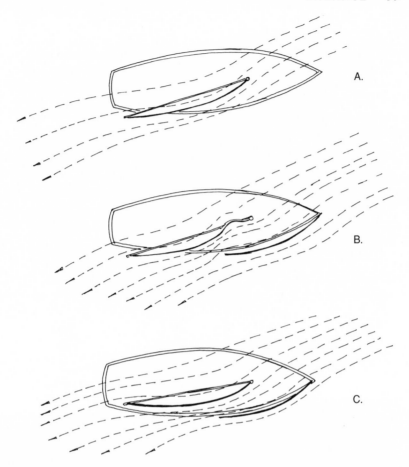

Fig. 4-3. *Airflow over the mainsail, and the main-jib combination.* A. *Mainsail only, trimmed properly.* B. *Jib set and trimmed properly. The mainsail, though unchanged, is now being backwinded by the jib.* C. *The main is trimmed properly for the apparent wind, coming off the jib.*

This will include the hull (below the waterline), keel, and rudder. (The rudder should really count only partially, since you can manipulate it, but this will be good enough for our purposes.) Crease the cutout lengthwise, parallel to the waterline, so it is stiff enough to hold its ends out straight (fig. 4-4B). Now place the crease gently down over the head of a pin, moving the pin forward and aft until the cutout balances (fig. 4-4C). Mark that point, unfold the cutout, and draw a vertical line (perpendicular to the waterline) that passes through that point (fig. 4-4D). That is, more or less, the center of lateral resistance of the vessel. In approximate terms that is the pivot point of the vessel and is comparable to the pivot point of the wind vane.

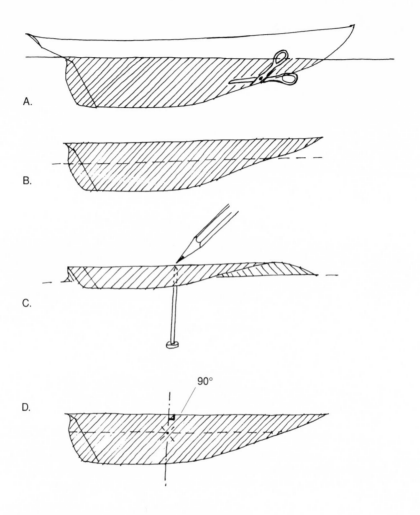

Fig. 4-4. *Finding the center of lateral resistance (CLR).*

Next, look at the sail plan and think about which sails are in front of, and which are behind, the CLR (fig. 4-5). On a ketch, the jib is out front, the mizzen out back; the main straddles it. In very approximate terms then the sail plan should balance. If the mizzen were much too big, it would act like the tail feathers of the wind vane and the boat would head up. If the jib were too big and the mizzen too small, the vessel's head would be blown off, downwind. The designer would not make a mistake like that, so one can reasonably expect the vessel to balance, as long as she is sailed properly.

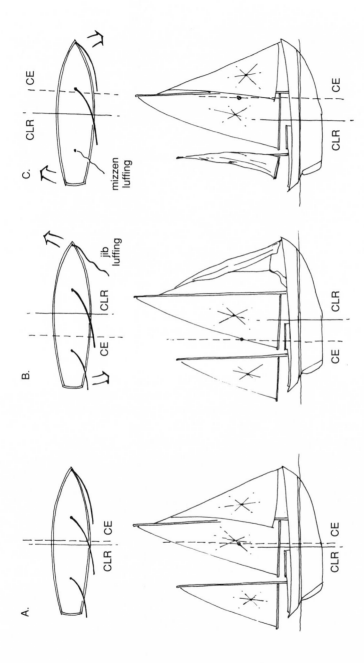

Fig. 4-5. Balance under sail. A. All sails drawing well; vessel is balanced. B. Jib luffing; center of effort (CE) shifts aft; vessel wants to head up. C. Mizzen luffing; CE shifts forward; vessel wants to head off.

Suppose we let the jib carry a luff, so that it is not drawing well. The mizzen will now be having more effect than the jib. The power of the sail plan, taken as a whole, will be shifted aft. What we are now talking about is the center of effort (CE) of the sail plan. This could be found by mathematically averaging all the force vectors from all the sails and finding the one resultant force of the whole plan. (See appendix I for a method of establishing the actual center of sail area of a sail plan.) But we do not need to know it so accurately. It will serve us well simply to understand that as we de-power the jib by letting it luff, we shift the CE aft, whereas if we de-power the mizzen, we shift the CE forward.

As the CE moves forward and aft (as we change the trim, or power, of each sail), we alter the balance of the vessel. If we allow the jib to luff and sheet in the mizzen, the boat heads up. This is because the CE moves aft of the CLR, creating a moment about the pivot point. The mizzen forces the vessel's stern to leeward and the slack jib allows her bow to come up into the wind. You can look at it in two ways, and you should grasp both. Letting the jib luff has taken some pressure off the bow, allowing it to head up into the wind. Or, letting the jib luff has shifted the CE aft, allowing the mizzen to take charge and forcing the stern to leeward. You may need to utilize either of these two viewpoints. If you suddenly need to get the bow to head up, slack the jib. If you need to get the stern to move to leeward, again let the jib luff. All maneuvers under sail are assisted by these moves. Maneuvering by rudder alone is inefficient and sometimes will prove to be impossible. The power of the rudder to steer can easily be overcome by the sails' own power to steer.

So what happened to the vessel who blew out her mizzen? Initially, she was well balanced because her designer balanced the sail plan so that the CE was very close to the CLR. The mizzen was doing its part to maintain the overall balance, so when it blew out, the CE suddenly shifted well forward of the CLR. This produced a powerful moment which allowed the jib to take charge, blowing the bow to leeward. Simultaneously the sudden release of pressure from the mizzen allowed the stern to jump to windward. The vessel took a quick swerve to leeward.

Now let us continue this scenario, and assume the worst—that there is an obstacle right in front of you, to leeward. What to do? Turning the rudder hard over to try to force the vessel to head up will have little effect without taking the proper steps to restore the balance of the vessel. She is hopelessly unbalanced with the CE way forward. It must come as an instinctive reaction to slack the jib sheet immediately. This will dump the power from the jib, allowing the CE to move back to the approximate center of the mainsail, more nearly in line with the CLR, restoring, or nearly restoring, her balance. The rudder now regains control and can steer the vessel to windward, clear of the obstacle. Before, she was so overpowered by the jib that the rudder would do little but stall in the water stream, in turbulence.

From this example it should appear that without a firm understanding of balance one can easily be overpowered by the sails. The same principles apply to any sail plan, from a sloop to a four-masted barque. These principles also apply to situations other than emergencies. Sail balance should be utilized to handle your vessel at any time when turning or maneuvering under sail. Docking, undocking, mooring, anchoring, heaving-to, even tacking in a light wind or in a tight spot—in all cases you can make the forces around you work for you, rather than against you, to your great advantage.

VARIATIONS OF SAIL PLAN

A sloop has a main and a jib, with a spinnaker for downwind work. That does not offer many choices, but there will be decisions to be made regarding which to set first, strike last, and when to reduce or increase sail area. Those decisions should be well thought out. Most of us learn to set the main first when getting under way, then the jib, and this is certainly the appropriate process for most occasions. But there are occasions when the opposite would be more advantageous, and the skipper who understands sail balance will know when.

Suppose you are in a crowded anchorage with little room to turn around for a downwind departure. If you set the main first, then set the jib as you break out the anchor, you will never get turned around before you are charging off on a reach. The mainsail, even with sheet slacked way out, presents so much wind resistance abaft your CLR that it will resist your efforts with the rudder to head off. It would be better to weigh anchor, set the jib, and use it to spin you around and sail out downwind. Once clear of the anchorage, you can round up (strike the jib to do so if necessary) and set the main.

On vessels with two or more masts, the options increase. On a schooner or ketch, you really must have a clear understanding of all the options, so that you are making your decisions wisely. A poor decision may mean poor efficiency, or it may mean disaster.

When under way and not maneuvering, you will still need to be aware of the balance of center of effort and center of lateral resistance. Your choice of sail combination must take balance into account. On a ketch the jib, main, and mizzen will balance. As the wind builds, or if you are shorthanded, or if you want to level the boat for a quiet lunch, a reduction in sail to mizzen and jib, or a reduction to mainsail alone, makes sense. Both are balanced sail plans, but there are other considerations besides balance here. Under mainsail alone, you will be able to handle your vessel more easily since you have only one sail to think about, and a self-tending one at that. But the mainsail is taller than the jib and mizzen combination, and so will produce a greater heeling force. It is also a bigger sail, which may be too big for you to handle comfortably by yourself if you should have to strike it or jibe it.

For coming into a harbor where maneuvering is the concern, you must think about tacking and jibing. You must consider the handling characteristics of the vessel under the sail combination you choose. If you will be making a downwind approach through a crowded harbor, you may not want that long main boom hanging out there to snag on other vessels. Furthermore, as you near the mooring, it will be handy (if you are under just mizzen and jib) to strike the jib at the last minute and be left with the mizzen only, providing the ultimate wind vane effect to help round you up quickly without gaining any headway. If you had the main up for this maneuver, it would be producing a great deal of forward drive as you round up, which might cause you to overshoot the mooring.

If on the other hand you are coming to anchor, perhaps you would prefer to have the jib down and furled before you make the final approach, leaving the foredeck clear to work with the anchor. In this case, it would be impossible to sail the boat without the mainsail up. The question would then be whether she would balance sufficiently under mizzen and main or if you would have to strike the mizzen and come in under main alone. It can be nice to have the mizzen back there to help you round up and to keep her headed into the wind once you have the anchor down.

PRACTICE

Try out different combinations when you have the time and the sea room, so you will know what works for your vessel. It is surprising how much you can learn in a single afternoon of practice maneuvers. Everyone on board learns from such a drill, especially if you rotate the positions. Set aside several hours on a day with a good breeze. Throw a marker of some kind overboard, anchored if possible so it does not blow away. Then practice making approaches to the mark from every direction. Round up to it as if it were a mooring. Sail up alongside it as if it were a dock. Heave-to alongside it as if it were a man overboard. Each of these techniques will be covered in subsequent chapters.

Do not feel that you must be at the wheel for each maneuver. You can learn at least as much by watching others and observing as they succeed or fail. You and your crew will learn a great deal about sail handling, tacking, jibing, and helmsmanship by such an exercise, and a learning experience is more challenging than a mere afternoon sail around the bay. The increase in your level of confidence will be noticeable by the end of the afternoon.

Further reading (see bibliography for details): Chase, *Introduction to Nautical Science,* chaps. 3 and 4; Glénans Sea Center, *The New Glénans Sailing Manual,* chap. 8; Henry English & Associates, *Trim for Speed* (videocassette); Ross, *Sail Power,* chaps. 5–8.

CHAPTER FIVE

BASIC MANEUVERS UNDER SAIL

TACKING

In its simplest form, on a sloop, tacking involves heading up, slacking the taut jib sheet, steering across the wind, and sheeting in the opposite jib sheet. Under less than ideal conditions, however, it may involve a carefully timed sequence of rudder changes, backing of various sails, and even backing of the vessel herself to bring a vessel about. This can happen under critical conditions, such as off a lee shore in a steep sea, when a single mistake would jeopardize the safety of the vessel.

In order to understand fully the sequence of events we must recall the discussion of balance, involving the location of the center of effort and center of lateral resistance. We will begin by tacking a ketch, watching the various forces at work as we go. The principles covered will be applicable to all other kinds of rigs, with some variations according to the number, size, and location of sails involved, with balance always the key.

The vessel is proceeding on the starboard tack, full and by (sails full, and sailing by the wind), with good headway, in a moderate sea. Jib, fore staysail, main, and mizzen are set and drawing well. The skipper gives the command "ready about." This instructs the crew to get ready for the maneuver. Probably all that they will need to do will be to check that the leeward (taut) jib sheet is coiled and ready to run and that the windward (slack) jib sheet is clear for hauling. If the jib is a big genoa, one or two crew will move to the foredeck to be ready to help drag the jib forward around the forestay. (If it is a roller-furling jib, this is simplified by rolling it up, then resetting it on the other tack.)

While the crew is getting ready, the helmsman should bear off a little to gain some extra headway. This precaution may prove critical in the tack, and will cost a negligible amount of ground to windward.

When all is ready, the skipper will order "hard alee." On high-performance vessels all that will happen here is that the helm will be put over, and all other activity will await further orders. This is because the jib will still be providing some lift as the vessel begins to head up, and there is no point in losing this power before the sail spills its own wind. At that point (which will be called by the foredeck crew), the command "break" will signal the leeward jib sheet tender to let the sheet run. On heavier vessels, especially those that have a hard time coming about, it may be better to let the jib sheet run immediately, at the "hard alee" command, to release the pressure on the bow, allowing it to respond more easily to the rudder. If the jib is held, it will be working against the rudder (it is keeping the CE way forward) and may be a hindrance to letting the bow come up.

The use of the rudder is also an important point here. If the rudder is put over too quickly, with great force, it will reach its stall point in the water, causing the waterstream to break into turbulent flow, creating unnecessary drag and reducing its effective lift. Remember it, too, is a wing, and you must keep it within the bounds of smooth hydrodynamic flow to get maximum effectiveness from it. Use the feel of the wheel or tiller as a guide; put the rudder over quickly, turning it until you feel a substantial resistance, then pause. As the vessel comes up into the wind and loses headway, that resistance will ease, and you can put it over some more. Continue this process until it is hard over. You will maintain maximum headway through the turn this way. On a very handy vessel, you may not even need full rudder. Experimentation with your particular vessel will refine this process.

If all is going well, the vessel will come quickly into the wind and across it, the jib will be helped across, all the other sails will luff their own way across on their travellers, and the jib crew will begin sheeting in the jib on the new tack. This moment is also important. The jib is luffing as the vessel comes through the eye of the wind, and the crew are in a mad rush to try to get it sheeted in right away. They must be precise in this. If they sheet in too soon, the jib will catch some wind on the wrong side—and be backwinded. This means that right at the most vulnerable moment—when the vessel has the least headway and the rudder has the least effect—the bow will get a shove in the wrong direction. She is turning here, and she has angular momentum that you are relying on to carry her through this delicate phase of the tack. If you kill this momentum, you will probably end up in irons, or falling back on the previous tack (see figure 5-1).

On the other hand, the jib sheet crew should be prompt and start sheeting in as quickly as possible once the sail is through the eye of the wind. This action, timed well, will let the wind catch the sail on the proper side, which will assist completion of the tack by pulling the bow around. Besides, if the crew members are quick enough they will be sheeting in the sail while it is still luffing, rather than having to fight a sail full of wind. If they are quick enough for this, they must be watching closely so that if the wind shifts slightly and starts to catch it aback they can slack off, to prevent it from getting aback.

The tack we have just covered was a smooth one—all went well. Let us now look at one where things are going against you. Perhaps there is little wind,

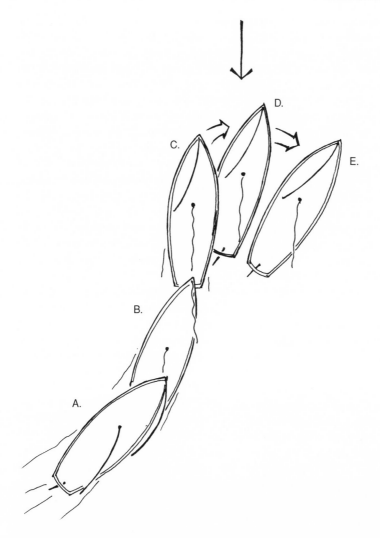

Fig. 5-1. *An unsuccessful tack. In this example, the jib was sheeted across too soon, caught aback, and forced the boat back onto the original tack. A. Sailing full and by. B. Leeward jib sheet is slacked off, jib is luffing. C. New leeward jib sheet is hauled in prematurely and the jib is caught aback. D. The jib, aback, forces the bow to fall off on the original tack. E. No amount of rudder will regain control until the boat is once again moving forward.*

and you are afraid the vessel may not have the momentum to get through stays (across the wind). You can employ your mizzen to help here. On a sloop or a schooner you would use the main. On a square-rigger you would use whatever fore-and-aft sail you had farthest aft, presumably the spanker. The idea here is to employ a sail well aft of the CLR to push the stern around. It will function just like the rudder, only in the wind instead of the water.

As you give the order "hard alee"—as the jib sheet is cast off—have the mizzen boom pushed to weather (to windward), perhaps by leaning into it yourself. Picture the sails now. The jib is luffing. It has released its pressure that was holding the bow off the wind. The fore staysail and the main are still drawing, but the staysail is small and not very far forward and the main is more or less straddling the CLR. These two are still providing a little drive, which will help keep the headway up, allowing the rudder to function. The mizzen, however, is now pushed up to windward. Your body is leaning to windward holding (with some difficulty) the mizzen boom up into the wind. The rudder is trying to shove the stern to leeward, so the bow will go to windward and make the tack. Picture your feet on the deck. What are they doing? All the force that you are feeling as you lean into the mizzen boom is being delivered to the boat through your feet, and they are shoving the stern to leeward. Literally, your body (with a little help from the mast and rigging) is delivering the force of the wind to the stern of your vessel in a complimentary direction to the rudder. If you are a windsurfer, you can probably relate this process to that of tacking a sailboard (see figure 5-2).

If the vessel should lose headway due to a steep head sea or because the crew let the jib get caught aback, or because there just is not enough wind to produce the headway you need, this maneuver will almost always get you through. It is quite possible for one or two people to significantly assist an 80-foot schooner through a tack by leaning on the main boom in this fashion. If the strain is too much for a few people to accomplish this, it can be done by rigging a quarter tackle from the sheet bail to the windward rail and hauling the boom to windward as you begin the tack. If you are headed into a tack under questionable circumstances, you should have this technique in mind and have people or tackles ready for the job.

Meanwhile, up on the foredeck, once your bow is pointing directly into the wind, you can have the jib sheet that was just let go—the one that was to leeward—hauled back in. This will back the jib, allowing the wind to help push the bow around. Note that this is not the same as sheeting in prematurely on the new tack. That effort will catch you aback on the new tack, shoving you back toward the old one. What we are talking about now is deliberately getting the jib filled aback while still on the old tack and having it help the vessel over onto the new one. If it is not convenient to back the jib, it may be simpler to have someone haul the staysail aback instead. If the staysail is set on a club, or boom, this may be the simplest move. If you anticipate difficulties in the tack, you might secure the staysail club to leeward with a preventer before you start the tack. Then the staysail will automatically fill aback as the bow comes into the wind. A word of caution, however: be sure your crew secures the club with a knot that can be slacked off gently, because it will have a great deal of strain on it. If the club is released suddenly and someone is in the way, that person could be hurt or knocked overboard (see figure 5-3).

True wind
direction

E.

D.

C.

B.

A.

Fig. 5-2. *"Windsurfing" a ketch through a tack. The crew member is pushing the mizzen boom to windward, which is helping to push the stern of the boat to leeward. A. Sailing full and by. B. "Hard alee." Jib sheet is slacked, rudder is put over. C. The mizzen is pushed to windward, forcing the stern to leeward. D. The jib is sheeted in, helping to pull the bow around. E. Under way on the new tack.*

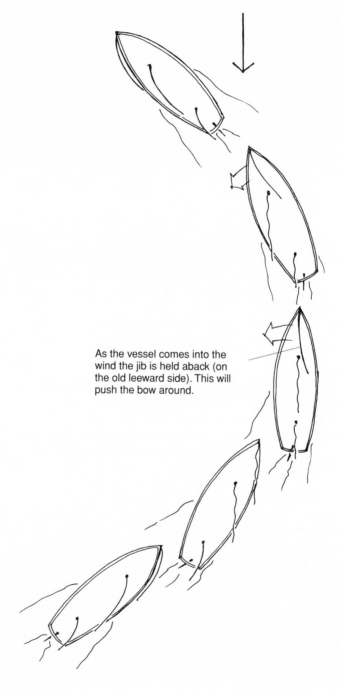

As the vessel comes into the wind the jib is held aback (on the old leeward side). This will push the bow around.

Fig. 5-3. *Backing the jib to assist with a tack.*

Once the bow is through the eye of the wind and the jib is filling, there is often a tendency for the person at the helm to steady up too soon—a mistake. Unless the vessel has maintained good headway through the tack, let her fall well off before easing up on the rudder. Most vessels are designed with a small amount of weather helm, which causes them to want to head up. This is normally counteracted by the rudder, but when the vessel is stopped (or nearly so) by the process of tacking, the rudder will not be able to counteract the tendency to head up. This problem is most evident with the schooner rig, whose large mainsail—located well aft—is so overpowering. Just when you thought the tack was complete, she will drive right back up into the wind and you will find yourself in irons. Therefore, let her fall off to a close reach before relaxing on the rudder; then, as she does head up, she will be gaining momentum and the rudder will have regained effectiveness before she gets into the wind. If you have really lost headway, you may have to slack off the mizzen and/or main sheets, shifting the CE well forward, allowing the jib to swing the bow off the wind in order to get headway started.

All of these points are based on balance. If you can fix the concept of the wind vane, with centers of effort and lateral resistance, in your mind so that they become intuitive, you will have the tools with which to become an expert in shiphandling under sail. Remember, the rudder cannot work without headway, but with a little wind you can use the sails as rudders in the air.

Practice these techniques. When you have time and a little sea room, try stalling your vessel in mid-tack; then use these methods to force her to fall off on the tack you want. Tack back and forth in quick succession—quickly enough so she cannot get any headway built up in between. Then you will have to use the sails, since the rudder will be useless. Once you have done it a few times, you will realize how much control you actually have, with or without headway. It may save you embarrassment (or more) someday.

JIBING

Jibing is a delicate operation at any time. It must be done carefully so as to keep the mainsail well under control throughout the jibe and, in a stiff breeze and a good sea, there is little margin for error. The principles that apply to small vessels apply equally to large vessels—only the stakes are higher. Offshore in a blow, it will often be inadvisable to jibe at all, and the skipper will resort instead to tacking—going the long way around. Since in a heavy sea tacking itself may not be feasible, good seamanship may well dictate striking the main before a jibe becomes necessary. Without the main (on almost any rig), jibing is not such a problem. It is the size of that sail, with its boom and gaff (if fitted), that makes it dangerous.

To accomplish a jibe safely, the main must be sheeted in virtually flat, jibed, and then let run out as quickly and smoothly as possible. On a ketch or yawl, this process will not affect the balance of the vessel nearly as much as it will on a schooner or even a sloop. On a schooner particularly, you must be very aware of your balance as you execute the maneuver. We will go over such a jibe on a schooner, offshore, in a moderate breeze and sea.

When running dead before the wind (or nearly so) on a schooner, the main, due to its enormous relative size and location so far aft, will virtually blanket the rest of the sails. Therefore, it is not uncommon to sheet the headsails in flat to prevent them from slatting around. This can be done with little or no adverse effect in preparation for a jibe. Then you will not have to concern yourself with them during the main event. The foresail, too, can be sheeted in, unless conditions are such that you feel it is safe to let it jibe all standing (untended).

Once these preparations are made, sufficient hands are gathered to sheet in the main. The helm should be given to an experienced person who will be able to feel the response and balance of the vessel as the jibe progresses. If it is rough, the helmsman should let the vessel come up to a broad reach so as to prevent all possibility of accidentally jibing while the crew is handling the sheet. However, you must think about where the CE is at this point. With all the forward sails blanketed, the entire effort of the rig is in the main, well abaft the CLR. She is dying to round up, and will do so given the slightest chance. If this happens, the rudder will have no power to prevent it, being greatly overpowered by the huge mainsail. Thus, the helmsman must strike a balance between keeping the vessel up enough to prevent an accidental jibe and keeping her off enough to prevent her rounding up. In a steep following sea this requires skill, concentration, some strength, and a good feel for the balance of the vessel, as felt through the rudder. At night the crew will be working almost entirely by feel. They must be able to feel where the wind is coming from on the backs of their necks. The helmsman must keep the vessel on a steady course relative to the wind, not the compass, shifting that course immediately if the wind shifts.

Once the main has been sheeted in flat (and the helmsman's job becomes more difficult the flatter the main is sheeted), the lead person on the sheet must get several turns around the bitts and all the others must get well clear of the line. If they have not disturbed the pile of line on the deck (where they have piled it as they hauled it in), it will not require coiling. This will save considerable time, but only if they are certain they have not disturbed the pile. (The line is going to need to run out rapidly and smoothly, without fouling around itself, or anybody, which could have disastrous results. Therefore, if the pile does get disturbed, it must be recoiled before proceeding.) The vessel is now running off on a very broad reach, with all sails sheeted in flat. Steering may be difficult under any circumstances, but in a rough sea, she will have a very strong tendency to round up. If she should get a start, it will be almost impossible to stop her and the only recourse will be to let the main sheet run and start the whole process over.

If all is going well, and all hands are ready, the skipper should now call "jibe-ho." The helmsman will bring her stern carefully, slowly, across the eye of the wind. When the wind does get around to the other side of the mainsail, it will come across with great authority, and a couple of things must happen immediately. The person tending the main sheet must give it all the slack it wants—let it run freely, but without losing the turns around the bitt. You must retain control, being very careful not to get a rope burn in the process. At the same time the helmsman must give a good deal of correcting rudder to stop the vessel from rounding up. The momentum of that mainsail slamming across (the slamming can never be completely prevented) will drive the vessel's stern around quite hard, and she will heel and commence an abrupt turn toward the wind, on the new tack. (The heeling of the vessel moves the center of effort out over the leeward side. This causes it to develop a strong moment that forces the vessel to turn into the wind.) The combination of slacking the sheet and correcting with the rudder will prevent her from coming too far before you regain control.

While the mainsail is jibing, other crew members can be bringing the other sails over, usually with a good deal less trouble.

This jibe is described for a schooner, because it is the most difficult rig to jibe, having the largest mainsail. Other rigs should be dealt with in much the same way, but will generally be less troublesome.

SETTING AND STRIKING SAIL

The evolution of setting and striking sails will be done quite differently when offshore and when in the harbor.

Starting in the harbor, at the mooring, it is usual to start setting sail from the aftermost one and work forward. On a ketch or a yawl, the mizzen will be a great help to steady the boat, keeping her head to the wind like the tail of a weather vane, while other preparations are being made. On some yawls, this is the primary function of the little mizzen or jigger. (There are yawls that were designed as cutters or sloops, with a very small mizzen added far aft to be used principally for this purpose.) Some vessels may get restless once the mainsail is set since it is not only large, but is also located close to or astride the center of lateral resistance. Therefore, on these vessels, it will be prudent not to set the main until all else is ready to go. In some cases you may want to set the headsails first: if, for instance, you were going to sail off downwind and wanted to pivot quickly 180 degrees after dropping the mooring.

In the usual case, though, you will set the aftermost sail first and sheet it in flat before moving to the next sail forward. It is important to keep that aftersail (even if it is the mainsail) sheeted as flat as you can get it, so as to keep it from developing any forward drive. You want it to luff, and if the vessel swings enough to fill it, you want it to look as little like a wing as possible. It should just push the stern back downwind, without developing any aerodynamic lift.

The next sail forward (on a sloop—the jib; on a schooner—the foresail; on a ketch or yawl—the main) can be set now, and the sheet for this one should be let fly, to give the sail full freedom to luff and not to fill. Remember this sail will have its CE forward of (or very close to) the CLR, and it will want to turn the weather vane downwind or drive the vessel ahead. You do not want this to happen until you let go the mooring. As the last (foremost) sails are hoisted, the mooring is let go and the vessel drops astern. You will now slack the sheets aft and haul in the sheets forward, thereby shifting the CE well forward, causing the vessel's head to fall off until you can settle onto the intended track. We will discuss the rest of this maneuver when we talk about mooring and anchoring (see pp. 81–85).

Setting sail at sea will normally require a completely different approach. You are already under way, not secured by a mooring; you will probably be rolling and/or pitching; and you may well be dealing with much greater wind speeds outside the shelter of the harbor.

Since you are already under way, you will not be trying to stabilize the vessel by use of the mizzen, as you were at the mooring. You will be on course, and in light winds you will simply set the new sail with the sheet slack, allowing it to luff until fully hoisted, when you will tension the sheet and go on. No problem.

The problem comes in the stronger winds and rolling seas that you will often encounter offshore. Luffing is hard on a sail, which beats itself back and forth, straining every stitch and fitting. In the sheltered harbor this is not normally a problem, but at sea it is often significant.

Heading up into the wind will always cause luffing, so this action, which is generally appropriate in sheltered waters, will no longer be a good option. How then can you set or strike a sail without it being either full of wind or luffing? For the mizzen or the main there is no alternative. You will have to let them luff, at least partially, in order to get them up or down. But for everything forward of the main on any vessel (assuming the main is set), you can head off. This might at first sound like a strange move, but doing so will blanket the forward sails in the lee of the mainsail. In a gale of wind, you can set or strike a sail in the lee of another with ease.

There is an added advantage here. By heading off and running with the wind abaft the beam, you have dramatically decreased the apparent wind, as well as the apparent speed of the approaching waves. It is amazing how a wild gale and a rough sea seem to smooth right out when you run off before it. The bow is no longer leaping over and diving into the seas, the screeching wind seems to ease right off to a breeze, and the jib that was straining at every seam suddenly goes limp in the lee of the mainsail, or foresail. If you have a bowsprit, you will now be able to climb out on it to furl the jib in relative safety, whereas a moment before it would have been quite dangerous to do so.

When hoisting (or lowering) sail in a rolling sea, you will have to worry about the boom. On a gaff-rigged vessel the gaffs too will be a major concern. When the sail is set and drawing, these are well under control, being under constant pressure from the sail. But during the hoisting or lowering phase these can become dangerous. The boom can be controlled to some extent by the sheet, but the gaff will be virtually uncontrolled while hoisting and lowering. It will swing around overhead, with some potential for damage to the sail, the rig, or the crew.

The best way to minimize the danger from booms and gaffs is to keep some wind in the sail. By putting the vessel on a reach when you hoist or lower a big sail, and by adjusting the sheet to spill most but not all of the wind, you will maintain some pressure on both the boom and gaff, which will limit the amount of the vessel's swing. When hoisting, this will mean keeping the sheet in tight until the sail is nearly up. When lowering you will sheet it in very soon after you start lowering. The use of quarter tackles on the main boom—tackles which lead from the port and starboard quarters (on deck) to the main sheet bail (on the boom)—will be very helpful to keep the main boom in control during this procedure. A peak downhaul on a gaff sail—a single line from the peak of the gaff to the deck—can be used to help control a gaff. This line may in fact be necessary to haul the peak down when a big sail is full of a breeze and should be left rigged when sailing offshore, since it cannot be rigged when it is needed.

Downhauls in general are not often used in coastwise sailing but are important to have rigged offshore. As we have seen, it is often not safe to head up or luff to strike a sail, so it may have to be hauled down while still somewhat full of wind. This holds true for all sails, and all sails may need downhauls for the purpose. They are simply a single part of strong line secured to the head of the sail, whose other end runs to the deck where it can be gotten hold of when needed.

REEFING

Reefing a sail involves reducing the area by any one of a number of means. Traditionally, the sail would be lowered partially and then reset with the lower part secured. Or, in the more modern application, the sail is rolled up around a spar, a stay, or inside the mast.

Traditional sails are equipped with reef tacks and clews, which are reinforced securing points along the luff and leech, respectively (fig. 5-4). These get secured to the boom when reefing and take the place of the regular tack and clew as the point of attachment for the lower corners of the sail. Also fitted are reef points, which are small lines run through grommets in the sail, spaced evenly along the sail between the reef tack and clew. These get tied together around the reduced portion of the sail, to secure it.

The first step to tie in the reef will be to secure the reef tack (forward, lower corner of the reefed sail) to the tack fitting on the boom. Next, a reef tackle is used to haul the reef cringle (the fitting secured to the sail at the location of the reef clew, the after lower corner of the reefed sail) out as far as it can go on the boom, within reason. (On some vessels, a reefing pennant—a single part of strong line—is left permanently rigged from the reef cringle, down and through a cheek block on the boom, and forward, where it can be easily reached from on

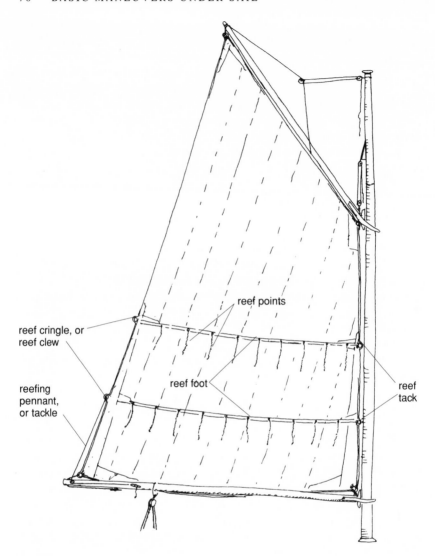

reef points

reef cringle, or
reef clew

reefing
pennant,
or tackle

reef foot

reef
tack

Fig. 5-4. *A traditional gaff sail showing reefing gear.*

deck. The reef tackle is then secured to this pennant, saving the crew from
having to climb onto the boom to reach the cringle, a dangerous practice.)
Herein lies another common misconception. The reef foot is not intended to be
hauled extremely taut, and doing so can damage the sail. It should be hauled
taut enough to hold the foot straight along the boom, without being stretched.
Now a lashing is passed to secure this clew to the boom, and the unused lower
portion of the sail is furled up tight and tied with the reef points. These should

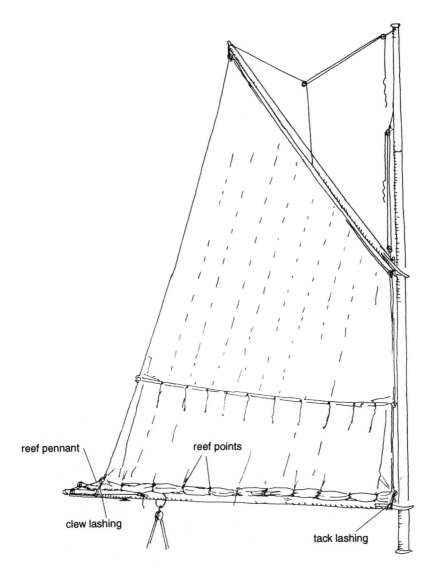

reef pennant

reef points

clew lashing

tack lashing

Fig. 5-5. *The same sail, reefed.*·

be tied together, one from each side, passing between the real foot of the sail and the boom, not under the boom. (This is not possible if the sail is fitted with a boltrope on the foot, slid into a slot in the boom.) This permits a little give. If tied under the boom the reef points become too firm and may over-strain the sail. The reef points are there to keep the lower, reefed, part of the sail from flapping in the breeze and are not intended to hold a substantial part of the load of the sail. The sail can now be hoisted as usual (fig. 5-5). If you have two sets of reef points and you have tied in the first, or lower reef, watch very closely as the sail goes up to ensure that no one has inadvertently tied one of the upper reef points, as you will rip the sail if one of these should come up tight. If you subsequently decide to tie in a second reef, leave the first tied in. You will want that first reef again later as the wind eases.

The secret to tying in a good reef is timing. It is well said that the time to tie in a reef is the first time you think of it. Too often skippers postpone the inevitable until the sea is too rough to do a good and safe job of it. The process necessarily involves some risk, as your crew will be balancing on the cabin top while tying the reef points, and reaching out to the end of the boom while tying in the reef clew. If this work is done before the gale is howling, you can watch the onset of the blow with a feeling of some guarded smugness. If you wait until conditions become severe, you will endanger your crew, and end up with a sloppy reef.

There are many newer reefing systems in use now, most of which are fairly straightforward versions of the above. Slab reefing is very popular and consists essentially of the traditional reef without the reef points. In this case, the reef tack and clew are secured as with the traditional method, or with various labor-saving variations, but the reefed portion of the sail is left unsecured. (An improvement on this, called jiffy-reefing, has the lines for securing the tack and clew permanently rigged so they are at the ready to simply haul down.) The sailcloths in use now tend to be stiff enough so that they do not flog as much as cotton would. This method does, however, require that the cloth be strong enough or reinforced to handle the full strain of being supported only by the two corners, as a loose-footed sail would be. Roller reefing involves rolling the sail up around the boom, the stay (in the case of a jib), or around a rod inside a hollow mast. Each of these has its advantages. They are all simplifications in terms of manpower, though the roller-furling mechanism represents a complication in gear.

Roller-furling gear is well loved by all who have used it without having it fail. But if gear failure occurs, it is terrifying to watch your entire jib, or main, suddenly appear in the teeth of a booming gale just when you thought you had everything snugged down and secure. The good versions of this gear are quite good, and expensive, and the poor versions are very dangerous. If you have any doubts at all, you should add stops around the furled sail to prevent its coming unfurled accidentally. A quick solution is to take a spare halyard and wind it around the furled sail (fig 5-6). This can be done from the deck in a matter of seconds with little difficulty, and undone just as easily. To do this around a furled jib, take the end of a spare jib halyard and walk forward to the base of the jib's stay. Slack the jib's sheets enough so that you can bring them to the same spot, and then simply wind the halyard around the furled sail.

Further reading (see bibliography for details): Maloney, *Chapman Piloting,* chap. 10; Chase, *Introduction to Nautical Science,* chap. 4; Glénans Sea Center, *The New Glénans Sailing Manual,* chaps. 8 and 9.

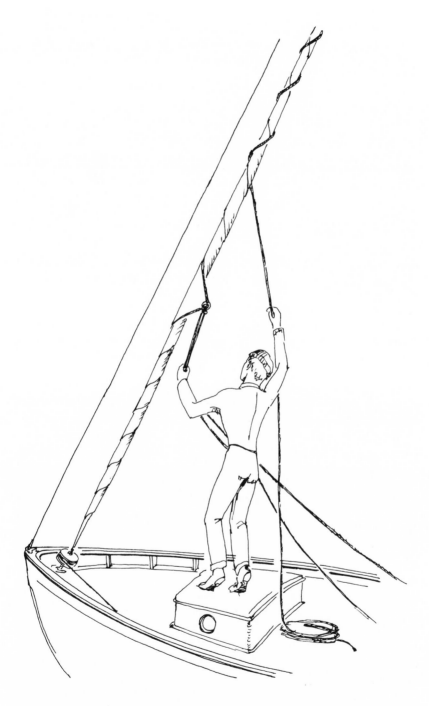

Fig. 5-6. *Passing a spare halyard around a roller-furled jib adds an extra measure of security.*

CHAPTER SIX

ADVANCED MANEUVERS UNDER SAIL

Having discussed setting and striking sail and some basic maneuvers, we can move on to the more complex ones, where it will become even more apparent how important it is to have a thorough understanding of your vessel's center of effort, center of lateral resistance, and balance. While the new sailor may be intimidated by the prospects of docking a vessel under sail for the first time, she should discover from this chapter that the principles of the maneuver are easily grasped. The sailor should then make a practice of watching others perform the maneuvers, observing, analyzing, and trying to predict the commands of the captain and the movements of the vessel.

A text entitled *Shiphandling*, by King and Noel, lists four phases through which a shiphandler passes. Although this text was written for masters of large merchant ships, the same process is observable aboard smaller ones. In phase one, the novice shiphandler has an exaggerated respect for the forces involved, amounting to timidity. All maneuvers are accomplished very slowly and cautiously. In phase two, confidence wells up prematurely, and is also exaggerated. The shiphandler becomes brash and reckless, and may start showing off. Phase three comes with an accident or a near miss. It is a sobering and humbling (if not disastrous) experience, but leads to phase four, when the person has acquired wisdom through experience. Confidence returns slowly, care and thoughtfulness go into every maneuver, and precision is the goal. Following phase four, the shiphandler is afforded the respect and confidence of her juniors and seniors. The trick, of course, is to avoid the second and third steps.

This chapter discusses anchoring, mooring, and docking under sail, in that order. Of these, anchoring is generally the simplest, because normally no great precision is required in the placement of the anchor, so the skipper need not stop the vessel exactly at a given spot. She will of course have a spot in mind, but an error of a boat length or two is not generally critical, and whether or not the vessel is moving at 1 or 2 knots is usually immaterial. When picking up a mooring, the situation becomes more complex, because the vessel must be stopped or nearly stopped at a precise spot, although the exact heading will not normally be critical. Also, the heading on which you will approach the mooring will usually be the ideal approach direction for stopping, that is, upwind. Docking, however, requires that everything be right. You must stop the vessel at exactly the right spot, on exactly the right heading, and that heading will not necessarily be the ideal approach heading in terms of wind and current, as it will be determined by the lie of the dock.

As in all sailing maneuvers, there are many ways to approach any berthing problem, and the best one will be different for every combination of skipper, vessel, wind, current, and berth. There is no single best method to anchor, moor, or dock any particular vessel under sail, but a few situations will be examined that highlight some of the practices involved in these maneuvers.

ANCHORING

The approach to an anchorage may be from any direction (relative to the wind direction), but we will look at the upwind and the downwind approaches. The points to consider are controlling your speed, maintaining steerage and control, establishing a sail striking sequence, and stopping the vessel with precision.

In an upwind approach, it will generally be easy to control your speed, which you do by luffing the sails to slow down and filling them to speed up. To reduce speed on a downwind approach, you usually can sheet in the sails more or less flat, thus presenting the smallest possible sail area to the wind. This can be very effective, though on a schooner it can make your steering difficult for the same reasons discussed under jibing. Speed can also be reduced by striking sail, but control does not only imply slowing down. It may mean speeding up, and it may mean utilizing your sails to help steer or maneuver the vessel. The words steer and maneuver are used here to differentiate between turning while moving, using mainly the rudder (steering), and turning while stopped or nearly so, when the rudder is ineffective (maneuvering).

The order in which you will strike sail will be critical to maintaining this control. You must strike any sails that will hamper your maneuverability while keeping those you will need for the particular maneuver. For instance, you will probably strike the jib first. It is so far forward it will shift your CE—changing your balance—every time it fills, luffs, or gets blanketed. The mizzen, if you have one, seemingly fits the same description, but you will want it at the end of the maneuver to help round up and keep your head to the wind once the anchor goes down. On a schooner the main will serve this purpose.

Stopping will generally mean coasting to a halt, though there are ways to brake your vessel using the rudder, the sails, or, of course, the anchor itself. The rudder is a moderately effective brake, applied by shifting it from hard over on one side to hard over on the other, back and forth, called "cycling" the rudder. Sails can be hauled aback—literally stuck out into the wind—as a substantial wind brake. And, finally, as long as your speed is not excessive, the anchor can be dragged, or set, and the chain or rode surged (allowed to slip, under control) to slow and stop you.

Of the above braking techniques, the use of the sails bears amplification. This can be a very effective technique for use in a downwind approach. We will step through such an approach on a schooner to illustrate several points.

Assume you are aboard an 80-foot schooner running downwind into an anchorage area with limited maneuvering room (fig. 6-1). If you have any light air sails, such as jib topsails or gaff topsails, you will want to take them in well outside the anchorage. Since the jib and fore staysail are already blanketed by the main, you will strike them while still outside as well, so they can be tidied up and given a temporary furl (save the finished furl for later), before you begin your maneuver.

With the foredeck clear, you can now swing out your anchor and make it ready to let go, hanging from the rail or the cat head, just above the water's edge, so it will not drag through the water and bang up your topsides. The crew that was involved in all of this is now free (with the exception of one to stand by the anchor) to man the foresail halyards and the fore and main sheets. You may or may not be running wing and wing, that is, with fore and main on opposite sides. Set up a preventer on the foreboom. This line will lead from the outboard end of the boom to a solid securing point well forward on the foredeck, holding the boom in place with the sheet opposing it (see figure 6-1A). This combination means the foreboom cannot move, but will stay boomed well out regardless of what direction you turn. This will become your brake.

You will make your approach to the side of your anchorage spot, leaving it to leeward; that is, passing it on the same side as that which your main boom is on and leaving enough room to easily accommodate your turning circle. As you approach a point abeam of your anchorage spot, you will make preparations to jibe the main, sheeting it in tight. Just after you pass abeam of the spot (the exact distance will require knowledge of your particular vessel's characteristics for turning and headreach), you will put your helm over and jibe. Do not let the main sheet run after the main jibes; hold the main in flat. That huge sail will act as a giant wind rudder to help your turn. It will be extremely effective (fig. 6-1B). (It is also possible to make your approach from the other side, leaving the anchorage spot to windward and rounding up without jibing. In this case the turn will be slower and your turning circle will be bigger, since in the jibing scenario the forcefulness of the jibe drives your vessel around quite hard.)

Two things will now happen to stop your vessel, even if you have a good deal of headway. First, the tight turn will consume much of the energy of your speed. Second, the foresail will now go to work as a wind brake. As you round up, the foresail—still held out by the preventer—will fill aback (see figure 6-1E). You must be sure the preventer is strong enough for the task. As the vessel slows you will ease this off, either to retain a little headway to get to your desired position or to prevent its pushing your bow off the wind. You must be sure you have had it secured with a belay that can be slacked off under strain.

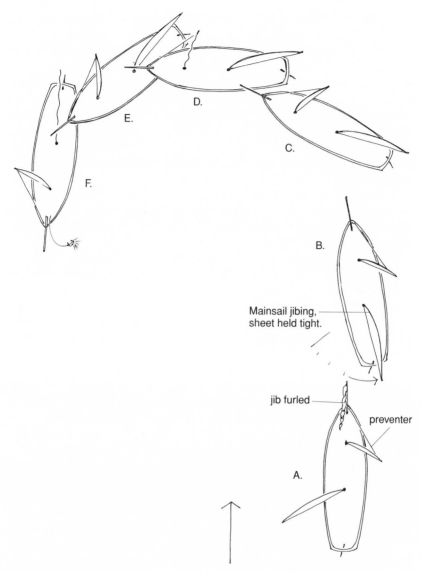

D.

E.

C.

F.

B.

Mainsail jibing,
sheet held tight.

jib furled

preventer

A.

Fig. 6-1. *A schooner making a downwind approach to an anchorage, using the foresail, on a preventer, as a brake.*

The anchor will be let go at the desired point and can be used as an additional brake if needed. If quarters are very tight it could even be let go at about the same time you turn into the jibe (at the location shown in figure 6-1B), but you must be aware that you will be placing quite a strain on the anchor, chain, and windlass by doing so. In moderate conditions this works fine and can enable you to jibe, turn, and be anchored in a very few moments, with only a ship length or so of turning room. It is impressive when done right, and embarrassing or disastrous when it has been misjudged—so practice.

To do the same thing on a ketch, put the preventer on the main or the fore staysail (although this will provide a relatively small braking force). On a yawl, you can use the mizzen for the push through the jibe, but using the main for a brake may not work. Because it is so large compared to the little mizzen, it may just shove the vessel's head off the wind again. (You must always think of the balance of the sails, and which sail will dominate in the present configuration.) In this case you might be able simply to use the turn to kill your headway, with the option of making two complete round turns if your vessel carries her way well.

On an upwind approach nothing quite so spectacular will happen, though the various sails may still be used as brakes by hauling them to windward as you approach. This will require brute strength rather than the finesse of the downwind approach technique.

The upwind approach will be simplest if the last tack before the final leg is made a little late. Then the final approach can be made on a very close reach instead of hard on the wind, leaving a little allowance for last-minute wind shifts, avoiding mooring buoys or boats and changes of plan. This will also allow the headsails to be taken in early, since you will not need all sail to gain ground to windward. It is a big help to get the headsails down and cleared away well outside the anchorage, giving the foredeck crew a clear deck to work on when preparing the anchor. The rest of the crew will then have fewer sheets and halyards to cope with. When making an approach on a close reach you can regulate your speed well by slacking your sheets and luffing or hauling them in to produce drive. Be careful not to allow too much headway to develop.

Stopping on an upwind approach is generally just a matter of losing momentum by letting the sails spill more and more of their wind until you coast up to the desired spot with all sails luffing. The anchor is then let go and the main (on a ketch or yawl) or the fore (on a schooner) is either lowered or the sheet let run, while the mizzen (ketch or yawl) or the main (schooner) is sheeted in tight. This will shift the CE as far aft as possible, so that the vessel will continue pointing into the wind like the weather vane.

On a sloop, the jib still may be struck early, unless it is felt that you need the extra pull to get to the anchorage. Once the anchor is let go, the jib must be struck, or you will find the vessel sawing back and forth with every luff of the sails. Get the jib down and the main sheeted in flat. If your vessel is still too restless (because the main is straddling the CLR and may want to fill away on alternate tacks, even though it is sheeted in flat), you will just have to strike it quickly. On sloops where this is a problem, the solution may be to strike the main early and sail in on just the jib. This can work particularly well if you have a roller-furling jib, in which case you can furl the jib a little at a time to adjust speed in the final approach.

MOORING

The approach to a mooring is essentially the same as the approach to an anchorage, except that now you must have a much more precise feel for the stopping characteristics of your vessel. The best way to get this feel is to practice often. Establish what you plan to do in case you miss the mooring. Depending on the layout of the mooring area, you may be able to keep going, fill away, circle around, and try again, or, lacking room for that, you may have to jibe or tack around quickly, in a tight circle, and get back out the way you came in.

To turn your vessel around when you have little or no headway requires that you fully understand sail balance (see figure 6-2). Simply turning the rudder will not work, and relying on this may put you in a dangerous situation. With no headway, the rudder has no effect, and the sails will completely dominate the maneuver. You must make them work for you rather than against you. To head off, you must get the CE forward. Remove all effective sail area aft by slacking the sheet on the mizzen (ketch or yawl) or main (schooner). (On a ketch or a yawl, back the mizzen to help push you around, as shown in figure 6-2B. Alternatively, you may even want to strike the mizzen, to remove any possiblility of its preventing you from falling off.) Load the sail area forward. To do this, since you have probably struck the headsail(s), you will need to reset them quickly (fig. 6-2B,C). This is one reason why they were not given a permanent furl. On a schooner, get the main out as far as you can by overhauling the main sheet—forcing slack into it—and physically pushing the boom out. Simultaneously, have the crew set and sheet in the headsails. Back them if necessary to get the maximum push to leeward. Even slacked way out, the main may be so big (relatively) that it will prevent you from falling off beyond a beam reach. You had better know this before you start, and plan accordingly.

When you are aware of possible difficulties, your plan should include having the main engine running throughout the operation, just in case. You must realize that in some cases even the main engine cannot overcome the power of the sails when they decide to take charge. If this should happen you will have no alternative but to round up and start over, or, in an emergency, to drop the anchor.

DOCKING

The most important decision you will make in a docking maneuver under sail will be whether or not to try it. If you do try it, and cause some damage, there will be little sympathy from those who have suffered the damage. It will be difficult to justify your attempt if the only reason for it was to see if you could succeed. However, if you have engine trouble, and anchoring or mooring off is not an option, you will have a good reason for docking under sail and will be glad you have learned how to do it.

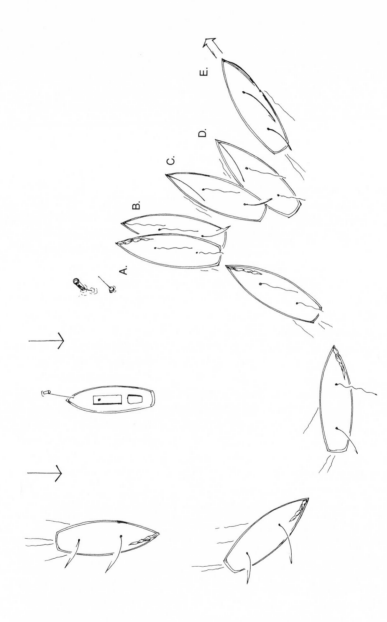

Fig. 6-2. A vessel, missing a mooring, falling off to make another attempt. Note the moored vessel to port. This obstacle makes it dangerous to fall off in that direction. A. The mooring has been missed. B. The jib is backed. C. The jib is reset; the mizzen is backed. D. The jib is backed. E. The vessel is again under way.

Fig. 6-3. *Observing the strength and direction of the current flowing past a buoy.*

Docking uses the same principles of balance and control discussed for anchoring and mooring. Now, though, you must get the vessel stopped at just the right spot and on just the right heading—parallel to the dock. There is no need to reiterate the same set of concepts and techniques. They just have to be a little more precise, and this comes only with practice. Finding the time and place to practice is the trick. You will not want to practice at the town dock, with fancy yachts to bump into. Instead, try setting out several buoys in a line to simulate the dock edge. If you use a real dock use plenty of fenders, on the boat and on the dock. Because it is difficult to get this practice, most sailors never get enough experience to want to attempt a docking under sail. There is nothing wrong with avoiding this—it is prudent. But if you can find the time and the place to work on it, you will hone your sailing skills to a fine edge that will set you apart from the crowd.

The best way to learn is to begin trying to dock in a small vessel and progress slowly upwards in length and displacement. If you commit yourself to this kind of program, you will become a very fine sailor indeed. As a paid captain, however, you should not take such risks without the owner's blessing.

There are several important points to consider. First, realize that the wind may be flukey around the dock, blowing around the wharf and the buildings on the waterfront. Second, the current may be flukey there as well, as it flows around the wharf and the shoals at the harbor's edge. Watch carefully for the

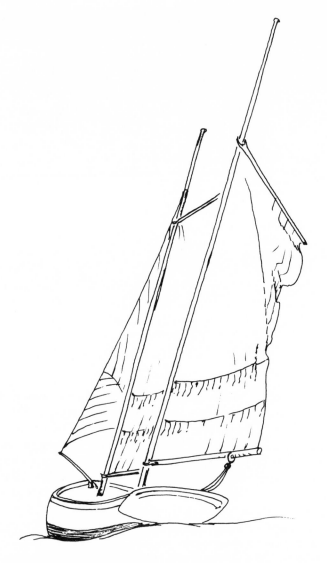

Fig. 6-4. *A gaff-rigged sail, scandalized.*

telltale signs of these changes—the flags and pennants near the dock, the lobster pot-buoys, moorings, or seaweed floating in the vicinity (see figure 6-3). A dry run, passing as close as possible to the dock, might be in order to investigate such things. Or send a crewmember in the dinghy to look the situation over.

Think about your main boom. Will it overhang the dock when you come alongside? Will your main sheet snag on something there? If those are possibilities, you may want to strike your main and come in without it. Will your sail combination provide sufficient speed to maintain control, yet allow you to stop when you get there? Will it be quick and easy to strike once you get your lines ashore?

On a yawl or ketch, you may want to strike the main and jib and come in under mizzen and staysail. This combination will generally give you good control, balance, and moderate speed and will be quick and easy to strike. On a schooner which will sail under foresail and staysail, that may be the best combination, because if you need the mainsail to sail her, you will have a handful when you get alongside. You may not actually have to strike a big sail to kill it. Under most circumstances you can just drop it a little way, letting it remain in a very loose, baggy state called "scandalized." It will luff and flog a bit if there is a breeze, but it will not fill. With a gaff-rigged sail you can lower just the peak halyards, about halfway, to accomplish this (see figure 6-4). In both cases, be sure to bring the boom under control with the sheet.

On a sloop, come in under mainsail or jib, but probably not both. Again, if you have a roller-furling jib, it will allow you very precise control of your speed, as you roll it up a little at a time during your final approach. When you finally come alongside, with a quick tug on the furling line you will have no flogging sails to deal with as you pass your docklines.

CHAPTER SEVEN

HEAVING-TO

THE PROCESS

The goal in heaving-to is to stop the vessel. There are various reasons for doing so, such as stopping for lunch or a swim on a nice day, or reducing the strains on the vessel, crew, and rig in a gale. The aim is to achieve a balance of opposing forces that will hold the vessel as nearly in one place as possible.

Sir Isaac Newton said that an object in motion stays in motion, and an object at rest stays at rest, until acted upon by an external force. A boat is constantly subjected to external forces, and these forces are constantly changing, so it is virtually impossible to keep a boat completely at rest. The best one can do is to minimize movement with a well-adjusted balance of forces.

First we will discuss the rudder. Securing it hard over to windward will cause the vessel's head to come up into the wind when she gains headway. This will cause the sails to spill the wind, killing that headway. If she starts to back down, the rudder will then force her stern to windward and her bow to leeward. The motion developed is much like that of a leaf falling.

The only problem with this rudder arrangement is that many vessels could gain enough headway to carry right through the wind and tack. Once tacked, the rudder (still being secured on what would now become the leeward side) would steer her off the wind, so that she would continue to gain headway until she finally jibed over and headed back up. This could be dangerous and would definitely be uncomfortable. Therefore, the sails must be adjusted to prevent this from occurring. The solutions for the different rigs are discussed next, but in general all require sails forward and aft counteracting one another. The after sails are sheeted to leeward, snugly, and the forward ones are sheeted to windward. The effect of this combination is illustrated in figure 7-1. (Note that although these diagrams represent a ketch, vessels with other rigs will respond in a similar way, with different sails performing the various functions. These sail combinations are discussed next.)

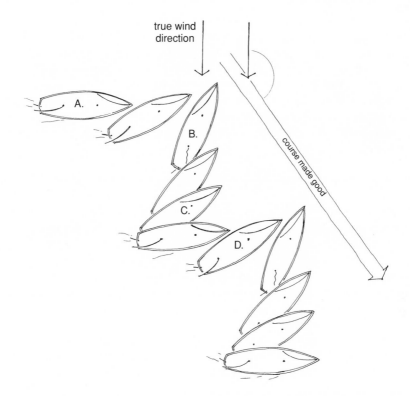

true wind
direction

course made good

A.

B.

C.

D.

Fig. 7-1. *A ketch hove-to. The motion is comparable to that of a leaf falling. The resulting course made good will generally be somewhat forward of directly to leeward.*

In figure 7-1A, the vessel is broadside to the wind. The pressure on the mizzen is trying to drive the vessel up into the wind, and the pressure on the jib is trying to drive the vessel off the wind. If the mizzen takes charge, it will drive the boat's head into the wind (with or without the assistance of the rudder) until it starts to luff.

Figure 7-1B shows that the jib is aback and the mizzen is luffing and no longer exerting any driving force. The jib will take over, forcing the bow to fall off. Since the boat's headway died off as soon as the driving power of the mizzen was lost, the rudder no longer has any effect and so allows the vessel to fall off.

Figure 7-1C shows that since the jib is aback, it will not develop any forward thrust. Rather, it will be pushing the boat backwards, acting as a brake.

Finally, in figure 7-1D, as the mizzen fills again and develops forward thrust, the process is repeated. The boat gains headway and heads up, the mizzen luffs, the jib pushes the bow back, and she falls off again.

The effects of this process are quite noticeable. The boat will pull ahead, round up, luff, stall, fall off, and start over. In the process she will also sideslip, more or less, depending on her underbody shape and the amount of windage aloft. Since there is some headway involved in the process, the boat will make good a course that is somewhat forward of dead downwind. The actual direction will be different for every vessel and every different combination of wind and sea conditions, but for an example, an eighty-foot, sixty-ton, gaff-rigged schooner of traditional design can be expected to make good a course of about 130 degrees (+/– 15 degrees) off the wind at about 1.5 knots (+/– 0.5 knots) in a gale with 10- to 15-foot seas, riding under storm trysail and backed jib or fore staysail.

SAIL COMBINATIONS

The actual sail combinations used in heaving-to will vary from one boat to another and, in different conditions, aboard a single vessel. But the principle is always to have a sail set to leeward aft, and one backed to windward forward.

On a sloop, there are not many choices for the "after" sail, but you can either set a full mainsail, a reefed main, or a trysail. Forward, you will set a jib or a storm jib sheeted aback (fig. 7-2). On a cutter, a club staysail is the usual choice because the club makes it easy to secure the sail aback. When you heave-to on a nice day to chat with a passing boat or to pick up your hat in the water, you can even heave-to with a big Genoa set. The only problem is that it will be chafing against the windward shrouds. You will want to be certain to have checked that there are no sharp edges on the spreaders or elsewhere that might tear the sail.

On a yawl or a ketch, the mizzen will normally be the choice aft, and the jib or staysail forward. On a big ketch in a stiff breeze, the full mizzen may be too much, and you might want to reef it down. (An over-large mizzen could drive your vessel's bow into and through the wind, causing her to tack.) One of the major advantages of the ketch rig is the ability to balance your sail plan under so many different combinations. If you wanted to ride a little farther off the wind—that is, with the bow pointing more downwind—you might want to try striking the mizzen and setting a trysail on the mainmast (or a reefed main) and a backed staysail (or jib). This combination shifts most of the sail area forward of the center of effort, thereby causing the bow to fall well off. You then rely on the rudder to bring her up into the wind. This will mean you will also maintain more headway than leeway, which could, under some circumstances, be desirable.

On a schooner in heavy weather, you will normally set a reefed main or trysail aft and a backed staysail and/or jib forward (fig. 7-3a). Schooners have such large mainsails that even if they are reefed, a small staysail could not balance them. Therefore, the jib, or the foresail, may be left up. Either of these will work, if kept lashed aback. It is possible to heave-to under four lower sails on a schooner in a moderate to light breeze, when stopping for some reason other than heavy weather (fig. 7-3b).

Fig. 7-2. *A sloop hove-to with Genoa aback. This is fine for a short time in good weather, but the sail will be chafing against the windward shrouds, with potential for damage.*

Once you get set up for a certain sail combination, watch and see how the boat rides. If she wants to tack, your center of effort is too far aft. Your first and simplest correction should be to slack the sheet of the aft sail. This will allow her to fall off the wind farther, and that sail will luff sooner as she starts to head up, killing the headway that was driving her across the eye of the wind. If this is not sufficient you will have to set more sail forward (sheeted aback), or shorten sail aft by reefing or changing to a trysail.

The boat will settle down slowly. You must give her time to establish her pattern. It will probably surprise you how comfortable and steady she will be. If it is blowing a gale, the relief on you, the crew, and the vessel is extraordinary.

Once the pattern is established, you should try to estimate your set and drift. You must maintain your position fixing just as carefully as if you were

Fig. 7-3a. *A schooner hove-to under storm sail. The storm trysail is set from the mainmast, sheeted to leeward, and the fore staysail is sheeted to windward, aback.*

under way—because you are under way. You will be making a knot or two (possibly more), and the direction of your drift will be somewhat forward of dead to leeward. If you are in a gale, and it blows for a day or two, your vessel can cover a substantial distance. Watch the weather and the set of the currents in the area. Your direction and rate of drift will depend on these. If you should need to cut down on your drift to leeward, running the engine ahead will direct the drift farther forward, which may suffice.

There are many reasons to heave-to, besides heavy weather. It is unfortunate that more sailors do not appreciate the usefulness of this technique for circumstances such as waiting for a berth, the tide, or daylight; for a swim call; or for a smoother lunch on a rough day. If something needs your attention below and you are not comfortable leaving the sailing to the guests, heave-to.

Fig. 7-3b. *A schooner hove-to under four lowers. This combination is suitable only for light to moderate conditions.*

Think of it as putting on a parking brake, but one that does not hold you completely stationary.

Further reading (see bibliography for details): Chase, *Introduction to Nautical Science,* chap. 4.

CHAPTER EIGHT

MAN OVERBOARD

The most terrifying sound on board any vessel is the cry of "man overboard!" This is true on power vessels as well as on sailing vessels, though there are several reasons why the risk of falling overboard and the difficulty of retrieving a victim are greater under sail than under power. First, because sailing vessels routinely sail at steep angles of heel, with their lee deck edge near or in the water, movement on deck is dangerous. Second, the necessity of handling flogging or jibing sails while standing on an exposed deck invites accidents. Third, the difficulty in stopping and turning a sailing vessel in a fresh breeze makes finding and recovering a person from the water difficult. As shown in the discussion of maneuvering vessels under sail (see pp. 55–63), one often cannot simply put the wheel over and expect the vessel to turn around. Sail trim and balance usually have to be considered. Valuable time will be lost while getting sufficient crew on deck to handle sails to make turning around possible.

JOB ONE: STAY ON BOARD

It is absolutely imperative that all persons aboard get training in the kinds of safety procedures that will prevent them from falling overboard. "All persons aboard" is deliberately phrased. Safety is a subject in which crew, passengers, guests, and dignitaries alike must receive training. The members of the ship's company who know the least about sailing will be most at risk when moving about on deck, and those same people may well be needed to assist if a vital member of the ship's crew is in the water.

As with most emergencies, there is no knowing when this one will strike, so training cannot be put off until some convenient time. The time to begin man overboard training is before you leave the dock. In fact, the very process of getting under way with a new group of students, guests, or crew is one of the most dangerous times (in this regard) of the whole voyage. A large number of people in an unfamiliar environment, with excitement and adrenaline running high, is a perfect recipe for an accident. One of the most important parts of your predeparture pep talk should be to convince everyone to take it easy, relax, and be careful. Your job, as a mate or master, will be to plan a departure that keeps confusion to a minimum.

The most important aspect of the man overboard issue is keeping people on board. The most important aspect of keeping people on board is keeping their attention level up. And the most important safety device available to help us with both of the above is the safety harness. Its purpose is twofold: it not only keeps people physically attached to the vessel, it also reminds them to be careful. If you are clipped to a lifeline by your harness tether, you must take the deliberate step of unclipping and moving that tether any time you want to go anywhere. That very act makes you think before you move, and that thought process should keep you in touch with the safety procedures you have been taught. Harnesses themselves do not keep people on board; they only keep people attached to the boat, and being dragged along by a harness is no joyride.

MAN OVERBOARD! THE FIRST RESPONSE

It is widely believed now that the single most important step in successfully recovering a person who has fallen overboard is never to lose sight of him. If you lose sight of the person, the chances for recovery drop steeply, due to the extremely poor visibility of a person afloat. This concept may not be obvious to people at first, and it is therefore important to impress it upon them during emergency discussions and drills.

When you hold a man overboard drill, throw something over that approximates the size and color of a clothed person, perhaps a blue workshirt stuffed with a pillow. If you do not put any flotation inside, it will soon become waterlogged and sink, and this feature gives the crew a very sobering sense of the kind of urgency that should accompany these drills. If you do in fact lose "Oscar" (the international code flag O, or Oscar, means "man overboard," and consequently all man overboard dummies have come to be so named), your drill has not failed. It may be the most indelible drill you will ever conduct. People will joke about losing poor Oscar, but encourage them to spend a few minutes contemplating the fact that they just lost a shipmate. After a drill in which Oscar is lost, a genuinely uncomfortable look will be observed on the faces of the entire crew. The lesson teaches itself.

The challenge then becomes, "How do we avoid losing sight of the person?" The solution is simple, though it comes with no guarantees. Do not take your eyes off the victim. If you see him go over, do not take your eyes off him for a second. Until you fully understand how critical this is, you will fail, and your shipmate's odds for survival will plummet. Shifting your eyes for two seconds is just as fatal as not throwing a life ring. This cannot be overemphasized and will probably not be taken seriously enough by your crew until you prove it to them by demonstration.

If you hold all your man overboard drills on a calm, clear day, you will do more harm than good, because you will train your crew to believe that it is easy to find Oscar. Throw something the size of a person's head (a melon is good) overboard on a rough day and prove your point. Have the crew lined up and watching as you throw it over. Have them watch it until it is a few hundred feet away and then tell them to turn around in a complete circle and try to find it again. Do not let them talk to each other, or point, and see how many are able to find it again. It will be a very chilling experience for all of you, and you will accomplish two things. First, the crew members will learn what it takes to keep their eyes really glued on the person and, second, they will become much more interested in the proper use of safety gear such as harnesses, strobe lights, lifejackets, reflective tape, man overboard poles, and life rings. They will be determined not to slip overboard.

Having placed adequate emphasis on this point, if you *do* lose sight of a victim, do not lose hope. And if you are the person in the water and realize that your shipmates have lost sight of you, do not lose hope. There are plenty of stories of remarkable recoveries of people who went overboard long before they were ever missed. A carefully executed search can have good results. The person in the water must not lose hope and must work on keeping himself alive and functional; then, when the rescuers do reappear, the swimmer will be able to attract their attention.

This brings up the topic of position. You should record a position and a time as quickly as possible after a person goes overboard, but do not count on that position for much. Even with the accuracy of GPS (Global Positioning System), you will be disappointed by your attempts to return to a floating object by navigation alone. The person is drifting, so you will need to account for set, drift, and leeway, all of which will be difficult to estimate for such a small object. But a position is needed to provide a starting point for planning a search pattern, if it comes to that.

THE RESCUE

The rescue process begins the minute a person is discovered to have fallen overboard. Whoever sees the person go must do several things immediately, and simultaneously, if possible. Assume that you are the one who sees the victim fall. You are that person's lifeline. You should throw some sort of flotation to the person, alert the rest of the crew, and fix your eyes on the person.

The more floating gear you and others throw in, the better, for two reasons. First, it gives the person more chances of getting a hold of something. Second, it will give you more objects to see if you should lose sight of the person. Additionally, if you continue to throw items over as you sail away, they will provide a trail of objects leading back to the person. In the fog especially, this could be very useful.

Immediately after those steps, you should station yourself wherever you can get a good view, and do not budge. Let the rest of the crew worry about handling sails, etc. If you are at the helm, make someone relieve you immediately, or let someone else take over the lookout.

If you are needed somewhere else on board, you can turn over the lookout to others, but only if you are absolutely certain they can do as good a job as you. For example, is their eyesight as good as yours? Do they wear glasses? If it is raining or foggy, glasses will get wet and vision will be obstructed. Remember that you, as the initial point of visual contact, are the person's lifeline, and you will feel terrible if another person loses sight of him. You will always wonder if you could have done better.

This information should be impressed upon all persons aboard. Anyone aboard might be the one who witnesses the accident, and that person must fully understand and appreciate the importance of this part of the process. The rest of the process will require more training and, depending on the size of your crew, you may or may not need to train the passengers in the rest of the evolution.

The next steps will involve getting the vessel stopped, turned around, and back to the scene. The method you employ here will depend on whether or not you have an engine, whether or not you have a suitable rescue boat, and whether or not you have some sort of recovery/retrieval system such as the Lifesling system.

UNDER POWER

If you have an engine that can be readily started, and is powerful enough to be effective in the existing conditions of wind, sea, and current, you should use it. If you have a reasonably powerful engine and no fancy sails up (ie., spinnaker, square sails, mizzen staysails), your best tactic will be simply to power your vessel around in a circle, completely ignoring your sails. There are obvious limitations to this method, and there will certainly be occasions when it cannot be employed. However, when conditions permit, it is the quickest and best maneuver. There is no point tying up the crew handling sails when they can all be put to use as lookouts, rigging the rescue boat, or otherwise preparing to recover the person. Furthermore, if you are on a reach or a windward leg, if your engine starts quickly, and if you drive your vessel through the wind without touching a sheet, she will end up hove-to and drifting just to windward of the swimmer and quite close by. In some conditions you may be able to do this without the engine.

RESCUE BOAT

If your vessel is equipped with a rescue boat (which is recommended for any vessel, and required for some), your goal will be to stop the vessel quickly and launch the rescue boat with at least two people aboard. The ideal rescue boat is an inflatable, preferably hard-bottomed, with an appropriately powerful outboard. The operators should be experienced boathandlers, strong, and should have at least basic rescue training, if not actual EMT (emergency medical technician) training. They should wear personal flotation devices and, in cold waters, should be in appropriate exposure suits. The driver should not be in a full exposure suit except in very cold conditions, as she will need to be very agile. A float coat or Mustang suit (a brand of flotation suit that provides some hypothermia protection) would be better. The other rescuer, however, may have to get in the water to assist the victim, and therefore should be buoyant and protected from the cold, with a proper exposure suit. The rescuers should also be equipped with a walkie-talkie (for giving and receiving directions and/or instructions), oars or paddles, and flares, in case they become visually separated from the vessel.

The inflatable-type boats are ideally suited for this purpose as they are very seaworthy and stable, while having very low freeboard and soft sides. This allows for dragging the person up over the side out of the water. If the victim is wearing a survival suit or Mustang suit which is full of water, you must be aware of the weight of water trapped inside the suit. First, this will make the person very heavy to lift. Second, if the person is dragged over the side on his belly, as the knees come over the side, the weight of the water in the lower legs could bend the legs forward at the knees, causing a dislocation.

HOISTING ABOARD

The toughest part of man overboard recovery, after getting back to the person in the water, is getting him aboard the vessel, either from the water or from the rescue boat. At some early stage in your crew training you should try to haul a real person, fully clothed, out of the water. It is remarkable how heavy a person is, especially if unconscious. Various systems and techniques have been devised, using halyards, special tackles and davits, and other gear. Try it on your boat, as the system that works well on one boat may not work at all on another. Merely relying on brute strength will not work. If the victim is injured or hypothermic, both of which are likely, you will have to work fast and carefully.

The Lifesling System
The patented Lifesling system has proven effective in most vessels. This employs the use of a long line, secured to the stern of the vessel and attached to a sling-shaped life float at the outboard end. When a person goes overboard, the life float is thrown over (it is unimportant that it gets anywhere near the victim with this system), and towed behind the vessel as you start a long turn around the victim. You continue to circle the victim, slowly, in a decreasing circle until

Person Overboard Rescue

⚓LIFESLING®

- **Stop the boat**
- **Keep victim in sight!**

Deploy the Lifesling and circle the victim until contact is made, or...

Carefully approach the victim and throw the Lifesling when close by

When Lifesling reaches victim, stop the boat immediately

Pull and secure victim alongside boat

Rig hoisting tackle or other lifting device

Hoist victim aboard. If unable to retrieve, call or signal for help

See Lifesling manual for complete instructions

Fig. 8-1. *Lifesling. Courtesy The Lifesling Company.*

the towline comes in contact with the victim, at which time the person allows it to slide through his hands until the float is reached. The float is slipped on and, with the boat now stopped, the person can be hauled back in. In the meantime a tackle is rigged for hoisting the person aboard. This system of course relies on the victim being conscious. If the victim is unconscious, a rescue swimmer or boat will need to help.

Under Sail

If your boat is strictly a sailing vessel, or you are unable to start the engine, you will need to complete the maneuver under sail, and this will require practice under a variety of conditions. Although many techniques have been advocated, none can be considered universally applicable. There are simply too many variables—wind strength and relative direction, sea height and type, current, nearby navigational hazards, other traffic, crew size, sail plan, number and type of special sails set, whether you have a preventer rigged—all of which must be considered when choosing the maneuver to be used.

The best advice for returning expeditiously to a person overboard under sail is to be the most capable sailor you can be, with the best crew you can hire, on the best equipped and maintained boat you can put together. You should perform many drills under a wide variety of conditions. Every one of these variables is under your control as the master or mate. If you feel your boat is not well equipped, improve it or do not sail. If you feel your crew is lacking in skills, train them. If you are uncertain of your own skills, practice.

In a general sense, though, your goals are just the same as when under power. Get the boat turned and/or stopped as quickly as possible, without losing sight of the victim. Stopping a boat under sail will generally involve heaving-to. As mentioned earlier, if your present sail plan will allow it, you may be able simply to turn the wheel hard over to windward, tack, and end up hove-to, having left the jib sheets alone. This will leave you close enough to get the rescue boat overboard.

If you cannot turn around immediately due to your sail plan (say you have a square sail, a mizzen staysail, or a spinnaker set), you may have to continue under way until help arrives from below. In this case, one standard tactic is recommended in most circumstances. This involves turning immediately to a beam reach. Under almost any sail combination you can do this simply by turning the wheel. Note this new course on your steering compass and steer it very carefully, steering by the compass, not by visual cues or by the wind. You will probably lose sight of the victim during this maneuver, so that person's life now depends on your ability to steer a straight course and return along it exactly.

When the crew is on deck, they will take in sail as necessary to get the boat under a controllable sail plan and, when ready, you will perform a Williamson turn (fig. 8-2). This maneuver involves turning the vessel 60 degrees in either direction, using maximum rudder, and shifting the rudder at that point (when you reach 60 degrees) to hard over in the other direction. The result of this turn will be to swerve one way, then swerve back around completely to end up on the reciprocal of your original heading, and almost exactly on the same track line you were on initially. If you do not do this, but simply turn around instead, you will be off your original track by the diameter of your turning circle, which may be just enough for you to miss seeing the victim on your return pass. (This is a good place to point out the simplest way to compute your reciprocal course.

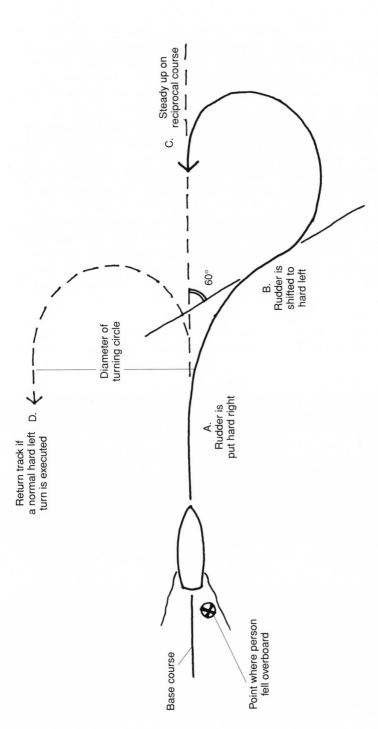

Fig. 8-2. *The Williamson turn. A. Rudder is put hard right. B. Rudder is put hard left. C. Steady up on reciprocal course. D. Return track if a normal hard left turn is executed.*

Especially in the confusion of an emergency, a simple job like subtracting 180 degrees from your base course—the course you were steering before starting the Williamson turn—might prove difficult to do in your head. The trick that is used by the mathematically challenged is to subtract 200 degrees from your base course, then add 20 degrees. This also works by adding 200 degrees, then subtracting 20 degrees. If you try this a few times, you will quickly realize its simplicity.)

Coming to a beam reach immediately after the person falls overboard enables you to steer the precisely reciprocal course on the way back, under sail, with complete maneuverability and good speed. Your goal should be to steer a perfectly straight track on the way out, so you can be fairly sure of following the same track on the way back. Do not forget to record the time the person fell over and evaluate your speed, so you will know how far to run back.

With a little luck and a constant watch you should regain visual contact with the victim on the way back along your track. You will have to consider the wind when estimating the victim's drift. A person in the water is affected very little by the wind, while a vessel is affected a good deal. Both will be affected by the current. Once the person is back in sight, you will generally want to maneuver to heave-to just to windward of him if possible (or a little aft of that, to allow for fore-reaching as you drift), for two reasons. First, you will form a lee with your vessel, providing smoother water to effect the rescue. Second, your vessel will drift to leeward faster than the person in the water, so you will drift toward him. This is not always desirable, depending on the shape of your hull sides, but on most boats you can safely drift right up to the person if he is approximately abeam. Obviously, you should avoid this if you feel there is any danger of rolling down on top of him. If all goes well, you will drift down to him and be able to pull him aboard with whatever tackle arrangement you have rigged for the purpose. If all does not go as planned, you will have to depend on your seamanship skills to revise the plan.

Recovery under sail is a great deal more risky than under power. You will probably lose sight of the victim on the way out if you have to strike much sail, and the maneuvering once you find him takes skill, luck, and time. Therefore, if you have an engine, use it.

EQUIPMENT

It should now be obvious that recovering a man overboard is difficult at best. Luckily, some excellent safety products are available to to help. Unfortunately, they are generally expensive, but if you think they are too expensive, reread this chapter. You may not need all of this equipment, but you need a package that makes you feel comfortable that the odds for recovery of a crew member or passenger are the best you can make them.

Harnesses are the first line of defense and *should* be required on any vessel on which the laws do not already require them. You need not wear them on a calm day in the bay, but they should be available for use when appropriate. Not all harnesses are created equal, and some can be downright dangerous. When you try one on, make sure it rides up high under your armpits, around your chest. If not, it may break your back if it fetches up below your rib cage. Harnesses should be easily adjustable so they can be made comfortable. Otherwise they will not get worn. The tether should have rugged clips at *both* ends—not just one. In 1986, when the *Pride of Baltimore I* sank following her knock down, some of her crew were hauled underwater by their harnesses as she went down. They could not reach the ends of their tethers to unclip them, and were lucky to have another crew member nearby to cut them loose.

Life jackets (now known by the Coast Guard acronym PFD, for personal flotation device) have come a long way over the years. There are as many different types and styles now available as there are of running shoes. There are jackets, coveralls, coats, and vests, and then there are the inflatable ones. The possible choices may be confusing, but many of them have become relatively comfortable and unconfining to wear.

Inflatable life jackets (similar to what you see demonstrated in airplanes, or what divers call BCs, for buoyancy compensator) have recently been gaining in popularity. They have the advantage of being very compact, and are often integrated into a harness. The only drawback is that they must be properly maintained to be reliable. Corrosion can destroy the inflation mechanism, and deterioration of the air bag material can cause them to leak or burst when inflated. For this reason, the U.S. Coast Guard has not yet approved any inflatable life jacket to take the place of regular PFDs. This does not mean you cannot wear one, but you should not think of it as a substitute for one required by regulations.

There are several categories of PFDs, as published by the Coast Guard. Type I is approved for offshore work, where you could be in the water for a long time waiting for a rescue. Type I will definitely turn an unconscious person upright and support the head above the water. Type II is intended for near-shore work, where rescue should not be too far away. It will turn *most* unconscious people upright, but will not necessarily support the head above water. Type III is the most comfortable and most common sportsman's vest, and is only intended for recreational use where there are lots of other boats around to pick you up fairly quickly. This vest will assist a *conscious* person in turning himself upright. Type IVs are the throwable ones, such as boat cushions, and type Vs are the hybrids such as float coats and coveralls that are designed to be worn, but not to be pulled on in a hurry in an emergency situation. These must be *worn* to be effective, not stored ready for use.

Life jackets do no one any good if they are stored below. To be effective they must either be worn or be ready at hand, and this means on deck, in a deck box with a lid that will float open or away if the vessel should capsize or sink. In this case the PFDs will float to the surface after the accident and be available to the crew. The best solution to the storage problem is to have a slatted floor in the box, so water can flow in from underneath. Then the combined flotation material of the PFDs inside will push the lid off and they will float free. These deck boxes should also be well marked so everyone on board will know where to find them. This arrangement of deck storage may not be practical on smaller yachts, but steps should be taken to make the life jackets as accessible as possible.

Reflective tape is a modern marvel with light-reflecting qualities that are astonishing. A Coast Guard search and rescue helicopter pilot has informed the author that he prefers to search for victims at night, if he has reason to believe they are wearing reflective tape. The searcher can scan the sea surface with a spotlight and even a tiny (eight-square-inch) piece of tape stands out like a beacon, whereas by daylight a life jacket in a rough sea may be almost invisible. All your life jackets, and some of your clothing, should display this tape. Foul weather gear, harnesses, and coats are all items that you might be wearing even if you are not wearing your PFD; so, decorate them with tape.

Whistles and small strobe lights or chemical lights are also important. Your voice will give out quite soon, and a whistle is more shrill than most voices, anyway. The little strobe lights that are attached to the offshore PFDs are battery operated, and many are activated by contact with salt water. Chemical light sticks contain two chemicals that glow when mixed and are activated by bending the tube, thus breaking the vial inside, allowing the two to interact. They are quite bright, and last for about forty-five minutes. These are so effective they are often used for other purposes; so make sure the boat's emergency light sticks are kept for emergencies.

Throwable devices have become more sophisticated. Where vessels used to carry a simple life ring, they now carry quite a combination of devices strung together. As long as they deploy properly, they are extremely effective. Life rings, especially those near the helmsman, are often connected to a long line, a water light, a man overboard pole, a dye marker, or a smoke bomb. Any combination of these is effective, as long as they can be ejected without tangling. The man overboard pole is perhaps the most important piece. This should have a weighted end and a float, which in combination holds a tall pole and flag, well up in the air. The pole may have a radar reflector on it as well. Put some reflective tape on the pole or on the flag for night work.

All of this gear is only as good as the crew that backs it up. No amount of gear will take the place of training and practice, but the gear can definitely increase the odds that the training and practice will pay off.

Further reading (see bibliography for details): Glénans Sea Center, *The New Glénans Sailing Manual,* chap. 14; Maloney, *Chapman Piloting,* chap. 4; Van Dorn, *Oceanography and Seamanship,* chap. 29.

CHAPTER NINE

MOTORSAILING

The majority of sailing vessels today, especially those in commercial service, are equipped with auxiliary engines. The professional skipper should know how to use the engine to maximum advantage. Too few sailors appreciate what the engine can do for them while under sail. Furthermore, the same people often do not understand that they are wasting fuel by not using their sails while motoring.

The combination of sails pulling and an engine pushing gives a result that is greater than the sum of the parts. The increase in speed produced by the engine provides an increase in the apparent wind, which allows the sails to produce greater aerodynamic lift. This not only provides more speed, but will also take some of the load off the engine, significantly improving fuel economy.

The increase in fuel economy is no small amount. In 1984 the Japanese built a small oil tanker with auxiliary sails to test the theory that sails were a valid fuel-saving device for commercial cargo ships. The designers predicted a 10 percent fuel savings over the long run. In actual practice, according to Paul Priebe in his book *Modern Commercial Sailing Ship Fundamentals*, they realized fuel savings of up to 50 percent.

Since the increase in boat speed will cause the apparent wind to shift ahead, it might seem impossible to enjoy this benefit when trying to get to windward, since the sails will be luffing. This is not always the case. When motorsailing, you are not relying on the aerodynamic lift of your sails to provide the primary driving power for the vessel. They are merely giving some extra boost. You will find that you can sheet your sails in virtually flat—as flat as you can get them—and steer remarkably close to the wind. As long as the sails maintain some aerodynamic shape, they will provide some benefit. A large, gaff-rigged schooner that under sail alone could sail no closer than 55 degrees to the wind, will be able to make good about 35 degrees to the wind when motorsailing. Her speed will be commensurate with her motoring speed, or a knot or two better, and her fuel economy will be greatly improved.

Your choice of sails will be determined by how close to the wind you want to run and by how flat you can trim them. Jibs may not work well, as they cannot be trimmed as close to amidships as the main, staysail, and any other boomed sails. A sloop may work best (to windward) with only the main set. If you are off the wind a bit, set anything that can be kept full.

There will be occasions when this technique will not be the right choice. If the true wind is abaft the beam, motorsailing may not make sense. The speed provided by the engine will be decreasing the apparent wind, so the technique will pay off only if there is enough wind to keep the sails full. In that case you would almost certainly be sailing instead. Also, there will be times when you will need that one mile dead to windward, in spite of the motion and the fuel cost. Then you will be taking all your sails down (except what you might want for steadying against the roll). You certainly do not want to steam into the wind with sails luffing, as you will only add windage and damage your sails. But if you motor dead to windward for an hour, and then bear off and set some sail, you will be amazed at how much more comfortable the vessel will be with the sails drawing.

For some vessels this will not be the right choice. Square-riggers have so much rigging, and such a tremendous head rig (the entire rig forward of the bow, including the bowsprit, etc.), that they simply can't be driven to windward effectively or safely in a substantial head sea, under sail or power. There is too much windage, the rig can't take lunging into a head sea, and the head rig is too vulnerable to being driven into the face of a wave—an action that could easily break your bowsprit or jibboom. Smaller vessels that tend to sail at substantial angles of heel may not be able to run their engines at such angles. You should be certain to check the engine manufacturer's recommendations on maximum heel before motorsailing. Some engines cannot lubricate themselves effectively if the boat is heeled past 20 or 30 degrees.

When does a sailor decide to utilize the engine? Most would say when speed under sail, either through the water or toward their goal, drops below a certain arbitrary point. Let us say you are on a large schooner, making an extended voyage of several weeks' duration, and you have laid out your schedule based on a conservative average speed of 4 knots. It would be wise to say that (at least for the first half of the voyage, until you have some miles "in the bank"), if your speed drops below 4 knots, you should start the engine. More discussion about these choices will take place in the chapter on passage planning, but for now let us work with this figure.

You are sailing close-hauled, and the wind is failing. As boat speed drops below 4 knots, the watch dutifully gives up, drops sail, and starts the engine, running at sufficient engine speed to attain 7 knots. With no sails set, they assume it makes sense to head directly toward the destination, which is dead to windward. The wind is light, blowing about 5 knots.

Steaming directly into the wind at 7 knots will produce a head wind of 12 knots, not an insignificant breeze considering the drag of all of your rigging and masts. All of this windage will hurt you in two ways. It will slow you down, and it will burn up fuel.

How much windage is there? By a conservative estimate, on an 80-foot schooner with no topmasts, a 45-foot foremast, and a 60-foot mainmast, counting masts, standing rigging, and running rigging only (not counting the hull, furled sails, and any deck gear or people), there would be about 400 square feet of "sail" area, which you will be pushing to windward. This is the equivalent of a 20- by 20-foot sail held square to the 12-knot wind.

How does this make the case for motorsailing? The wind—apparent, true, and relative—is there. You cannot avoid it, so you should use it, even when under power. In the same example as above, set your main, foresail, and fore staysail. Leave the jib down, because you cannot sheet it in as near to the centerline as the others. With these three sails set and sheeted in flat you will find that while maintaining the same engine speed you can sail to within about 35 degrees of the apparent wind, as previously explained. You will now enjoy substantially better fuel economy, probably a little more speed, and a better motion, as the thrust and inertia of the sails will dampen the vessel's tendency to pitch and roll.

The trade-off here will be that you are no longer heading directly for your destination. To determine if the trade is a good one, a simple calculation can be performed to compare your speed made good toward your destination under power alone (heading directly toward your goal), and under the combination of power and sail while heading off a few points. Do not fail to consider the improvement in vessel motion—and the consequent comfort to the crew—when weighing the difference.

Vessel motion when motorsailing improves more than just comfort, although saving crew energy is an important consideration on an offshore passage. A vessel pitching in a head sea is very hard on her gear. The shock loads of the masts alternately stretching their backstays, then lurching back and snapping their headstays tight, is a recipe for breakage. Likewise, when the wind and seas are more abeam, similar loads are placed on the shrouds and chainplates as the vessel rolls. With sails set and drawing, however, the loads become much more steady and consistent. Anything you can do to eliminate or reduce shock loads of this kind will greatly prolong the life of all of your gear.

The advantages of motorsailing disappear when the wind fails completely. In a flat calm, when there is not enough wind to fill the sails at all, you should strike them and proceed under power. You might choose to leave something set to help steady the vessel, but consider that that sail will take a beating by continuous luffing. A little time spent powering directly toward your goal when the sea is calm will allow you to spend more time under sail later when there is some wind. This will be covered in chapter 19 on voyage planning.

Further reading (see bibliography for details): Priebe, *Modern Commercial Sailing Ship Fundamentals.*

CHAPTER TEN

SAILING VESSEL STABILITY

THE BASICS OF STABILITY

The stability of a vessel is its tendency to return to an upright position when inclined by an outside force. If you push a boat over, it should pop back up. Why? There are a few underlying concepts that must be understood to answer that question.

The first concept is center of gravity (CG). The CG of a vessel is the theoretical center of all the weights that make up the vessel. If you could support a vessel by a single (sturdy) pin, run horizontally through the center of gravity, the vessel would be perfectly balanced in all directions. You could push it over with your finger in any direction and it would remain at the angle you left it. It would have no tendency to return to the upright position, or to any other position. It would be in perfect equilibrium. This point will not move around on the vessel as long as you do not move any of the weights on the vessel. Locating this point requires a tedious process of adding up all the known weights on the vessel, including every piece of material that went into building her, and figuring their moment. The moment is the product of a weight times its distance from a particular reference point. For present purposes, suffice it to say that the CG will be calculated by the naval architect, and we will be concerned only with changes caused by moving weights on board, by loading weights, or by discharging them. Since we are dealing with moments, it is not only the weight that is important, but also the distance that weight lies from the calculated center of gravity.

A second important concept is buoyancy—and the buoyant force. A vessel floats because there is a force pushing her up in the water that is exactly equal to the force of gravity that is pushing her down. This force is produced by the pressure of the water she has pushed aside. The weight of the vessel will cause her to settle into the water—to try to sink. As she settles, she must push the water aside to make room for her. The water pushes back. (Remember Newton:

For every action there is an equal and opposite reaction.) The more she tries to sink, the more water she pushes aside (displaces), and the more that water pushes back. When the force of the water pushing back (buoyant force) exactly equals the force of her weight pushing down (gravity), the boat will stop sinking and float. She is again in equilibrium. She is displacing an amount of water (by weight) that is exactly equal to her own weight, and this is known as displacement. It may be measured in pounds (or kilograms) for small vessels, or in tons (English or metric) for larger ones. If you wish to calculate a vessel's displacement, you need to calculate the volume of the underwater portion of her hull. This is the volume of water she must displace when she is floating. It then follows that if you take that volume and multiply it by the weight of seawater—at 64 pounds per cubic foot (or 62.2 pounds per cubic foot of fresh water if you are in a lake)—you will get the weight of your vessel.

A third concept is the center of buoyancy (CB). This is, for practical purposes, the geometrical center of the submerged volume of the vessel. This, too, is calculated by the naval architect. What the center of buoyancy represents is the center of the buoyant force. The sum of all the support the vessel is getting from the water surrounding her is theoretically represented by a single force acting at the center of buoyancy.

Remember that if you could support the vessel at her center of gravity on the head of a pin, she would be perfectly balanced. The buoyant force is that support, and the head of the pin is the CB. The force of gravity always acts straight down, so no matter how the vessel leans over, her weight will always be pushing straight down. The buoyant force is a reaction to gravity. Newton said that for every action there is an equal *and opposite* reaction; in this case, the action is gravity and the reaction is the buoyant force. Therefore, it must be opposite to gravity. If gravity always acts straight down, the buoyant force must always act straight up.

INITIAL STABILITY

You have so far managed to get your vessel balanced on the head of a pin, so that she is in perfect equilibrium. Unfortunately, this is not desirable, because if you lean her over she will stay there; she should spring back up. One way to accomplish this would be to design a vessel so that her center of gravity lies below her center of buoyancy. The CG would then be below the pinhead, so she would not be floating in equilibrium. The weight would be hanging below the supporting pinhead. The buoyant force is holding the boat up from a point above the gravity force which is pushing her down. She will now float upright with a tendency to return to the upright position whenever she is inclined away from it. The strength of this tendency to return upright will depend on how far below the CB the CG is.

By way of an example, think of a rod with a weight on it, such that the weight can be moved along the length of the rod (see figure 10-1). The CG of

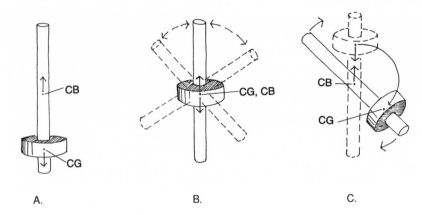

A.   B.   C.

Fig. 10-1. *Stability simplified.*

the rod/weight combination will be located approximately at the center of the weight. The rod is supported at its mid-length. This support will mimic the buoyant force. In figure 10-1A, the rod is stable, since the weight (CG) is located well below the CB. Any force that attempts to tip the rod will be resisted by the tendency of the weight to pull the lower part of the rod back down. This rod is said to be stable. A force may tip (heel) the rod (boat) over, but as soon as that force is removed the rod (boat) will return to its original position.

In figure 10-1B, the weight (CG) is moved to the middle of the rod. The CG is now in the same position as the CB. The rod may rest at any angle, with no tendency to return to its original position, or to move to any other position. The rod is now said to be in a state of neutral stability. A force may incline the rod, and when the force is removed, the rod will remain in its new position.

In figure 10-1C, the weight (CG) is moved to a point above the CB. The rod is now unstable. If the CG and the CB are perfectly aligned vertically, the rod will remain upright (a delicate balance), but if a force is applied now, the rod will incline, and even when the force is removed it will continue to incline until it comes to rest in a new, stable condition. It will tip over, or capsize, tipping until once again the CG ends up below and vertically aligned with the CB.

In the case of your boat, however, there is more than just the weight and a single point of support holding it upright. The boat in fact has many points of support. The hull is wide, not narrow like the rod. Because of that width, it has supporting points out to each side of the center of gravity. This will even allow the design of a boat that has its center of gravity above the center of buoyancy to still float in a condition of positive stability. It is as though the rod has legs, giving a stable base to the rod/weight combination.

Now look at a boat at rest in the water (fig. 10-2A). This boat does not have a deep lead keel, but instead derives her stability from her width. This boat's CG is above her CB. She might appear inherently unstable in this condition, and in imminent peril of tipping over. But look at what happens as soon as she begins

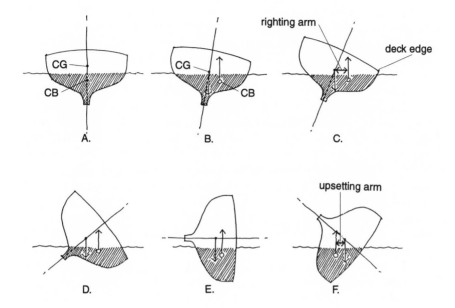

Fig. 10-2. *Stability of a sailing vessel.*

to tip—even a little bit. As she leans, she lifts some of her hull out of the water on the high (windward) side, and presses more of her hull into the water on the low (leeward) side (fig. 10-2B). This means there is now more hull in the water to leeward, so her CB must be moving that way (remember, the CB is at the geometric center of the underwater portion of the hull). If no weights on board move, the CG will not shift on board the vessel, but it will move with the vessel as she heels. The amount that it moves will be small compared to the amount the CB is moving. The result will be that almost immediately the CB will be out of alignment (vertically) with the CG, but in a favorable way, such that the CB is pushing the vessel back upright. The horizontal separation between the force of buoyancy and the force of gravity is known as the righting arm. It is figuratively the "arm" that is pushing the boat back upright. Furthermore, the CB will continue to shift to leeward as the boat heels more and more, lengthening the righting arm, giving us a stronger and stronger push back upright as she heels more (fig. 10-2B,C). To a point, that is.

As the vessel continues to heel over, there will come a point when the shift of the CB will stall and then begin to shift back toward the center again. This change will begin when we put our deck edge underwater (fig. 10-2C). Note that up to the point of deck-edge immersion the submerged portion of the vessel has been "growing" to leeward. This has been causing the CB to shift dramatically to leeward as well—to our advantage. But once the deck edge is immersed, the vessel has no more width to put in the water. The vessel is now "shrinking" to leeward. The CB must, sooner or later, start shifting back toward the centerline and toward the CG, thus reducing the righting arm (fig. 10-2D). When the CB finally gets back in line vertically with the CG, the vessel has lost her tendency to right herself—the righting arm will have been reduced to zero—and if she heels any further she will develop a negative righting arm—called an upsetting arm—and she will capsize (fig. 10-2F).

The angle of deck-edge immersion is an important angle, since it dictates the angle of heel at which stability begins to decrease. Actually, on most boats, the righting arm does continue to increase at that point, but the *rate* of increase begins to slow down. Thus, when sailing with the "lee rail under," be aware that the boat is gaining stability at a decreasing rate from that point on. We can get away with sailing boats beyond the angle of deck-edge immersion (with the lee rail under), because at those steep angles of heel the sails begin to spill their wind, and the more we heel, the more they spill. Nonetheless, deck-edge immersion is an important angle, and one you should normally use as a measure of maximum safe heel.

It would certainly be useful to know the point at which stability approaches marginal conditions, and it is not difficult to determine this. Again, look at the rod in figure 10-1. When the weight is far from the CB, the rod will snap upright with great force. When the weight is near the CB, the rod slowly and gently returns to the upright position. The same is true, and noticeably so, with the stability situation on the boat. If she has a relatively lively, snappy motion she is quite stable. If she has a long, slow, lethargic motion she has little stability. If you want to measure this, you can time the roll of your vessel. Note the time it takes for the vessel to roll from the end of one roll, over to the other side, and back to the point where she was when you started. This is called the rolling period, and is a direct measure of your vessel's initial stability. Again, a quick roll indicates a great deal of initial stability, and a slow roll indicates little initial stability.

An interesting rule of thumb is presented by Cyrus Hamlin in his book *Preliminary Design of Boats and Ships*, in which he states that for a small- to medium-size vessel—say between 30 and 150 feet—if the rolling period is greater than the beam of the boat in yards, or meters, then the stability of the boat is questionable. This is of course a crude measure, but for a seat-of-the-pants field test, it could prove very useful.

Is the answer to get all the weight as low in the vessel as possible and get rid of all the weight on top? This would certainly lower the CG, if that is what you want, but it is not as simple as that. You can overdo stability. If you have excessive initial stability your vessel will have a snappy roll all right. She will snap her rigging, spars, and the patience of all her crew. An overly stable vessel is a very uncomfortable vessel to sail on and can be very hard on her gear. Each roll is quick, even violent. A vessel in this condition is said to be stiff or cranky. In such a case, you would want to reduce your stability a little by raising your CG. Bring some heavy things up from the lowest stowage locations. Swap lightweight things stowed high in the vessel for heavy things stowed low. The roll will become slower and more comfortable. Be careful though—if you overdo these corrective measures you will be getting into a dangerous condition again and your indicator will be a very long, deep roll. A vessel in this condition is said to be tender.

THE SAILING RIG

A stable vessel will remain upright until inclined by an outside force, and after such force is removed will return to the upright position. Sailing vessels in general are very stable vessels because they are designed to withstand being acted on by just such an outside force—the wind—and it is often quite a strong one. The wind pushes on the sails, tries to blow the ship over, and she will heel over until her stability is sufficient to resist.

How much pressure comes from the wind? In the discussion of the aerodynamic forces involved with the sail, the total aerodynamic force was found to be approximately perpendicular to the chord of the sail. This force could be resolved into two vectors—one in the direction of travel of the vessel (straight ahead), and another at right angles to it. Looking at figure 10-3, note which vector is dramatically greater than the other. The big one is pushing directly abeam, to leeward. The short one (pointing forward), is known as the driving force, and the long one (pointing abeam), is known as the heeling force. If the drive from the sail is impressive, the heeling force is even more so.

Now observe that the heeling force is acting at a point well above the CG of the vessel. That height above the CG multiplies the effectiveness of the force. It develops a moment that is the product of that height and that force.

How high is the heeling force? Remember that it is one component of the total aerodynamic force (TAF) discussed in chapter three, where we found that the TAF can be represented by a single vector acting approximately at the

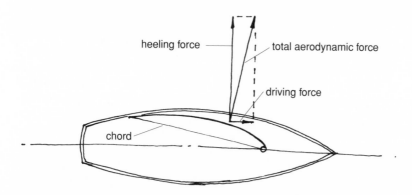

Fig. 10-3. *Heeling force.*

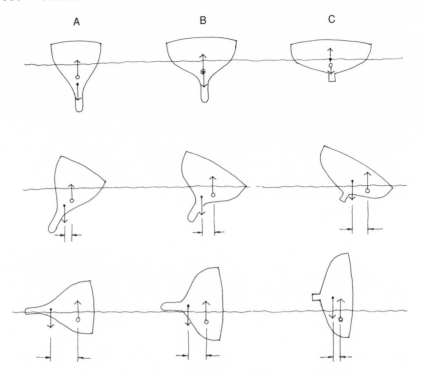

Fig. 10-4. *Comparison of different hull shapes and their stability.*

geometric center of the sail—the center of effort (CE). We discussed the CE when we talked about balance, but at that time we were only concerned with its horizontal location. Now it is its vertical position we are interested in.

Knowing the height of the CE and the strength of the heeling force, look at the power involved in heeling the vessel. The heeling moment is a very powerful force acting at the end of a very long lever, creating a tremendous moment. Your vessel has to resist this effort with her righting moment. The righting moment is made up of the weight of the vessel (displacement) times the horizontal distance (righting arm) between the center of buoyancy and the center of gravity. Looking at figure 10-4, notice that two factors can affect this. The first is the amount of shift of CB that occurs as the vessel heels. If the vessel's hull shape is such that her CB shifts well to leeward as she heels, the righting arm will grow longer quickly. If she is bowl shaped, the CB will shift little and she will gain little righting arm as she heels (see figure 10-4B). The boat in figure 10-4C is gaining her stability mostly from her width—her shift in CB. The second factor is the height of the CG. The lower the CG the longer the arm will become as the vessel heels. The boat in figure 10-4A (with a deep lead keel) is gaining most of her stability from the weight of her keel swinging to windward as she heels.

Designers of sailing vessels work with both of these factors to give boats the stability needed to sail safely. They try to get the vessel's CG as low as possible by putting lead keels on the boats and by locating heavy installations, such as engines, as low down as possible. They try to keep all gear aloft as lightweight as possible and they design the vessel's hull shape so that it provides more and more buoyancy to leeward as she heels. It is up to us, as the sailors, to work with the understanding and information we have to maximize our vessel's existing stability, without overdoing it.

WHAT TO DO ABOUT STABILITY

If a vessel is inspected by the U.S. Coast Guard, she will have met certain stability standards in order to pass that inspection. The captain's job is to make certain to maintain those standards. As a vessel operates, over time the location of various weights may change. New gear may be added, old gear replaced or discarded. New gear is often lighter in weight as technology advances. If this newer, lighter gear has replaced heavier gear below, the vessel's stability may have decreased. If the newer, lighter gear has replaced heavier gear aloft, the stability may have increased. Either situation may be detrimental.

In the first case, the vessel may now be noticeably more tender, unable to carry as much sail as before without putting her deck edge under. The indicators of a tender ship will be apparent. She will be rolling slowly, lethargically, and hanging on at the ends of the roll. Find the cause and deal with it. You may need to add inside ballast or shift some weights lower down.

In the second case, she may be getting cranky or stiff. You will notice that she seems to have developed a nasty motion in a sea. You will be feeling new stresses on the rig when the vessel is rolling, and if you have to work aloft under way, it will become increasingly difficult and dangerous. Pay attention to these signs and identify the cause. You should be quite certain of what you are doing before you take steps to reduce your vessel's stability, but that can be just as important for safety as increasing it. In either case you must be aware that if your vessel is U.S. Coast Guard inspected, significant changes in her stability, or any changes you might contemplate that could affect her stability, must be reported.

STABILITY ISSUES WHILE UNDER WAY

You, as a sailor, have control over more than just the weight distribution on your vessel with regard to stability. You have control over the force that is heeling the vessel. Your choice of sails to set will be your day-to-day stability job. Your choices will include: amount of sail area set, height of sails set, height of CE of individual sails set, amount of heeling force of each sail set, and the relative ease with which you can strike any sail if necessary.

In consideration of the height of their CE, some sails, such as topsails and flying jibs, are obviously set higher than others; but the shape of each sail must also be considered. The CE of a gaff sail will be considerably lower than that of a Marconi sail of the same area, because it is short and wide rather than tall and narrow (see figure 10-5A). Because of this, a gaff-rigged vessel may be able to set more total sail area than a Marconi-rigged vessel of similar size, depending, of course, on her overall stability.

The CE of some of the sails (mainsails, mizzens, foresails, even some staysails) can be lowered by either reefing or scandalizing. As already explained, when reefing a sail, we lower the sail to its reef. Sails that roller-reef around a stay may not substantially lower their CE, but those that roll into a mast generally do (see figure 10-5C, D). Scandalizing is a process used rarely on gaff-rigged sails. The peak halyards are lowered, leaving the throat where it is (see figure 10-5B). This is a very crude, but very quick and effective way of rapidly reducing sail area and lowering the CE. It may also destroy your sail with all the attendant flogging, and the swinging gaff is a hazard, but in an emergency it could be justified.

The amount of heeling force on each sail will be a component of the total aerodynamic force that sail is generating. We can control the TAF (and therefore the heeling force) by controlling the trim of the sail. In the simplest solution, we control this with the sheet (we can sheet in to maximize the TAF, or sheet out to luff the sail and spill its wind), but we can also use our knowledge of sail trim to reduce the power of a sail by any of the other adjustments we have available. We can, for instance, put extra belly in the sail by releasing the cunningham, downhaul, or outhaul.

Finally, we must think ahead to the possibility of an increase in wind (sudden or not) and consider whether each of the various sails presently set can be easily struck when the time comes to do so. Any that will be problematic should be taken in at the first indication of threatening weather.

Another stability consideration has become more of an issue with advances in rigging and sail technology. Formerly, the materials used for rigging and sailmaking were fairly strong; nowadays, the materials are incredibly strong. Dacron, Kevlar, Mylar, Spectra (all trade names for various materials used in sails and rigging), carbon fiber, and graphite fiber represent fabulous leaps forward in material strength. We continually pursue the unbreakable rig and rip-proof sail. Unfortunately, when hit with the ultimate gust of wind, something must give. In the old days the ship would generally lose her sails or her rig, but at least she might still be afloat. Now, if neither the rig nor the sails will give, the vessel will capsize. Alternatively, if something does break, it may be where least expected. Since all known stress points have been beefed up with stronger materials, the failure will occur where no one has predicted it. Sailors may or may not have control over the materials used on the vessel, but they must be aware of them, try to identify weak links where they exist, and use their seamanship skills to work the vessel safely.

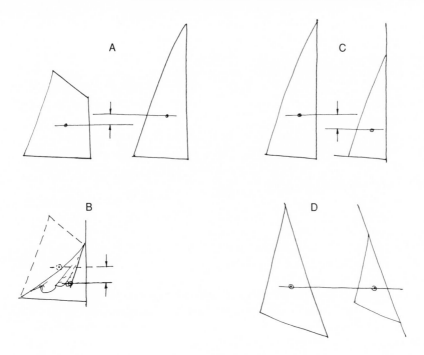

Fig. 10-5. *Different sail shapes have their centers of effort (CE) at different heights. A. A gaff sail's CE is typically lower than a Marconi sail of similar area. B. A gaff sail, scandalized. C. Reefing a roller-furling sail into a mast will normally lower the CE. D. Reefing a roller-furling sail around a stay might not change the height of the CE.*

Further reading (see bibliography for details): Chase, *Introduction to Nautical Science*, chap. 2; Hamlin, *Preliminary Design of Boats and Ships*, chap. 6; Kinney, *Skene's Elements of Yacht Design*, chap. 23; LaDage and Van Gemert, *Stability and Trim for the Ship's Officer;* Marchaj, *Sailing Theory and Practice*, Part 3, chap. 3; Phillips-Birt, *Sailing Yacht Design*, chap. 7.

CHAPTER ELEVEN

GROUNDING, FLOODING, FIRE, AND ABANDONING SHIP

GROUNDING

It is not unusual in a state of emergency for an inexperienced person to have an instinctive reaction that is inappropriate, and even potentially dangerous. This is when a professional, with proper training and experience, will earn her pay. In the case of grounding a vessel, the instinct might be to try to back off immediately, and except in minor cases this should not be attempted without careful investigation of several conditions. We will discuss these conditions one at a time, but when the event occurs they will need to be considered virtually simultaneously.

Most commonly, a vessel runs aground head-on, generally grounding on her keel, and driving up onto the shoal until she stops. The extent of the grounding is the first piece of information the skipper must determine. Where is she aground, and how hard? Her keel may have hit initially, but by the time she comes to a halt, she may be aground on her bilge or her rudder as well. In that case, an attempt to back off may do more damage than has already been done.

The keel of a traditional, full-keeled vessel, such as a schooner, is fairly rugged and will withstand quite a jolt. But the fin keel of most modern sailing vessels cannot take that kind of punishment without some damage. While even a fin keel can withstand a bit of a hit from ahead, to back or twist the vessel on it (especially if it has been weakened by the initial blow) may do a great deal more damage, even to the extent of tearing it from the hull.

Regarding the bilge, realize that as the vessel drives up onto a ledge she has inertia that drives her up and forward, and inertia that holds her upright, just as a person riding a bicycle stays upright while moving. When she stops that inertia is gone, and she falls onto her side (just as the bicycle rider does). If she has ridden far enough up the ledge she will fall, or at least come to rest, on one bilge. Bilges are not built for this kind of stress, and she may be holed here.

More important, though, is that the bilge might have survived this initial phase, but an attempt to back off, or be pulled off, may cause the bilge to be holed.

Rudders are always fragile. Again, even if it is not damaged on the way up, the process of backing, or dragging her back, may well do the damage from which you were spared initially. This is probably the most common casualty in an ill-conceived rescue attempt. Many rudders that were undamaged in the initial event are wrenched or torn off in the course of being "saved."

The key here is understanding that your momentum has quite likely carried you farther up onto the shoal than your shattered ego is prepared to accept. You must investigate before acting. Sound around the vessel with a lead line. Get in the dinghy and paddle around the vessel. If you have a snorkeling mask, put it on and try to see the situation underwater. If your vessel is not too deep, an oar or boathook may suffice to probe the ledge to determine the slope, the shape, and the extent of the rock. Find out in what direction the shoal slopes away. Perhaps you have bounced over the highest point, and the route off is to go ahead, not astern. Perhaps the route off is to one side.

If you are aground in sand or mud, damage will probably be minimal, but you may still be thoroughly stuck. Backing down hard with your engine, or getting a pull from another boat may simply pump more sand around your keel, leaving you more firmly stuck than before. (Also, you must be aware of the risk of sucking mud into your engine cooling water intake.) To avoid this, get your rescuer to pull you from the end of a long line. This will keep the rescuer's prop wash far enough away to prevent its contributing to the problem.

There is one advantage to a quick attempt at backing off that should not be ignored, but it should be attempted only in relatively minor groundings, after a quick assurance that there is no major damage and no hazard in backing off. By backing hard with your own engine your propeller will push a good deal of water under your hull, which may be just enough to float you off. But if it does not work in one try, it will not work any better in bullheaded repeat attempts. Note that the opposite effect will work against you if you should try to drive forward to get over the shoal. Then your propeller will pump water out from under the vessel, grounding you harder and harder the more you try. If you want to try to move ahead, do so with slow engine speed.

The state of the tide will be of utmost importance to you the minute you hit. With a rising tide, you will have time to prepare before acting. With a falling tide, especially if you are in an area with a substantial rise and fall, it will be necessary to think and act fast. You must still run through the many precautions we are discussing here, but you had better have them all sorted out and priori-tized so you do not waste any time, because a few minutes may make the whole difference between inconvenience and disaster.

You should know, at all times, several things about the tide in your area. Know the range. Is it 2 feet, 6 feet, or 20 feet? Know the tidal period. Does this area experience diurnal or semidiurnal tides (one high and one low, or two highs and two lows per day, respectively)? Or are they mixed tides, which give an almost random series of highs and lows of different heights. Most importantly, know the times of high and low water. This information should always be in the back of your mind. The time it takes, after you have run aground, to calculate the state of the tide may be all the time it takes to become hopelessly stuck on your ledge. Later, if you are still stuck, you will want to calculate the tides more precisely, because you will need to know at what stage of the tide you hit, and therefore at what time you can expect to float off again. If you had the misfortune of going aground at high tide, you will need to know if the height of the next high tide will be greater or less than the current one.

As you are sounding around your vessel and evaluating the situation with regard to your point of contact, look for surrounding dangers. There is no point in dragging yourself off the rock you are on if you end up inside a pocket, surrounded by more rocks. The path of least resistance may be the path into greater danger. On the other hand, this could be a prudent move if it will put you in a better position to ride out one tide, buying time to lighten the vessel so you will be able to get out for good on the next high tide.

Get a weather forecast. Get it from the radio, or develop one yourself. You will want to know more than simply if bad weather is coming. Bad weather may be your savior if it brings low pressure and consequently a higher tide. An onshore wind may blow you harder aground, but onshore winds also bring higher tides. An offshore wind may sound like a blessing since it gives you a lee, but it will blow the water offshore leaving you harder aground. If the forecast is bad for the next high tide, it may be necessary to take some risks now rather than wait.

Will bad weather come at the time of high tide? Is your position exposed to rough seas? If so, you will take a terrible pounding while you are partially afloat. If you have access to some old tires, these can be sunk and wedged under your bilge to cushion the pounding. If you have the storage space, these are good things to carry with you. Old tires have other uses as well, including tying them between two hawsers for your towline, acting as shock absorbers, and for use as rough-duty fenders. Bags of extra sails could be sacrificed for this purpose as well.

Other gear you will wish you had with you will include heavy timbers of any kind, to shore up and brace the vessel in whatever position you wish to hold her. Carrying a few big timbers, if space is available, is a worthwhile precaution; otherwise, you may end up sacrificing some spars for the job. There is no telling when such timbers may prove useful, and if nothing else they can be jettisoned to lighten the vessel. Better to jettison scrap lumber and old tires than fuel, water, stores, or valuable equipment.

Scuba gear is thought to be good to have, and it is, if you have a qualified diver in the crew. But this warning is extremely important: If you *do not* have a truly experienced diver aboard, having the gear could be a recipe for tragedy. If the equipment is there, the temptation to use it will be great, and salvage diving is extremely dangerous work—in no way similar to recreational diving, which is done under ideal conditions. In a grounding, there will be currents, obstructions, breaking waves, a pounding vessel of many tons overhead, and no buddy to dive with. As a skipper, you had better understand that you are asking a person to risk his life for this job. Consider exactly what you hope to gain by sending a diver down, and decide whether the risks to vessel and crew justify the risk to the diver.

Take soundings of your bilges. Ascertain whether or not you have been holed. It will be wise to take up some floorboards in each compartment and leave them up (unless the openings will present a hazard to people walking around below), so you will see immediately any change in bilge water level. If you are badly holed, the last thing you will want to do is get off the rock into deep water where you can sink. If you are in a bad spot with moderate damage, you may decide to get off the ledge and then find a safer place with a smooth or soft bottom to run aground again, where repairs can be made under safer conditions.

You may need to assess quickly approximately how much weight of the vessel is aground. For this you will need to know what your vessel's "TPI" value is. This stands for tons per inch immersion (or pounds per inch on smaller yachts) and refers to the weight required to immerse your vessel by one inch, when she is floating on her designed waterline. It is found with your vessel's stability information, and in order for it to be useful, you will have to have researched it before you run aground. If you can determine how far the new waterline is below the normal waterline, you can calculate approximately how much weight is aground. If the water is now 2 inches below where it was before you grounded, and your TPI value is 2.2 (the value for one particular 80-foot wooden schooner of 62 tons displacement), then you have about 4.4 tons of weight bearing on the rock. That is a good deal of weight to try to move without some careful consideration of the factors discussed above. Furthermore, the TPI value will tell you how much weight you will need to jettison to refloat the vessel if the water level remains unchanged.

It must be noted here that you cannot simply compare the new water level to the painted waterline on the hull. It is highly unlikely that the boat was floating at that level. Normally, the bottom paint is painted several inches above where the boat floats, so you must keep a mental record or a logbook entry of where she is actually floating. This will be easier on bigger vessels with draft marks, but even without them you can make a point of looking at the waterline every time you come alongside in the dinghy. Also, once she is aground she will probably not be level, so you will have to note the level on both sides, or fore and aft, and average them. At best it will be approximate, but better than nothing.

Another valuable piece of information you will want to look at in your stability information is your "MT1" value. This stands for the moment to trim one inch and represents the moment (weight times the distance from the tipping center) required to trim, or tip, the vessel by one inch fore and aft. Your tipping center (that point about which your vessel will tip, or trim in a fore and aft direction) can be assumed to be in approximately the same location as the longitudinal center of buoyancy (LCB), which should be indicated on your ship's plans. This is an exercise you should work out when you first join a vessel, because with some simple calculations you can learn what effect you can have by adding, discharging, or shifting weights fore and aft. This will not help much on a fin-keeled vessel, but on a vessel with a full-length keel that is aground aft, the simple act of having the crew (who perhaps were standing aft when you hit) run to the bow may be enough to lift her stern a critical inch or two. A large number of people crowding onto the bowsprit can have a remarkable lifting effect on the stern. You may also want to calculate how much weight of water you can pump into the forepeak, or the afterpeak, with your fire pump (if you have one), and what result that will have. On the same 80-foot schooner mentioned above, it is possible (by calculation) to raise the stern 4 inches in ten minutes by pumping water into the chain locker with the fire pump, at 50 gallons per minute. The same effect could be had immediately if fifteen people were aft at the time of grounding and they were all ordered forward.

If your vessel is subdivided into watertight compartments, you should be aware of your vessel's floodable length curves, also from your stability plans. These tell you how many, and which, compartments may be flooded and still allow your vessel to remain afloat. If the wrong combination of compartments is holed, you will know that you cannot afford to get off your ledge.

On an inspected vessel, this information must, by law, be maintained aboard, usually with the ship's lines drawings, sail plan, and construction drawings. For an uninspected yacht, the information should be readily available from the designer or builder.

All of the information discussed so far is information you must have at your immediate disposal, and every item is important. When you feel the sickening lurch of your vessel grinding her way up onto a rock ledge, you may get the feeling that your career is being ground away beneath the keel. However, the actions you take in the next minutes and hours will quite likely have more impact on your future career than those of the past hour. You must already have thought the process through, made the calculations, and have the right information at your disposal, so that you can now go right to work to save your crew, your vessel, and your career, in that order. There is an old saying: "Any damn fool can run a ship aground, but it takes a real seaman to get her off."

Refloating

Having covered the immediate concerns, we can now discuss some of the techniques for getting the vessel off the rocks, or at least getting her stabilized. The first moves will consist of things like getting an anchor out into deep water, or to windward; or getting a line from the masthead(s) to the shore, or to an anchor.

To set an anchor, you will need an anchor that your crew can handle. Aboard a large vessel, your bower (main) anchors will most likely be too heavy for this purpose, so you will need to have a good kedge aboard. A 50- or 75-pound Danforth or similar anchor makes an excellent kedge anchor. It can be managed by one person, can be carried by hand or in a small dinghy, has exceptional all-around holding power, and can be stowed conveniently on deck or below. It should have a long (20 feet or so) length of chain attached. And it should have its own substantial rode, ¾ inch or greater, Dacron or equivalent, several hundred feet long. You may plan to use docklines for the rode, if they are suitable, but it is better to have a dedicated line for this purpose. You may well end up adding docklines anyway to get the length you need, or you may need them for other jobs.

The kedge can be run out to windward, to prevent being set further on to the ledge, or it can be set in such a way that you will use it to pivot and then pull the vessel off in the direction you wish to go. It may be set broadside-to, with a line run from the masthead to ensure that she will lean in the direction you want her to. There are many stories about using kedges and lines to trees to secure a vessel upright, so she will not lie over on her bilge when the tide falls. However, there seem to be an inordinate number of these stories that end with the vessel taking a terrible fall onto that very bilge when the strain becomes too great for the rig. It would therefore seem prudent, under most circumstances, to accept the inevitable and take steps to be sure that she will lean (gently) to the preferred side, and do what you can to cushion that side. You may not be certain whether she will refloat before she fills as the tide returns (which is a function of hull shape, beam, and freeboard), but in the vast majority of cases vessels rise before filling. You will improve the odds here by seeing to it that she leans toward the high side of the ledge, which will hold her up a little higher. You should take steps to make the hatches, vents, and ports waterproof, so she will not fill through them as the water rises on the low side.

While she is still partially afloat you may be able to heave her over on to her side, lifting her keel off in this way. The kedge, with a line to the masthead, would be used here. This will work only if she is not very hard aground, but this method can be very effective if that is the case. A pull from a helpful vessel may accomplish the same effect. Use a good line from the masthead, but give some thought to the amount of strain you feel your rig can support in this effort. Do not pull your rig down in your enthusiasm.

Whatever the scenario, if your initial efforts do not succeed, or if you have gone aground on a very high tide, you will need to move on to more extraordinary measures. This may involve unloading your vessel completely—removing everything you can move. Assuming there is a place to take it all, such as ashore, or to another vessel, start with the heaviest gear (anchors, chain, boats, rafts, spare sails, and spars) and continue down the list as far as you can get before the next opportunity to refloat. Unbend your sails and remove your booms and gaffs if you can. Even personal gear, mattresses, and stores should go. Remember, every successive tidal cycle is another opportunity for her to pound and do more damage, so go at it with a vengeance. Never mind if it seems like overkill. Better to overdo it than underdo it and have to go through another pounding while the tide goes again and returns.

In the end, it may be this expenditure of energy toward saving a bad situation that not only saves your ship and crew, but your peace of mind as well. It is bad enough to find yourself aground, but it would be far worse to lose the vessel and have to live with wondering if a little more effort might have saved her.

FLOODING

Flooding aboard a sailing vessel and the procedure for coping with it are not significantly different than they are aboard any other type of vessel. Therefore, there is seemingly no reason to cover the subject in this text—it should be left to a general text on the subject. Unfortunately, there is, apparently, no such text available, except those written for large merchant and naval vessel operators and for naval architects. Small-vessel flooding (this statistic is derived from fishing vessel accidents, as reported to the U.S. Coast Guard in Portland, Maine, for the northern Gulf of Maine) accounted for approximately one-third of all reported accidents during 1993 and 1994. The problem is obviously significant, and the need for more information on the subject is apparent. What follows was prepared with the help of Jeffrey Ciampa, of the U.S. Coast Guard Marine Safety Office in Portland, Maine, who has been doing considerable research—and teaching—on the subject.

If your vessel's hull is holed at sea, you will have to make an emergency repair under the most adverse conditions. There will be no time to plan a repair carefully or execute it neatly. The repair will have to be fast and strong, and the result will probably be quite crude, but the object will be to stop a leak or prevent further failure of the hull structure. You will have to utilize the materials and tools you have on hand, and you may sacrifice some valuable pieces of your vessel's equipment to accomplish your repair.

There are many possible ways in which a vessel can become flooded at sea, besides capsizing or being inundated by a wave. (In these cases, unless there has been associated damage, the problem will be solely one of pumping her out, which will be discussed later.) A collision with another vessel, or a piece of floating debris, can puncture your hull. A severe wave can damage the hull, deck, or cabin structure. A broken piece of the vessel's own rig or equipment can puncture these as well. The vessel's hull can simply fail from material failure or faulty construction. A sea cock, also known as a through-hull fitting, is a piece of plumbing that penetrates the skin of the hull, for sink or head intake or discharge, engine cooling system, or other purposes. The sea cock, or the internal piping connected to it, can be damaged or destroyed, leaving an unprotected opening through the hull. A propeller or rudder shaft can break, or its internal connection to the vessel can fail, and the shaft can then fall out of its stuffing box, again leaving a hole in the hull. Galvanic corrosion—which can be caused by a stray current from a loose wiring connection becoming grounded in the bilge water—can corrode a fitting, causing it to fail. (This is often referred to as electrolysis, though that word technically refers to the actual chemical process involved.) A crew member, or a passenger, can accidentally (and possibly without even knowing it) step on or bump into, and dislodge or loosen, a hose connection to a sea cock. There are numerous ways for flooding to begin, but it may come as a surprise that the majority of flooding accidents are not the result of a major disaster, such as a collision. Many are the result of a seemingly small problem, which rapidly grows into a larger one as the circumstances gradually progress out of control. In the event of any of these failures, there are several techniques for temporary repairs that a sailor should be aware of, equipped for, and practiced in. Drills should be held for damage control, just as they are for other emergencies.

Most mariners will dramatically underestimate the amount of water flooding into their vessel through an opening. More importantly, they will also dramatically underestimate the *weight* of water entering their vessel through an opening. This is a very important point. Your vessel is afloat due to the buoyancy of the submerged portion of the hull. The rest of the intact portion of the hull, that which is above the water, is known as reserve buoyancy. This is your safety margin. When sea water is flooding into your vessel, she is settling deeper into the water due to the added weight, and she is losing her reserve buoyancy at the same rate. As you lose reserve buoyancy your deck hatches and companionways are getting progressively closer to the sea level. Assuming these openings are not watertight (they are usually *weathertight*, not watertight), if they reach that point they will begin adding, exponentially, to the flooding problems. To get an idea of what you might actually be dealing with, a 2-inch opening, 2 feet below the surface of the water, will allow approximately 111 gallons of water to enter your vessel *every minute*. This relates to almost *1,000 pounds per minute* (954.6, to be exact) of added weight, or lost reserve buoyancy. If this same size opening is 8 feet below the surface, this value doubles, to almost *1 ton* per minute. (See table on page 128 for flow rates of water through various openings at various head pressures.) In any case, the goal of the damage control process should not be to stop the flooding completely, but rather to bring it under control. You must not allow yourself to become fixated on trying to make a perfect patch, when an imperfect one will reduce the flow sufficiently to permit you to move on to other urgent jobs, such as investigating further to see if any other leaks need your attention. It is entirely too easy to become fixated on a single problem, while allowing another, equally important one, to go undiscovered.

Flow Rates (Q) in Gallons Per Minute

Diameter of hole, in inches	Head of water, in feet				
	2	4	6	8	10
1	28	39	48	56	62
2	111	157	192	222	248
3	250	353	433	500	559
4	444	628	770	889	994
5	694	982	1202	1388	1552
6	1000	1414	1732	1999	2235
7	1361	1924	2357	2721	3043
8	1777	2513	3078	3554	3974
9	2249	3181	3896	4499	5030
10	2777	3927	4810	5554	6209

Flow rate (Q) is calculated by the formula: $Q = 19.636\,(\sqrt{h})d^2$, where h is pressure head, in feet, and d is the diameter of the hole, in inches. Weight of sea water is approximately 8.6 pounds per gallon.

Once the accident or failure has occurred, and the crew have recognized the need for and the urgency of a repair, they will require some basic repair materials and tools. The need for these, and a discussion of which are appropriate for your particular vessel, should be addressed during the planning phase of a trip.

The first step, for any significant underwater hull damage, will be to slow the leak enough so you can effect a proper repair. This is most effectively done by dragging a collision mat over the hole on the outside of the hull. A collision mat is a commercially available piece of heavy canvas or synthetic tarpaulin material, preferably waterproofed, generally in two or more layers, with heavily reinforced edges and corners. The corners will have strong eyelets, and there should be eyelets along the edges as well. If you don't have a specially made collision mat, you can use a sail, tarp, boat cover, or any other piece of heavy material you have available. It will be necessary to fold it, or use several pieces, to achieve at least two layers. One layer will probably leak too much to be very useful. The collision mat is applied by tying lines to the corners, and perhaps to the eyelets along the sides as well, and utilizing these to drag the mat down the side of the hull, on the outside, until it covers the opening. The pressure of the water trying to flood into the hull will hold it in place, once it is there. It might prove useful (and some of the commercial mats have this installed) to attach a piece of fairly heavy chain, or other weight, along what will be the lower side of the mat to weigh it down. This will cause the mat to hang vertically in the water as you maneuver it into place. Once this mat is in place, it should at least slow the leak enough to make a more permanent repair possible. The collision mat will not likely stay in place if you get under way, since there will be a flow of water over it, tending to peel it off the hull; therefore, a more permanent repair will be necessary. But it is a relatively quick solution that will at least hold the flooding at bay until you can get the materials and tools together for the next step.

For a more permanent patch on the hull, deck, or house, plywood is almost universally useful, and every vessel should carry as much of it, in as large sheets as possible. Carry a thickness that is manageable—say ½- or ⅝-inch thick, so that it can be bent to conform to the curvature of the hull. It can be applied in multiple layers to add strength, as necessary. Be sure you have a suitable saw to cut it. To attach plywood to a wooden hull, a battery-powered screwdriver (a drywall gun) with galvanized drywall screws is ideal. (If you don't have the electrical system to support power tools, a so-called Yankee screwdriver will save a good deal of wear and tear on your wrists. This is a geared, hand-powered screwdriver, that works with a push-pull motion.) Drywall screws require no drilling, are fast, easy to apply, and reasonably strong. They should be used generously. To help seal around the edges, and help the screws bond the plywood to the hull, a strong, flexible, underwater-curing marine adhesive is recommended. Lacking that, put almost anything soft between the plywood and the hull, to function as a gasket. Several layers of cloth, smeared with grease, or any kind of caulking material, whether it is a synthetic goo or a natural fiber such as cotton or oakum, will also do well.

For fiberglass hulls, the combination of plywood and marine adhesive is still appropriate, but you will want self-tapping screws instead of drywall screws, to penetrate and grip the fiberglass.

On a steel hull, you will not likely succeed in attaching anything to the hull. Covering the hole with a collision mat will work as well as with any other hull, but any further repair will have to be made with a patch of plywood, or what-ever you have, that is not actually fastened to the hull, but simply braced up against it. (It is possible that you will get a good marine adhesive to stick to the steel hull, but unless you clean the paint off it first, you are really just sticking your patch to the paint, which has only a tenuous hold on the steel.) This will require some stout timbers, at least two-by-fours, for a small repair in a small space, but probably four-by-fours or heavier for most repairs. These timbers must be cut to fit between the patch they are supporting and something solid, more or less opposite it. The piece of timber should be cut to be slightly longer than necessary, so it must be driven into position between the bracing point and the patch. This same technique is used to shore up a weakened bulkhead, to support it. In that application it is called shoring, and though it may appear to be just crude carpentry, there are many tricks to cutting, fitting, and bracing a good shoring job. It is a process that is well worth practicing.

For a truly quick solution to a large hole in a hull, a mattress makes a reasonable plug. Stuff it into the hole the best you can (from inside the hull), then place something solid over the inboard side of it, which you can then brace with timber. Other inventive solutions will occur to people in desperate situations. Whatever works, with the materials you have at hand, is a good solution.

Other leaks have their own solutions. A split or cracked pipe can be wrapped with rubber gasket material and clamped with hose clamps. A crack in a pipe, a bulkhead, or the hull itself (on a steel or fiberglass hull), can sometimes be stopped up by driving a soft-wood wedge into it. A pipe or sea cock that has broken off completely, or become disconnected, can be plugged with a softwood, tapered plug. (These plugs and wedges, in different sizes, are available in so-called "damage control kits." They are a very important part of a damage control plan, but don't let the name lead you to believe that they constitute a complete kit. As explained above, there are a number of materials and tools that make up a complete damage control kit.)

Another common source of flooding is the loss of a propeller or rudder shaft. Every propeller shaft and most rudder shafts must penetrate the hull of the vessel, and where they do, the watertight integrity of the vessel is preserved by a "stuffing box." These work in various ways, but in general terms they contain a packing material that is compressed into the gap between the shaft and the tube through which it passes, where it penetrates the hull. The lubricated packing bears hard against the shaft and the tube, allowing the shaft to turn inside it, but preventing all but a slow drip of water from getting into the vessel. (The slow drip helps to lubricate and cool the shaft and the packing, so it is important not to try to stop it under normal operating conditions.) As with any mechanical device, stuffing boxes can fail. They sometimes spit out their packing or fail in other ways, and when they do, they can allow a great deal of water to enter the hull. They also present a very challenging leak to plug, since it is a circumferential gap around the shaft. To plug one, you need to repack it. If the mechanism for holding the original packing has failed, then you will have to use whatever material you can find that can be forced into the gap. It is not easy to drive any kind of material into this gap when water is pouring in through it. Depending on the configuration of the inboard end of the stuffing tube, you may be able to hose-clamp a piece of rubber gasket material over the tube and the shaft to effect a seal. Any of these methods will prevent you from being able to use your shaft, and thus your engine, again, so unless you have a second engine, you will have to rely on your sails until you can effect a functional repair. With some vessels, it may be possible—after effecting a temporary repair to slow or stop the leak—to ballast her down far enough by the head to bring the stuffing box out of the water. If this can be done, it would then be possible to remove the temporary patch and replace the packing system properly. This operation should be attempted only in calm weather, since this condition of trim would probably leave your vessel in a tender condition of stability.

The rig of a sailing vessel can overstress the hull in heavy weather, to the point of starting either minor or catastrophic leaks. The most common failures in this case are the garboard seam and the deck-edge seam. The garboard seam is the lowermost seam in a planked, wooden vessel, where the garboard plank meets the keel. The problem here occurs when the compressive forces of the mast drive the keel down and away from the planking, causing that seam to leak. A deck-edge seam failure occurs when the sideways force of the mast—where it passes through the deck at the partners—overstresses the connection between the hull side (the topsides) and the deck. This is a particular problem in fiberglass boats, since their hull and deck are each cast in a single, separate, piece and then connected. This connection is often a weak link, especially in the cheaper production boats. Failure in either the garboard or deck-edge seams will be particularly difficult to repair at sea, since they are both very difficult to access. The leak will probably be in the form of a long, narrow crack, and the crack will probably pass behind one or more bulkheads and/or floors or frames. The best solution will have to be developed on the spot, to accommodate the particular problems of the case, but you will need to try to force into the crack whatever caulking materials will fit. Smear a generous amount of marine adhesive on the hull (and/or deck) around and in the crack, and on the caulking material, before you drive the material into place. Then back it up with some bracing to hold it in place. If it stays in place long enough, the adhesive will cure and the patch should hold.

All of the actions described above will be useful only if you know where the leak is. If you are not aware of the problem until the flooding has submerged the leak, you may have a very difficult time locating the source. There is no simple solution, and if it is more than a small leak, it may not even be realistic to try. You can start by checking the most obvious places, and then continue with a general search, hoping to see or feel the water rushing in. In the engine room, or space, start by shutting off the engine. This way, if the raw water pump is the source of the problem, you will no longer be pumping the water into the boat. Furthermore, with the engine shut off, you may be able to hear the sound of the water rushing in. Next, check the stuffing box and all sea cocks. Then check around the mast step and along the garboard seam. If one of those doesn't appear to be the source, then you will just have to keep searching until you find something. It can be very difficult, given that so much of the vessel's hull is hidden, from the inside, by joiner-work, ceiling planking, and what-have-you.

Pumps

While some of the crew are involved in the patching process, others of the crew will have to be operating and maintaining the pumps. This is rarely as simple as starting them and letting them run. Pumps will clog, especially if there has been an accident, and there will be a variety of things floating in the bilge that will plug up the strainer, if you're lucky, or the pump itself, if they get past the strainer. Soft material, such as rags, will plug up a pump, but hard or gritty material, such as nails or gravel, will destroy an impeller. For this reason, you must be certain you have a number of spare impellers for each impeller pump on board (other types of pumps have their own idiosyncratic ways of becoming disabled). To prevent such problems, assign someone to monitor the pumps and the bilges constantly, pick up any stray material that might clog the pumps, and clean the strainers periodically, if they are accessible. Shutting the pump off for five minutes to clean the strainer, on a regular basis, is a precaution that could easily save you a half-hour of impeller-replacement time.

Most mariners, who are, as we have said, apt to underestimate the amount of water flooding into their vessel, are also likely to overestimate their pumps' abilities to remove that water. Remember the amount of water that might be flooding in through a single, 2-inch opening, 2 feet below the surface—approximately 111 gallons per minute (GPM). The portable salvage pump described in chapter 15, which is a fairly substantial pump, will pump 120 GPM. That pump will stay just ahead of such a leak. If the leak is 4 feet below the surface, or is $^1/_2$-inch larger in diameter, that pump will not keep up. You must evaluate your vessel's pumping system to be certain that you can keep up with a substantial leak, even after one of your pumps has become disabled. There is no such thing as having too much pumping capacity on a vessel.

Commonly, one of the most powerful pumps on board a vessel is not a bilge pump at all. A water-cooled main engine's raw water pump is a very substantial pump and can be brought into service as a bilge pump in a serious flooding emergency in the engine room. It will require disconnecting the hose, or piping, from the suction side of the pump, somewhere along the plumbing between the pump and its sea cock. This may not be easy to do, unless it has been considered in advance, and some arrangements have been made to do so. If the engine room is flooding and the suction side of this pump is submerged, this pump will move a substantial volume of water for as long as the engine remains running.

Having covered the actions to be taken to try to save the vessel, it is equally important to stress the need for careful evaluation of the whole problem, to determine whether the vessel is in fact going to be saved. If you allow yourself to become overly involved in the patching or pumping process, you could lose sight of the big picture, which in fact might indicate that the ship really is sinking. Flooding is a progressive problem. The flooding rate increases as the leak(s) become submerged farther underwater, as shown in the table on page 128. Don't wait until the last minute to make preparations for abandoning ship, or sending Mayday calls for help.

On a vessel with watertight subdivision, you should know whether or not your vessel will remain afloat with a given compartment, or combination of compartments, flooded. But if you have no watertight subdivision (if the leak is anything more than a minor one) and if the leak is at or below the water level in the bilge you should be seriously considering abandoning ship. The difficulty of placing and securing a functional patch, underwater, is simply too great to be very realistic.

Jeffrey Ciampa provides three rules for damage control on small vessels:

1. *Don't make it worse.* In your enthusiasm—or panic—don't let your patching efforts cause more damage than already exists. It is easy to drive a wedge into a hole, only to burst out a larger section of the hull, or pipe, or whatever you were patching.

2. *Work fast, and watch your back.* Time is everything. You have only to look at the table on page 128 to appreciate that the problem will get progressively worse as time progresses, without effective patching. Be aware of the possibility of more leaks and of the need to prepare to abandon ship. Get calls out for help. You don't have to reach the Coast Guard—call anyone in the area.

3. *There are no rules.* Whatever works is what you need to do. Each person involved in an emergency will be inventing solutions, because no two problems are the same.

FIRE FIGHTING

A fire on board a sailing vessel, while certainly an extremely dangerous situation, is not significantly different from a fire on board any other vessel. Sailing vessels may be somewhat more at risk than other categories of vessels, however, since their sails are typically flammable, and many of the vessels themselves are traditionally built with flammable materials. We will not go into the processes of fire fighting here, as this subject is adequately covered in a number of other texts. The reader is specifically referred to the Maritime Training Advisory Board text noted at the end of the chapter.

It is important that the master and mates make a point of discussing the fire plan for the vessel with the crew and hold regular drills to practice the methods and familiarize everyone with the equipment available for fighting a fire. Every crew member should be familiar with the locations of every fire extinguisher, its type, function, and purpose, and the circumstances under which it should *not* be used (as with a liquid-discharge extinguisher on an electrical fire, or a carbon-dioxide extinguisher in an enclosed space, with people inside). They should know the locations of remote-activation devices for fixed extinguishing systems and shutoff devices for fuel supply lines and ventilation systems.

One of the most difficult aspects of a fire-fighting plan, on a vessel with more than a few people on board, is determining if anyone is inside the space which is on fire. The risk involved in entering a fire- or smoke-filled space is so great, it is imperative that you not enter—or send someone else to enter—such a space unless you absolutely have to. Therefore, you must make every effort to account for every member of the ship's company before anyone tries to enter the space. A system for doing this should be included in the fire plan and practiced at each drill.

ABANDONING SHIP

If a shipboard emergency gets out of control, it may become necessary to abandon ship. The decision to take this step is an extremely serious one, with extraordinary ramifications, and should not be made by anyone except the master, or the next in charge if the master is incapacitated. It is tragic, but true, that vessels have been found afloat, after their crews have abandoned ship and subsequently been lost. Your ship, in almost any condition, is generally a better platform for survival than the best equipped lifeboat or life raft. One need only talk to a person who has lived in a survival craft at sea to be convinced of that. Life in a lifeboat or raft is pure survival—there is no measure of comfort to be had. Seasickness can overcome the strongest stomachs; saltwater sores, dehydration, sleep deprivation, claustrophobia, and many other phobias will take their toll. Some shipmates will rise to the challenge (sometimes the most unlikely ones) and become leaders and caregivers, while others (again, sometimes the most unlikely ones) may break down in despair, fear, or sheer misery, becoming a burden on the others.

On board your vessel, even if she is in terrible condition, you have more to work with. If you get your lifeboats or rafts ready for abandoning ship, but don't depart in them, you will have the benefit of the survival gear they have to offer, with the added benefit of the larger platform that is your ship. You will have more room to spread out, more food, water, tools, and supplies of all kinds, and the crew will not have suffered the sometimes debilitating depression that has been known to set in when their ship sinks or is left behind.

Nonetheless, having emphasized the importance of staying with the vessel as long as possible, it is equally important to make preparations to leave, in plenty of time. Do not delay the preparations, if the possibility of abandoning ship is real. The more time you have for preparations, the better you will fare once the step is taken.

One of the first steps in preparation should be to transmit a distress call on the radio. This is preceded by the spoken words "Mayday-Mayday," repeated three times. After that, give your position, nature of the emergency, number of persons on board, description of the vessel, type of survival craft or gear you have, and any other details you consider important. Give the entire call, even if you don't think anyone is listening. It is just possible someone can hear you, but you can't hear them responding.

In an emergency situation, it is advisable to make a radio call before the problem turns into a distress situation. If you detect significant flooding, or a fire, it is a good idea to transmit the details of your situation right away, in case the problem gets out of control. In this case, you will not be transmitting a Mayday call, but a "Pan" call instead. A radio message preceded by the spoken words "Pan-Pan" (three times) indicates an urgent message, but not a distress message. Give all the same information as you would for a Mayday call, but be sure to indicate that the problem has not yet reached a critical stage.

The process for abandoning ship is one that should also be practiced. The circumstances of a real emergency will dictate how much time there is to prepare, and therefore how much equipment and supplies your crew will be able to compile. However, if each person has specific responsibilities, it is almost a certainty that you will find yourself in the lifeboat better supplied than if everyone had just grabbed whatever came to mind.

One of the things to take is the "ditch kit," or "grab-and-go bag," which you should have prepared before the start of the voyage. This is a bag, such as a duffel bag, containing a number of items that will be useful to supplement your lifeboat's equipment. A recommended list of contents for such a bag is included in the Blue-Water Checklist in appendix II.

Further reading (see bibliography for details): Knox-Johnston, *Seamanship*, chap. 3; Maloney, *Chapman Piloting*, chap. 11; Maritime Training Advisory Board, *Marine Fire Prevention, Fire Fighting, and Fire Safety.*

CHAPTER TWELVE

INTRODUCTORY METEOROLOGY
FOR SAILORS

Weather is essentially a huge engine in the atmosphere. Its fuel is heat, which is delivered to it in the form of radiant energy from the sun. This fuel warms the land, water, and air; imparts motion to the air; causes clouds to form and dissipate by evaporating and condensing water; and develops high- and low-pressure areas throughout the earth's atmosphere. These major functions produce our weather and determine the force and direction of the winds. An understanding of these causative and controlling factors helps to predict winds and to use them to best advantage.

Different substances on earth absorb energy differently. Water, for example, has much greater heat storage capacity than air or land. However, water also requires more time to store up that heat. Materials that absorb heat slowly also release it slowly, and vice versa. Generally, land absorbs and releases heat relatively quickly, though there are variations with different types of land. These differences between land and water are of significant interest to us, because of the contrasts they provide. The sun rises, warms the land quickly and the water more slowly, and then sets. Throughout the night, the land releases its heat fairly quickly, while the water releases its heat quite slowly. As a result we get areas of relative warmth adjoining areas of relative cool.

Since we know that hot air rises and cool air sinks, we can quickly see how the process of airflow develops. On a local scale, as warm air over the land rises during the day it draws air in from the sea. This air was cool, having settled as it cooled. As it flows over the land it warms and rises aloft, where it is drawn outward and down by the settling of the cooler air over the water. This is the process that gives us our sea breezes, meaning that wind (at the surface) is flowing in from the sea (fig. 12-1). The process is reversed at night, because the water holds its heat longer than the land, which cools relatively quickly. Late at night you find the air over land to be relatively cool and settling, flowing out over the water (a land breeze) where it finds the water to be relatively warmer.

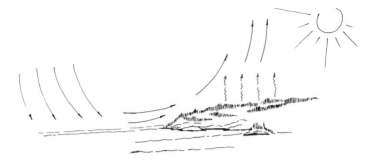

Fig. 12-1. *Sea breeze. The opposite cycle, occurring at night, is called land breeze.*

As it is warmed there, it rises and, when aloft, is drawn back over the land, cooled, and drawn down again.

This same process occurs on a global scale, with warm air rising at the equator, cooling and settling at the poles. It also occurs on a seasonal scale, as continents warm up during the summer and adjacent oceans remain relatively cooler. In winter the reverse happens and the land becomes cooler while the ocean remains relatively warmer. When one air mass rises and a neighboring air mass settles, a connected movement of air results.

The rotation of the earth produces an interesting phenomenon called the Coriolis force, so-called because it was discovered and explained by Gaspard Coriolis. The simplest explanation of this force, or effect, is illustrated by imagining the firing of a bullet from the North Pole toward a target on the equator. By the time the bullet reaches the equator, the target will have rotated with the earth, to the east, considerably. The bullet will miss the target, landing substantially to the west. To an observer in space, the bullet will be seen to travel in a straight line, but to an observer on the earth, it will appear to have been deflected to the right. From this overly simplified example, it can be seen that while there was no true force deflecting the bullet to the right, to an observer on the earth there certainly appeared to have been, and therefore we must take this "force" into consideration when making all calculations regarding moving objects. The Coriolis force is included in all calculations for firing long-range projectiles, for the prediction of ocean currents, and for predicting the movement of air (wind). Although the derivation of the actual formula which defines the effect of the Coriolis force is beyond the scope of this study, its apparent effects are simple to grasp.

- It deflects the wind to the right in the Northern Hemisphere and to the left in the Southern Hemisphere.
- The amount of that deflection increases as latitude increases (as you move away from the equator), and it decreases to zero at the equator.

(For practical purposes it can be assumed to be nonexistent within 10 degrees of the equator.)

- It increases in effect as the velocity of the wind (or current, or projectile) increases.

We will refer to this force periodically and will see its ramifications in several contexts, but these basic effects are important to remember.

THE PRESSURE GRADIENT

When looking at the winds in the atmosphere, we can view many different scales of wind patterns. We can look at the little cat's-paws, or puffs, of wind that rush across the cove, or the sea breezes that build in the afternoon along the coast, or the general counterclockwise circulation (for observers in the Northern Hemisphere) of winds around a low-pressure system, or the monsoons that blow seasonally on and off some of the continents. Or we can look at the global patterns of trade winds, doldrums, prevailing westerlies, and polar easterlies that blow more or less persistently year around. In all cases, the wind is the result of air flowing from an area of relatively high pressure toward an area of relatively low pressure, down what is known as a pressure gradient.

Air—that combination of gasses that makes up atmosphere—has weight. This weight may be difficult to perceive, but it is measurable. A barometer simply weighs the air above it. The more air above, the higher the pressure. The less air above, the lower the pressure. At sea level, this should theoretically be enough to displace about 29.92 inches of mercury in a standard mercury barometer. This translates to 1013.25 millibars of pressure. Any barometer reading higher than this indicates a high-pressure area, and a lower reading indicates a low.

Air is considered a fluid, and as such, it flows. It piles up in some places, causing higher pressure at the surface. In other places, rising air (caused, perhaps, by warming), is literally lifting the air's weight off the ground, creating an area of low pressure. Because of its fluid nature, air will tend to flow away from a high-pressure area, and toward a low-pressure area, in an effort to restore a general equilibrium. It is this horizontal flow of air that we call wind, the sailor's principal concern.

The flow of air from an area of high pressure toward a low is much like water flowing downhill. The higher the high and the lower the low, the more of a slope there will be between them. Likewise, the closer the high is to the low, the steeper that slope must be. This "slope" is called the pressure gradient. Just as with water flowing downhill, the steeper the pressure gradient (the more exaggerated the difference between the high and the low), the faster the airflow (wind) will be.

As implied above, one of the reasons for these areas of higher and lower pressure is often heat. Warmer air is less dense, and being less dense it tends to rise, lifting its weight off the ground and the barometer, causing (and causing your barometer to register) an area of lower pressure. This area of warm, rising air can be very local in scale (as with a small island that warms relatively more quickly than the surrounding ocean on a hot, sunny day); it can be continental in scale (as with the Indian continent heating up dramatically during the summer, while the adjacent Indian Ocean warms relatively more slowly); or it can be global in scale, with the equator remaining substantially warmer than the poles. In each case, there is a difference in temperature in adjacent air parcels, or masses (an air mass is a gigantic air parcel), which causes a pressure difference—or gradient—which in turn causes airflow, or wind.

GLOBAL WIND CIRCULATION

Drawing on an understanding of the pressure gradient and the Coriolis force, we can identify the global wind patterns, which include the famous trade winds and the equally infamous doldrums (see figure 12-2).

If we are to start with the clearest example of a heat-induced low, we must begin at the equator. The equator is without question an area of considerable warmth, worldwide. Here the warm air rises, with two results. First, there is virtually no wind, because rising air is not wind; horizontal airflow is. For sailors, this has historically made crossing the equator a challenge. Second, there is considerable cloud cover and rain on the equator. Rising air expands, due to the decrease in atmospheric pressure with altitude. Expansion is a cooling process, and the cooling of air causes it to condense out its moisture. This moisture then goes into suspension as minute droplets, which we see as clouds, and when enough of these get together, they form rain. This area has been known for centuries, by sailors at least, as the doldrums. It is infamous for having no wind (except for the occasional squall, coming from thunderstorms) and leaden, overcast skies with scattered thunder and lightning storms.

The trade winds are everything the doldrums aren't. They are a belt of steady winds and fine weather that extends north and south from the doldrums to, very approximately, 30 degrees of latitude. The winds are, at least over the major oceans, very persistent and reliable. They blow from the northeast in the Northern Hemisphere, and from the southeast in the Southern Hemisphere—hence their names—the northeast and southeast trades. The fine characteristics of the trades can be traced back to the rising air in the doldrums. That air rose and diverged, once aloft, toward the poles. Some flowed north and some flowed south (at this point, for simplicity, we will focus on the Northern Hemisphere—the same rules hold true for the Southern Hemisphere, as long as you remember that the Coriolis force works to the left there), but it had been drained of virtually all of its moisture as it rained down on the poor sailors in

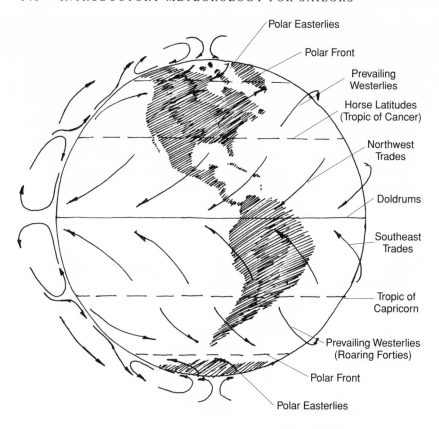

Polar Easterlies

Polar Front

Prevailing
Westerlies

Horse Latitudes
(Tropic of Cancer)

Northwest
Trades

Doldrums

Southeast
Trades

Tropic of
Capricorn

Prevailing Westerlies
(Roaring Forties)

Polar Front

Polar Easterlies

Fig. 12-2. *Simplified global wind circulation. This model ignores the effects of the land masses.*

the doldrums, and was cooled in the process of rising and flowing away from the equator. By the time it reached the latitude of about 30 degrees north, it was cool enough to sink back to the surface again. It did so, and two things happened. First, it dried out even more. (Remembering that the rising and cooling process wrings moisture out of the air, we can conclude that the sinking process warms and dries the air. Actually, the sinking process warms the air [by compressing it], and warmer air has a greater capacity to hold water. Since it now has increased capacity to hold water, but the water has long since been wrung out of it, it must end up as very dry, clear air.) Second, the sinking air must flow somewhere when it reaches the surface, so it divides. About half of it flows back to the south, toward the equator, where it eventually gets caught up in the cycle that began in the doldrums. So far, we have explained the reason for the clear, sunny weather of the trades, but we have depicted a flow of wind toward the south, not from the northeast. The easterly component of the wind is explained by the Coriolis force. The air would like to flow from 30 degrees north latitude, directly south to the equator, but it is deflected to the right by the Coriolis force, and ends up flowing toward the southwest.

The area of the oceans at about 30 degrees north has its own infamous name. It is an area of sinking air, which, like the rising air of the doldrums, is of no practical use to sailors. To make matters worse for the sailors who get becalmed there, the air is dry and clear—devoid of moisture. Apparently, as the story goes, a ship with a cargo of horses was becalmed long enough in this area that they were forced to throw their horses overboard, as their freshwater supplies dwindled. The region became known as the horse latitudes.

North of the horse latitudes, the air that flowed to the north from that area is also deflected to the right by the Coriolis force, and gives the region from 30 degrees north to about 60 degrees north a wind system that is roughly southwest (flowing toward the northeast). In the Northern Hemisphere, this region does in fact experience a prevailing southwest wind, but there are so many other meteorological influences affecting the weather here that we don't see nearly the persistence in wind direction that we do in the trade wind belt. Most of this variation can be attributed to the land masses and their widely varied temperature patterns. In the Southern Hemisphere there is much less land area worldwide, and the prevailing winds are more persistent there.

Finally, the region from about 60 degrees north to near the north pole experiences a prevailing wind from the east, known as the polar easterlies. This is the result of the very cold air at the poles sinking and flowing south along the surface. Again the Coriolis force deflects it to the right, and the result is a northeast wind.

Where the cold polar easterlies meet the relatively warmer prevailing westerlies (at about 60 degrees north), we again have an area of rising air—rising, cooling, and condensing. This is known as the polar front, and it is the breeding ground of the vast majority of low-pressure systems that we will discuss later.

The boundaries of all of the global wind systems and weather patterns described here are theoretical only, and in fact are altered dramatically, in some places, by the influence of land and its widely variable temperature patterns, and topography. In general terms, the farther you are from land, the more closely your observations will fit the theoretical model. The distribution of land masses on the earth is such that the Southern Hemisphere has about 20 percent more ocean than the Northern Hemisphere. As a result, the global wind circulation of the Southern Hemisphere is significantly closer to the theoretical model than that of the Northern Hemisphere.

LOCAL WINDS

In every part of the world there are different local wind and weather patterns with which one should be familiar when sailing in any particular area. These can range in scale from the winter and summer monsoons of the Indian Ocean to the way the local breeze tends to provide a favorable lift along one side of a certain bay. If we understand the basic principles of what is driving these variations, we can either deduce them for ourselves or at least make them easier to remember. We should also know where to find out about them. This would normally be in a local pilot book such as *U.S. Coast Pilot* or *Sailing Directions*. *American Practical Navigator*, by Nathaniel Bowditch (popularly known simply as *Bowditch*), describes a number of these local winds in the chapter on Ocean Winds and Weather. Many countries' governments publish similar pilot books about their home waters, and some countries have conducted very extensive research worldwide. (The U.S. *Pilot Charts*, published by the National Imagery and Mapping Agency [formerly the Defense Mapping Agency], provide extensive information on the whole world, but on a small scale.)

We described earlier the process that drives the land and sea breezes. This process can occur on a very local scale, and in some cases may appear to be slightly different from the theoretical model previously described. For instance, a variation from the norm might be found where a cold water current is flowing near shore. In this area in summer, then, you would find significant sea breezes developing during the afternoon when the land warms, but you would not find much of a land breeze developing at night, because the cooling land temperature might not fall below the temperature of the cold current along the shore.

Another local phenomenon is explained by drawing on our understanding of the Coriolis force. We know that wind will flow from high pressure toward low—and will blow harder the steeper the pressure gradient is—but as it does so, it is deflected by the Coriolis force, to the right in the Northern Hemisphere, to the left in the Southern. We also know that the amount of deflection depends on the velocity of the wind and the latitude. The stronger the wind, the more this deflection will be. At the surface, there is friction (aloft, there is no significant friction). The wind is slowed by the friction of the ground or the water. In general, the land (with trees, houses, hills, etc.) will develop more friction than the water. So we can expect the wind to speed up as it moves over the water. As it speeds up, the Coriolis force becomes greater and the wind is deflected more to the right. This deflection can amount to as much as 10 to 20 degrees. The wind blowing down the pressure gradient will be deflected between 50 and 70 degrees over land, and about 70 or 80 degrees over water. A sailor aware of this difference can sometimes plot a course to take advantage of this, by knowing when the winds near shore (where the wind is still under the influence of the land) will be favorable, or when the winds farther offshore (where the wind is under the influence of the water) will be more favorable.

Aloft, away from the frictional effects of the ground, the winds reach much greater velocities, and as a result the deflection due to the Coriolis force normally reaches a full 90 degrees. That is, although the wind is trying to blow down the pressure gradient, the Coriolis force deflects it so much that it ends up blowing parallel to the gradient instead. This will be important later when we look at upper-level weather maps.

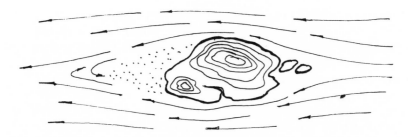

Fig. 12-3. *Wind flow around an island. Note the wind "bending" before it reaches the island; and the "dead zone" and eddies, to leeward.*

Now let us examine a third local phenomenon. Remember that air is a fluid, and it flows in exactly the same manner as described in the discussion of airflow around a sail. It will adhere to a curved land mass, such as a mountain, and flow around it, until the curve becomes too great, at which point it will break into turbulent flow. Here large eddies will form. We see this phenomenon on the leeward side of islands, where we may get a very different wind from that which is blowing on the windward side. There, the wind is deflected by its collision with the island obstacle. If we visualize the fluid flow around an obstacle, we can predict these wind currents and use them to our advantage. Note that the flow is not only affected on the leeward side of the island but to windward as well, where the approaching wind first gets deflected by the obstacle in its path (fig. 12-3).

Each of these particular local conditions is distinct in theory only. In real life, all of these separate conditions occur simultaneously, and our task is to determine which one will dominate in the final combination.

The development and movement of weather systems is a highly complex subject, but the following brief description will allow a sailor to get useful information out of a weather map as received over the weatherfax.

CYCLONIC AND ANTICYCLONIC CIRCULATION

Picture a low-pressure area as a small spot over the ocean. The wind tries to blow directly toward that spot, but gets deflected about 70 to 80 degrees to the right (in the Northern Hemisphere) by the Coriolis force. Since this will be happening on all sides of the low, a counterclockwise flow of air, or wind, will develop around and into that low. This is called cyclonic circulation. In the Southern Hemisphere it will still be called cyclonic, but it will be clockwise.

The reverse is true of a high-pressure area. The wind tries to blow directly out from a high, gets deflected about 70 to 80 degrees to the right (in the Northern Hemisphere) and ends up blowing in an outward, clockwise spiral. This flow is called anticyclonic.

In both cases, the air is blowing down a pressure gradient, but in real life it is rarely a smooth, even gradient. Instead, the gradient slopes differently in different directions. Looking at a barometric pressure map and comparing it to a topographic map of the countryside, you will see hills, valleys, gorges, cliffs, troughs, and ridges. The lines of the pressure map (called isobars because they connect areas of equal pressure) are comparable to the contour lines on a topographic map. The slopes represent the pressure gradient. The wind wants to fall down them, but as it does so it is deflected by the Coriolis force. So you do not have to find the center of the low to know which way the wind will blow; you need only know which way the slope is facing. Take any isobar, note which side of it has the lower pressure, start straight down that slope (at a 90-degree angle to the isobar) and then turn right about 80 degrees (if you are over water; 70 degrees if you are over land). This is roughly the direction the wind will blow at that point. (But do not forget that wind direction is given as the direction it is coming from, not going to, so a wind blowing toward the north would be described as a south wind.) From this simple step you can predict wind direction anywhere on a weather map, if the isobars are shown. And you can also estimate velocity. Wind strength will be a product of how steep the pressure gradient is. We can make fairly general estimates about wind velocity by noting whether the isobars are closely or widely spaced. Meteorologists have the means to measure it quantitatively, but it will generally be of sufficient value to us to be able to say it will be blowing very hard over here, or be quite light over there, depending on the relative spacing of the isobars. A study of surface analysis isobaric charts for a region will help to increase your understanding of this.

FRONTS

The next area of concern in forecasting is the front. A front is the leading edge of an air mass. An air mass is a large parcel of air with roughly homogeneous characteristics of temperature and moisture. An air mass that moves north and east from the Gulf of Mexico over the eastern United States will be relatively warm and moist, while an air mass that comes down from Canada will be relatively colder and drier. When these two meet, which they often do (this is the principle source of the weather we receive in the eastern half of the United States), there is an edge that divides them. This is the front. If the warm air mass is overtaking the cold one, it will be a warm front, because it will be the front edge of the warm air mass. If the reverse is true, it will be a cold front. These are drawn on weather maps using the symbols shown in figure 12-4A.

When warm and cold air masses meet, there is interaction. Warm, moist air, being lighter than the cold air, will ride up on top of the cold, and as a result will cool (rising air expands, which is a cooling process), causing condensation of its water vapor from the gaseous state (which is invisible) into its liquid state in minute droplets that we can see as clouds or fog.

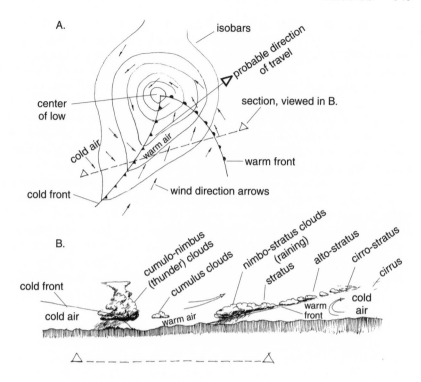

Fig. 12-4. *A typical low-pressure system, showing fronts, isobars, wind direction, and cloud patterns in plan view and in cross-section.*

At a warm front, air is forced aloft and cooled, and clouds are then formed by the condensation of the water vapor. If enough water is condensed, rain will occur. As the air continues to rise over the cold air mass, the water vapor is gradually condensed out, until finally there is none left. Thus the clouds are heaviest, with rain and fog accompanying them, at the base of the front, and they get thinner as they get higher. Looking at a cross section of this, we see the typical pattern of a warm front (fig. 12-4B).

As a warm front approaches, the first signs are the last of the water vapor being squeezed out, high overhead. This will appear as wispy, high cirrus clouds, popularly called mare's tales. As the front approaches, these will thicken and lower gradually, until within twelve to twenty-four hours the frontal base arrives in the midst of the low stratus and nimbostratus rain clouds and fog.

Once the warm front has passed, the warm air mass, of which the front is the leading edge, will arrive. This will be noticeably warmer, fairly humid, and mostly sunny, with scattered clouds.

Now picture that this warm air mass is itself being overtaken by a cold air mass. The leading edge of the cold air will be a cold front. Cold air being heavier than warm, it will be forcing its way under the warm air mass. The result is somewhat similar to the warm front; the warm air is forced aloft, cooled, and condensed. However, this process happens in an hour or two instead of a day or two. A cold front is very abrupt, and the whole process is very vigorous, sometimes violent. The reason is twofold. First, as the two air masses move along, they are literally dragging along the surface—the ocean or the land. Friction slows the movement of the air closest to the ground. Therefore, the air aloft over the warm front is able to slide out ahead, giving plenty of warning and making the whole process stretch out over a large area. At the cold front, however, as the cold air tries to force its way under the warm, that which is at the surface is slowed by friction, allowing the air above and behind to catch up, where it runs head-on into a wall of warm air that it must then slide under. This causes a pileup, so that a cold front is more nearly vertical. Thus the warm air must rise up a nearly vertical wall. The process that took many hours to happen at the warm front now takes place in an hour or two (see figure 12-4B).

Second, any mixing that occurs between the two air masses at the cold front will produce strong updrafts, because the lighter warm air will rise rapidly through the denser cold air. At the warm front, however, any warm air that gets mixed up in the cold will rise only until it hits the layer of warm air that has slid out ahead on top. This is why the clouds over a warm front are layered and flat—spreading out to cover the whole sky, whereas the clouds associated with a cold front are towering, puffy clouds containing strong updrafts. These are called cumulus clouds before they start raining, and when they are raining they are called cumulonimbus clouds. (The word nimbus indicates a cloud from which rain is falling.)

Because of the more abrupt, and potentially violent, nature of the cold front, there will be thunderstorms, lightning, and perhaps hail, tornadoes, and microbursts. It will pass very quickly and be followed by the cold, clear, crisp, dry air that came from the north. The cold front will be indicated on a weather map by the symbols indicated in figure 12-4A.

The examples given are for the U.S. East Coast, but similar processes occur in other areas. If the adjacent air masses are dramatically different in moisture content and/or temperature, the front will be more significant—if they are more similar, it will be less so.

EXTRATROPICAL CYCLONES

The warm and cold fronts described here are often tied together in a single cyclonic system, generally called a low, an extratropical cyclone, or simply a storm. (They are called extratropical because they occur outside of the tropics. Those that occur within the tropics are known as tropical cyclones or hurricanes. These systems are different and contain no fronts at all. We will discuss these in the next chapter.) The extratropical cyclone is an area of low pressure that is a system complete in itself. It is an area of enclosed isobars—that is, one or more isobars will completely enclose the low-pressure center (though it may be of almost any shape)—with a warm front typically leading off to the east or southeast and a cold front trailing off to the south or southwest in the Northern Hemisphere—in the Southern Hemisphere, this would be reversed (see figure 12-4). These two fronts enclose a sector of warm air to the south, which is drawn in by the southerly winds there. The air to the north will be colder, as it is drawn from the north by the northerly winds there (remember, the counter-clockwise wind flow around the low will mean that the circulation on the north side of the low will produce northerly and northeasterly winds there). Such a low will typically last for several days to a week before dying out. The dying-out phase begins when the cold front—which generally moves a bit faster than the warm front—gradually overtakes the warm front, eventually forcing all the warm air aloft. Once this happens, there is no longer a substantial temperature difference at the surface level, and the energy of the system is lost. (It is an important point that the energy fueling the storm is derived from the natural tendency of air, as a fluid, to want to return from a state of imbalance [tempera-ture differential, in this case] to a state of equilibrium.) This stage is called the occluded stage, and the front at this point is called an occluded front (fig. 12-5). The occlusion is the most violent stage of a low, but it is also the beginning of the end.

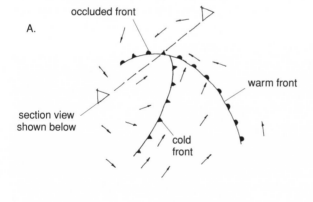

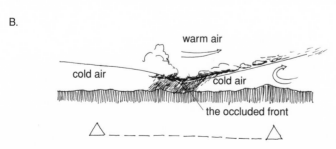

Fig. 12-5. *An occlusion.*

MOVEMENT OF LOWS AND WINDS ALOFT

Surface lows (there are lows aloft as well) travel more or less with the prevailing winds. In the prevailing westerlies they will travel from west to east. They are also attracted to other lows and shy away from, or veer around, strong highs. As a general rule, they move in a direction approximately parallel to the isobars in their warm sector (the warm area between the cold and the warm fronts). Furthermore, and more precisely, they will be steered by the winds aloft. This requires some explanation.

Well above the surface of the earth (20,000 feet or so), the winds experience very little friction. This allows them to blow extremely hard, and because of that it allows the Coriolis force to have its maximum effect (remember, Coriolis force increases with increased velocity). It deflects the wind a full 90 degrees to the right, so that it ends up blowing parallel to the isobars. These powerful winds provide the primary steering currents that drive the surface systems.

We can identify these winds by looking at a weather map that shows us what is going on aloft. This is found in the 500-millibar map. If we recall that the average sea-level pressure is just over 1,000 millibars, then we can see that 500 millibars of pressure will occur roughly halfway up through the atmosphere, at about 20,000 feet. (Since the atmospheric pressure changes at a decreasing rate as you go aloft, 20,000 feet is nowhere near halfway up through the earth's atmosphere by height. There is still measurable atmospheric pressure above 60 miles.) We can receive maps over the weatherfax that show the height of this 500-millibar surface. The nature of this surface is such that we can look at the height contours (called 500-millibar isoheights) and pretend we are looking at isobars. They look the same and they tell us the same thing. Where there is a low-pressure area aloft, the 500-millibar surface will be low, and where there is a high, the surface will be high. So we can look at these lines, pretend they are isobars, and note that the winds at this level will be blowing parallel to them. Which direction the wind is blowing along them is determined by remembering that the wind started down the gradient, then got deflected 90 degrees to the right (in the Northern Hemisphere). With this we can make an educated guess about the direction in which the surface lows will be moving.

THE MICROBURST

One of the most dangerous hazards to a sailing vessel is the microburst, or downburst, yet there is relatively little information available on the subject. Unlike hurricanes, which are carefully tracked and forecast, microbursts are such localized phenomena, and dissipate so quickly, that there is virtually no way for the National Weather Service to predict their occurrence, at least at sea. (On land, major airports are presently being fitted with special radar that will assist airport officials in trying to identify the atmospheric conditions that could spawn microbursts.) There are, however, some visual clues which can provide time to avoid a disaster such as the sinking of the *Pride of Baltimore I* in 1986 by a microburst, with the loss of her captain and three of her crew.

A microburst is a violent downdraft, ordinarily coming out of a thunderstorm, which, when it strikes the surface, spreads out in all directions. The implications to a sailing vessel are fairly obvious, but they have dangerous implications for any ship, as well as for structures and people ashore. They are practically instantaneous, usually lasting less than ten minutes, and can generate wind speeds of 150 knots. They can be so severe that, before they were fully recognized in the 1970s, the damage left by them ashore was usually attributed to unseen tornadoes. Microbursts do not always reach the surface, in which case they will not pose a threat to surface craft, but they are still potentially deadly to aircraft. This discussion of microbursts draws heavily from a book by Fernando Caracena et al., entitled *Microbursts—A Handbook for Visual Identification*.

The direction of the blast can be predicted by picturing it as originating from a downdraft blowing more or less straight down from the cloud and fanning outward once it strikes the surface. Therefore, at the surface, the blast will blow outward from the point of contact with the surface, in all directions. Furthermore, if the cloud is moving over you for the duration of the microburst, the wind will blow first from one direction and then from the opposite direction as the microburst goes by, producing a double whammy. The required precaution in all cases is to strike all sail and secure all watertight hatches and openings.

A typical visual indicator of a microburst is a characteristic "foot" shape in the rain shaft extending down from a thundercloud. The rain is being blown down out of, then out forward of, the cloud, and sometimes curls back upward at the forwardmost, leading edge of the rain shaft. This gives the "foot" the look of a jester's shoe, with the curled-up toe (see figure 12-6). Several people who have encountered microbursts (notably the surviving crew of the *Pride of Baltimore I*) describe the gust arriving as a "wall of water." This is because the downdraft is bringing the rain down with it from inside the cloud. Rain normally falls at a much slower rate, but the downdraft, falling at an extremely high rate, brings with it an inordinate amount of precipitation. Add to this the seawater that gets entrained in the blast when it hits the water, and the description is complete.

By way of a cautionary example, a microburst (as reported in *The Downburst*, by Theodore Fujita) passed over an anemometer at Andrews Air Force Base in Virginia on August 1, 1983, when the wind was recorded as increasing from an ambient wind of 12 knots northwest, up to 120 knots northwest, down to 2 knots, back up to 84 knots southeast, and then back to 5 knots northwest, all in the space of six minutes. (An interesting footnote to this story is that Air Force One had just landed there, with President Reagan aboard, five minutes before the microburst started.) Clearly, this is a phenomenon that must be taken very seriously.

Fig. 12-6. *A wet microburst on 20 May 1974, characterized by a well-defined foot shape on the left side of the rain shaft. (Photograph © 1974, C.A. Doswell III.) Note: This photograph is one of many excellent identification photos to be found on a poster entitled:* Microbursts: A Spotter's Guide *(see bibliography).*

Unfortunately, there is at this time no good way for the sailor to predict the conditions that are favorable for microburst development. It is, however, important to learn to recognize the characteristics of one in progress, because it is the large-scale atmospheric structure in the area that generates them, and if one has formed, it is likely that others will also. Nothing—at this time—will protect you from being hit by the first one to touch down, but if you see, and recognize, the first one at a distance, you may have time to prepare for one that might strike near you later.

Armed with this brief study of basic meteorology, you should now be able to look at a weather map and make some educated decisions with regard to planning your route, both for the rest of the day and for the rest of the trip.

Further reading (see bibliography for details): Bishop, *A Mariner's Guide to Radiofacsimile Weather Charts;* Bowditch, *American Practical Navigator,* chaps. 35–38; Caracena, *Microbursts—A Handbook for Visual Identification;* Fujita, *The Downburst;* Houghton, *Weather at Sea;* Kotsch, *Weather for the Mariner;* Lutgens and Tarbuck, *The Atmosphere;* National Ocean Service, *United States Coast Pilot;* Van Dorn, *Oceanography and Seamanship,* part 2.

CHAPTER THIRTEEN

HEAVY WEATHER SAILING

WHAT IS HEAVY WEATHER?

There is no single definition for what constitutes heavy weather, as it can be different for each vessel and each set of circumstances. Two vessels can be in the same weather system, just a mile apart, and one may be making reasonable progress in relative comfort while the other may be in serious trouble. This is fortunate, since it allows a vessel in dire straits to be rescued by another vessel that is able to operate in such weather. Furthermore, the same set of weather conditions may be a serious threat to a certain vessel while she is near shore—either because the seas are steeper there or because she is in danger of being set down onto the shore—and yet be perfectly survivable for the same vessel when well offshore.

The definition of heavy weather, then, depends entirely on a number of factors that are specific to the immediate situation, not just wind strength or wave height. Heavy weather may, in fact, best be defined as that condition in which you change your plans from trying to make progress to just hanging on and riding it out. You may heave-to to ride out the storm, you may run off before it, or you may strike all sail, stream some warps, and lay below, but circumstances oblige you to give up trying to make progress in your intended direction.

PREPARATIONS

Much of what determines how successfully you ride out a severe storm must be done before you ever leave the dock. Being prepared is probably the most important aspect of seamanship, and heavy weather sailing is the most vivid example of the need for it. Preparations must include maintaining the vessel, equipping the vessel, selecting the crew, training the crew, and preparing yourself both mentally and physically.

The vessel must be in good repair. Equipment failure might be disastrous at any time, but it probably will be if it occurs during heavy weather. The stresses and strains on your vessel will reach their maximum during a severe storm, and all parts of the hull, rig, and machinery will be severely tested. Equipment looks smaller in heavy weather. A shackle that looked oversized at the dock will start looking smaller as the weather builds, and any faults that existed before will begin to loom very large indeed. A fuel filter that looked as if it might need attention at the dock will become a source of desperate concern when you are being driven down onto a lee shore. So, don't accept a "good enough for now" attitude toward repairs to any of the systems or equipment on your vessel if you plan to venture far from home.

The vessel must be properly equipped. Proper equipment includes such things as storm sails, sea anchors, regular and emergency tools (such as bolt and wire cutters), survival equipment, man-overboard equipment, etc. It is possible to overequip a vessel. If you have too much of this gear, storage spaces will be overcrowded and none of it will be easily accessible. You should have appropriate, easily accessible gear, in good condition, and you should know how to use it. Having inappropriate equipment is no help. It can be too big or too small for your vessel or your route. If it is too big or too complicated, it will be difficult to use and may turn out to be more of a hindrance than a help.

The gear must also be well maintained. When you have a piece of emergency equipment, you will be mentally relying on it. The very fact that you know it is aboard will influence the decisions you make in coping with a situation. If that piece of gear is in disrepair when you need it, you may be in more of a jam than you would be if you had not been counting on it in the first place. For an extreme example, think of your bilge pumps. If you ever found yourself in a situation where you knew that none of your pumps was working, you certainly would not venture out into bad weather. If, on the other hand, you believed that all your equipment was in good order, you would sail confidently into a gale, only to find yourself in a desperate situation when you discovered that your pumps were not working, after all.

Finally, to be properly prepared, you must know how to use your emergency equipment, and you must make certain that your crew is trained to use it. Emergency drills should involve more than just talking about emergencies. You should make a point of bringing out different pieces of safety and emergency gear, talking about their intended use, and demonstrating them if possible. This will accomplish several things. First, it will show everyone where the gear is stored and how it works. Showing its location is more effective than just showing a diagram of storage locations. It will further demonstrate how easy or difficult it is to get it out of its storage location. You may be surprised to find that new construction on board has blocked access to emergency equipment.

ONSET OF HEAVY WEATHER

An old adage says: "The time to reef is the first time you think of it." Too many sailors resist shortening sail early, generally because they want to keep making progress, but in most cases a vessel will make as good progress after she is reefed as she did before, since most boats slow down when overpowered. They heel too far to present an efficient hull form in the water, and they spill as much wind as they use. When making the decision whether or not to shorten sail you should consider more than just speed. Crew safety and comfort should be your priorities. The safety issue is obvious, but crew comfort is less often accorded the importance it deserves.

Your crew are what will keep your vessel running. Handled efficiently, your vessel will be able to withstand a great deal of punishment. But your crew must be able to work efficiently, too. Heavy weather is exhausting. It drains people physically, mentally, and emotionally. Physically they will get tired, mentally they will get tired, and emotionally they can become depressed or frightened. Notice that the first two are givens. They will certainly get tired, the question is *how* tired. The third is not a given, and the extent of the first two will influence the third. When people become exhausted they are prone to depression, and with that can come fear. Any one of the above will severely limit their ability to perform efficiently under the harsh conditions of heavy-weather sailing.

You cannot always predict the storm's duration. Your crew has limited endurance, which can be exhausted quickly or slowly, depending on how you, as the master or mate, handle a situation. If you make the mistake of assuming the storm will last for only a day, you may squander the crew's physical reserves prematurely.

Physical exhaustion in heavy weather comes in several forms. Your crew will get tired from lack of sleep. Even with sufficient time off, sleep will be fitful and not fully restful. They will not get their "batteries" fully recharged during their watch below, and there will be a net loss of stamina over time. They will become tired from physical labor, as well as from simply combating the motion of the vessel. Both will wear their muscles down and, again, their time below may not be restful enough to recuperate fully between watches. The majority of sailors (even seasoned ones) will suffer some degree of seasickness. They may not only feel lethargic and uncomfortable, but they may also lose nutrition as a result of vomiting or loss of appetite. Furthermore, many of the available remedies for seasickness have debilitating side effects such as drowsiness or disorientation. Finally, with or without seasickness, nutrition may suffer if the galley crew is unable to provide full, hot meals at regular intervals.

The extent of emotional drain will have much to do with the crew's faith in their superiors. The master and mates can make a great deal of difference in this respect by keeping everyone well informed of the current situation and the plans for coping with it. The most frightening part of a severe storm can be the thought that you do not know what to do about it. Seeing and hearing that the captain knows what to do will have a very beneficial effect on those who do not.

All of this is directly related to reefing early. Taking that step will accomplish the following things:

- The reefing process will be easier earlier than later, when the weather is worse, and you will be able to do a better job.
- The vessel's motion will immediately ease, making everyone more comfortable.
- The improvement in motion may allow the seasickness-prone crew to get a little more rest or another meal before being stricken.
- All hands will see that you are taking charge of the situation and not simply waiting for it to take charge of you.
- You will ease the strain on the vessel and all her gear.

If you keep that old adage in your head (the time to reef is the first time you think of it), and apply it to all the aspects of dealing with heavy weather, you will gain the advantages shown above at every step of the way. Shorten sail early, change course early, and heave-to early. Conserve your own and your crew's strength.

PARTICULAR ACTIONS TO BE TAKEN: SHORTENING SAIL

Shortening sail is the most obvious action to be taken at the onset of heavy weather. There are many possibilities here, including reefing and striking sail in various combinations. The decision as to which sails to strike or reef will be based on the sailor's knowledge of balance and sail handling, as already discussed. The use of storm sails, however, bears some discussion here.

Offshore sailing vessels should be well-equipped with storm sails that suit the particular rig. Heavy-weather jibs, storm jibs (the smaller and stronger of the two), storm mainsails, and storm trysails are the common choices. These choices should be based on balance, versatility, and ease of handling.

When considering balance, consider where the center of effort of a particular sail will be. In severe conditions, especially when running before a gale through high seas, you will need to maximize your control of the vessel. To accomplish this, keep the sail area out of the ends of the vessel. It is true that sail area forward is effective for steering a vessel downwind, but it limits maneuverability, restricting you to sailing only downwind. If you should need to head up, you will not be able to. Therefore, a storm staysail will be a better choice than a storm jib. Carrying a storm staysail, however, will probably require that the vessel be fitted with running backstays, given that your staysail-stay probably terminates at a point on the mast where it is unsupported by the shrouds or the standing backstay.

Versatility is important as well. In storm conditions, there will be occasions when you will want your balance shifted forward or aft. You might blow out the sail you would normally want. Or you might damage or break a mast or a critical part of the rig. In any of these cases, you will be better off if your storm sails are designed to be versatile. For instance, a storm jib should be adaptable to be set from the main mast as well as from the headstay, and the storm trysail intended for the main should be designed to be set on the foremast, if necessary.

Given that storm conditions are difficult at best, the handling of storm sails should be carefully thought out. Because of its difficulty in handling, the use of the traditional, loose-footed, storm trysail has largely passed from favor with sailors of modern rigs, though it still has applications for the gaff rig. This sail is a small triangle of very stout sailcloth, well reinforced, with its head and tack secured to the mast and its clew sheeted to the deck on one quarter (either side of the vessel, back aft). The clew presents the problem. It is heavily reinforced, with a steel clew ring, and requires a block and tackle arrangement for its sheet, given the stress you can expect in these conditions. This hardware becomes lethal when tacking, if allowed to luff and flog at all. To avoid this problem, the sail must be struck and reset when tacking—a very cumbersome and time-consuming process. It is generally safer to set a triple, or very deep, reefed mainsail, which remains secure on its boom, using the existing main sheet and winch to control it. If you wish to use a trysail (to save wear and tear on the main), have one designed to sheet to the boom, eliminating the hazards described above.

For the gaff-rigged vessel, a trysail still makes sense, because it allows you to get the gaff down and secured safely. A deep reef in a gaff sail is almost useless, since the sail shape becomes an aerodynamically ineffective, low, flat quadrangle, with a marginally controllable gaff at the head. The idea of securing a trysail to the boom, versus having it loose-footed, becomes impossible given the rigging involved with the gaff sail. The peak halyards, topping lifts, and lazy jacks would interfere with such a scheme. That same rigging also interferes with the process of tacking the trysail. There is one method that will help, however. Once the mainsail is struck and well secured in preparation for setting the trysail, pass a line from the mast, aft around the main throat and peak halyards and lazy jacks, and back to the mast again. Then slack away on all that gear, drawing them in to the mast with the line just passed. (You may want to leave the topping lifts set up to support the boom end.) With these lines secured to the mast, you will have the space above the main gaff cleared to allow you to pass the trysail over to the other tack. With this arrangement it will still be recommended to strike the trysail to tack it, so as to avoid the flailing of the heavy clew and its gear, but clearing the halyards and lazy jacks will make it a good deal easier to pass.

OTHER ACTIONS

Offshore lifelines should be rigged around the deck. These are not the same as the 36-inch regulation lifelines that are required by law. For average-size adults, a 36-inch lifeline will hit below the center of gravity and will provide security only in moderate weather. If you fall against such a lifeline when it is rough, you could simply tip over it. A rough-weather lifeline should be more nearly chest or shoulder high. The added measure of security is amazingly comforting. With it you will feel enclosed, instead of exposed. A stout line or wire (a line is more comfortable to lean against) strung taught between shrouds, backstays, davits, or whatever you have, will do the job. Make it as tight as you can. This line may or may not be the line to which you will connect your harness. If it is, then the fewer connecting points the better, so you can travel farther along the deck without unclipping. One popular and effective solution for attaching your harnesses to is to stretch a length of nylon webbing along the deck on each side of the house, strongly secured at each end. This lies flat on the deck when not in use, so it presents no tripping hazard and requires no intermediate attachment points. Therefore, once your harness tether is secured to it, you are free to walk the length of the deck without unclipping.

Require harnesses to be worn and clipped in by all. Many vessels now require harnesses even for near-coastal work, and this is a good idea. But for offshore work harnesses are a must. On larger vessels with chest-high bulwarks they may be unnecessary in good weather, but on every vessel in rough weather they are vital. Given the extreme difficulty of retrieving a man overboard in bad weather, you must take all precautions to avoid letting that happen. The harness must be properly made and properly worn. (See chapter 8 for a further discussion of harnesses.)

Since crew members on deck are vulnerable, all but those actually needed should remain below. On deck, the most hazardous place is the foredeck, since the motion is more violent there and it is also more likely to be swept by seas. Prohibit everyone from going there except for essential functions, and then be sure someone else is watching them while they are there. For the same reasons, prohibit anyone from going aft. Lifelines may not fully enclose the stern, and a person there may be out of sight, since most of the crew on deck will be clustered around the wheel, looking forward. If a person slips over the side forward of the helm, there is a good chance he will be seen, but someone going over from back aft could be long gone before anyone notices, and could even be dragging along by his harness.

Access between the deck and below should be limited to the hatches that are most visible from the watchstanders' station (the helm, usually), so the watch can monitor who is on deck at any time and see whether the hatch has been properly closed. Other hatches should be dogged down. Off-center hatches in particular should be secured if possible, as these are the most vulnerable in the event of a knockdown. This is because as the vessel heels, the last part of the vessel to be submerged will be the high side. Since we cannot predict the side to which she will be knocked down, the centerline is the safest place on deck.

Put extra lashings on all deck gear and on furled sails. You do not need the added danger of having to go forward (or worse, aloft) to refurl a sail that has shaken itself out of its gaskets, nor do you want the almost inevitable damage to that sail. The securing of emergency equipment on deck is particularly important, and care must be taken to ensure that while it is well lashed down, it can still be easily deployed if needed. Life rafts generally come with their own effective securing system, which includes a quick-release mechanism and an automatic releasing device that will deploy the raft if the vessel should sink. Other gear, however, must be secured by the crew, and it must be done with a quick-releasing method in mind. The rescue boat is the most obvious example. It will require a substantial lashing to hold it in the event of being swept by a sea, but that lashing should be finished off with a slipknot, or preferably with pelican hooks or other similar devices. If all the lashings end at a pelican hook, they can be drawn extremely tight, yet in an emergency a blow to the pelican hooks with a hammer will release them. If no such devices are readily available, then a good, sharp knife (preferably with a serrated edge) should be kept handy to cut the lashings loose. Every crew member should carry a good knife anyway, but it is appropriate to keep one, for emergency use, at the watchstanders' station, probably by the helm.

Emergency cutting tools should include a stout pair of wire cutters and bolt cutters stored where they can be easily reached. These may be needed for any number of emergencies, chief among them to cut away the rig in the event of dismasting. (Be sure your cutters are suited to the type of rigging they will be expected to cut.) Once a mast is down, it can do a great deal of damage to the vessel or to her personnel if allowed to drag along by its rigging, beating against the hull as the ship rolls.

In all weather, a regular boat-check routine should be maintained, but during heavy weather this routine should be made more thorough and perhaps more frequent. Furled sails should be checked to make sure gaskets are not coming loose, sails set should be checked for chafe or signs of undue strain; standing and running rigging should be inspected for chafe, as well as security of belays and coils. (Imagine the main halyard coil being washed overboard, thus allowing the end to become tangled around the propeller.) Hatches should be examined for watertight integrity, and security of lashings on boats should be checked. The engine room checklist should be compiled by the engineer. The bilges of each compartment should be inspected for leakage, oil spillage, or debris collecting there that could later plug a bilge pump, and each compartment should be examined for smoke, fire, or anything else that needs securing or attention. The thoroughness of these rounds will be complete only if you, as master or mate, insist on it. With such a system in place as a matter of course, many small items will be corrected before they have a chance to become major problems.

RIDING IT OUT

There are as many ways to ride out a storm as there are storms and boats, but most are variations on a few themes. These are:

- Heave-to under shortened sail.

- Run before the storm, with or without any sail set, and with or without drogues or warps streamed.
- Lie-to under bare poles.
- Use the engine in combination with any of the above.

Which technique to employ will depend on the following variables:

- How severe the forecast conditions are, in relation to the seaworthiness of your vessel.
- What sort of rig the vessel has, such as a bowsprit and jibboom.
- What other hazards you have to worry about, such as land, shoals, or other traffic.

Generally, heaving-to is a simple and effective way to deal with most storm conditions. Under a good storm sail configuration (such as trysail or deep-reefed main and staysail), you should be able to ride out all but the most extreme storms. Choose the sail configuration that provides good balance with a relatively low center of effort, using your strongest sails, as discussed in chapter 7. You will generally find it to be quite comfortable, especially for those below.

As the storm becomes more severe, even the small amount of sail you are carrying while hove-to may prove to be too much. In this case you may wish to run off under bare poles (fig. 13-1a). This means you will strike all sail and run downwind under the windage of the rig alone. Running off before a storm has the additional advantage of reducing the relative speed with which the seas are sweeping down on you. This will give the vessel more time to rise to those seas and allow her to ride up and over them instead of having them sweep over her. On the other hand, it will also expose her stern to the seas, and vessels are generally built to withstand more punishment from ahead than astern. Hatches and companionways are generally more exposed on their aft sides and may not be able to withstand the force of being pooped (swept by a wave over the stern).

When running before a storm under bare poles, it may be surprising how fast (and therefore how far) you will go. If you cannot afford to travel that far downwind (because of dangers to leeward), you may have to lie-to, or lie ahull. This differs from heaving-to in that you will not set any sail. You will still drift to leeward, but with no sail set you will drift less. You may lie broadside to the wind and sea and roll deeply. How your particular vessel will lie-to will be determined by where the bulk of her windage is (the CE of her bare rig), and what her underwater shape looks like (where her CLR is). (See chapter 4 for CE and CLR.) Some vessels will lie-to in reasonable comfort. Streaming warps (such as docklines) from the bow or the stern in big loops will serve either to keep your head more nearly to the wind or to slow your run downwind, respectively. A sea anchor will provide a great deal of braking effect and is normally

Fig. 13-1a. *A ketch, running under bare poles, streaming warps.*

set from the bow to hold your head to the wind and sea to limit your drift (fig. 13-1b). But the more nearly stationary you hold your vessel, the less she can respond and lift to a big sea. If you are riding to a sea anchor and being swept by the seas, you should consider bringing in the anchor and letting the vessel ride it out on her own. It is amazing how a vessel will rise up at the last minute and ride over a sea that looked as if it surely would break over her. For this reason smaller vessels can often survive sea conditions that would do substantial damage to a large, deeply loaded ship that is simply too heavy to rise.

If you must minimize leeway, running the engine while hove-to can be helpful. You will not make any gain to windward, but you will cut down your losses to leeward. However, this is hard work for the engine. If the vessel is pitching substantially this can be very stressful for the shaft and drive train, as

Fig. 13-1b. *A ketch, lying-to under bare poles, with sea anchor streamed.*

the propeller alternately comes out of the water and races, then plunges down and digs in again. If you find yourself caught off a lee shore, this may be your only recourse.

Determining which of these courses of action is appropriate will depend on your evaluation of the variables listed previously. How boldly you will push on will depend not only on the severity of the forecast, but also on how much faith you have in the seaworthiness of the vessel, the crew, and the passengers. An unfamiliar or delicate boat (be it old, or just lightly built), or a new crew, will definitely require taking all possible precautions. A well-found and well-proven boat with a good crew, however, should be able to push on without undue concern.

The type of rig you have will affect your heavy-weather strategy. A tall, delicate, yachty rig will require a much more conservative approach than a shorter, sturdier rig that was designed for offshore work. With a tall rig you will focus on keeping rolling to a minimum to reduce the shock load that results from the mast whipping back and forth. If you have a gaff rig and no storm trysail, you should consider going to bare poles earlier than otherwise, to alleviate the stresses of having the gaff swinging around aloft.

The hazards around you, such as land, shoals, or traffic lanes, will play an important role in your planning. You will need to evaluate how far you can expect to drift, and in what direction, whether hove-to under reduced sail, motorsailing under reduced sail, lying-to, or running before the storm under bare poles. The obstacles around you may force you to take a more aggressive approach than if you had ample sea room. For this reason, one of the first steps at the imminent approach of heavy weather may be to push hard to gain sea room before the weather deteriorates enough to require heaving-to. It is all part of thinking ahead—one of the greatest and most fundamental attributes of a good seaman.

Further reading (see bibliography for details): Coles and Bruce, *Heavy Weather Sailing;* Van Dorn, *Oceanography and Seamanship,* part 7; Knox-Johnston, *Seamanship,* chap. 1.

CHAPTER FOURTEEN

HURRICANES AND
HURRICANE MANEUVERING

Hurricanes (known by other names around the world, such as typhoons, willy-willies, cyclones, tropical cyclones, and baquios) are the most dreaded storms at sea, for several good reasons. They not only produce some of the strongest winds and highest seas likely to be encountered, but they have certain unique characteristics that present particular problems that other storms do not.

The most unique feature of a hurricane is the "eye." This is the center of the storm, an area of fewer clouds and relatively calm winds in the midst of the otherwise maniacal tempest. To explain the eye, we must explain the structure of the storm. (We will do so only briefly; for more detail the interested reader should refer to any of the various sources listed at the end of the chapter.) The hurricane forms when a low-pressure cell develops over the ocean in the tropics, causing the air to rise. How that cell first forms is still something of a mystery, but once it does develop, it draws the surrounding air in. The in-flowing air is deflected to the right (in the Northern Hemisphere) by the Coriolis force, and so begins a counterclockwise circulation. That rising air, being very humid and warm, will condense as it rises (remember rising air cools by expansion, causing it to condense) and will become ever more buoyant as it does so. This process draws more air in, causing the air to rise faster, causing more air to be drawn in, etc. The result is that the air flowing in moves ever faster toward the center. Due to the characteristics of the Coriolis force, the faster the wind blows, the more it is deflected to the right. At some point it is deflected a full 90 degrees to the right, so that it blows around and around the center, but never quite reaches it. This is what creates the eye. The strongest winds of the hurricane are right at the eye "wall," or edge, but just inside that area it is relatively calm.

But what about the seas in the eye? Since the seas are generated by the wind, we would expect the seas to be highest where the wind is strongest, at the eye wall. Unfortunately, the seas don't die down there—they carry on into the eye. In fact, since the wind is blowing in a circle around the eye, and because

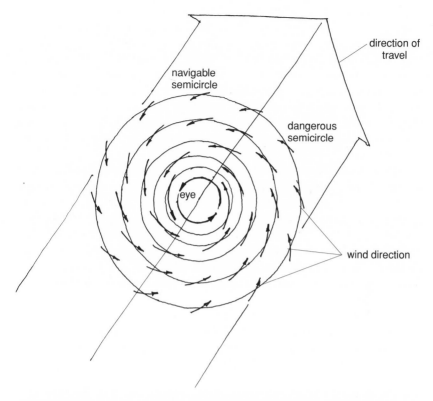

Fig. 14-1. *The dangerous and navigable semicircles and wind directions of a hurricane.*

the eye may be only 20 miles in diameter, the seas will not only be mountainous there, but will be horribly confused, since across a distance of just miles the wind is blowing with terrible force in opposite directions.

The eye, then, is one of the particular characteristics of a hurricane that is so menacing to vessels. When a vessel passes into the eye, the wind will drop to virtually nothing, though the seas will remain mountainous and quickly become very confused. This makes it very difficult to find a heading which best protects the vessel from the breaking waves. What's more, in a short time, the sailor must prepare to receive the full force of the winds back again, except from the opposite direction. This is especially dangerous when you consider that, as you entered the storm initially, the wind and seas were building gradually, giving you time to make some adjustments—both mentally and physically—to its intensity. When you meet the other side of the eye, however, it will come on from the opposite direction with its full force, all at once.

There is another feature that exists with all storms but is much more pronounced in a hurricane due to its circular form. Picturing a circular storm formation with an arrow drawn through its center indicating its path of travel, it can be seen to have a right side (or semicircle) and a left side. The wind is blowing counterclockwise around the center. The winds on the right side of the track are blowing in the direction of the storm's movement, while those on the left are blowing opposite that direction. If, for example, the storm's winds are blowing at 80 knots around the eye, while the storm is advancing at 20 knots, the winds on the right side will be blowing over the surface (and your boat) at a combined speed of 100 knots, while those to the left are blowing over a vessel there at a much more bearable 60 knots. The right side of a hurricane, for this reason, is known as the dangerous semicircle, while the left side is known as the navigable (or safe) semicircle (see figure 14-1).

There is one more reason why the right semicircle is more dangerous than the left. Again look at the direction of the wind blowing around the storm center. If you are caught on the right side, and especially if you are caught in the right, forward quadrant, the wind's direction will be drawing you into the eye. It is easier to make way downwind, or on a broad reach, in heavy weather, than to make any way to windward. Therefore, the vessel caught on the right side of the storm will be drawn into the eye, while a vessel on the left is able to put the wind on her starboard quarter and make reasonable headway out of the storm on a broad reach.

Therefore, a vessel must take every precaution to avoid the right, or dangerous semicircle. As a skipper, you will be doing everything in your power to avoid such a storm altogether, but once one catches you (and hurricane forecasting is still far from an exact science), you will need to rely on every bit of seamanship you have learned to make the best decisions at the right times.

The methods of hurricane avoidance are not complicated—they are only imperfect. The National Hurricane Center will give, in its hurricane advisories (which you can receive by radio, satellite phone, or weatherfax), the location and predicted track of the storm for the next several hours. It will also give the radius out to which hurricane, storm, and gale-force winds are predicted for the same time period. Plot both the storm's position and your own on a plotting sheet, or small-scale chart, and then plot the predicted storm track and the radius of various wind speeds. Given the circular nature of the storm, you can draw the approximate outline of the system, and from your knowledge of wind flow into and around a low, you can draw in the anticipated wind arrows (note the wind arrows in figure 14-1). Plot the predicted future positions of the storm as given by the forecast. Take that information as an educated guess only, and consider the very real possibility that the storm may change direction before the next forecast. With this information, you can decide what route to take. That decision may be a difficult one, and you must always be ready to make a change if the forecast or local cues warrant.

The account that follows, a true story, describes in vivid detail some of the difficult decisions a skipper may have to face. Capt. Philip Sacks had over twenty years of seagoing experience under his belt when this voyage took place, but this was the first time he was fully involved with a hurricane. The story is told in the captain's own words.* It is more than just a story about a storm at sea. It tells about the tremendous weight of responsibility that a master of a vessel at sea bears on his or her shoulders. A moment such as this one is a defining moment in a person's career, and Captain Sacks's solution is a fine example of how the professional sailor should bring his or her complete understanding of the many facets of seamanship to bear to solve a specific problem. He incorporates the principles of meteorology, heavy-weather sailing, stability, shiphandling; stress and strain on the ship, her rig, and crew; motorsailing, sail trim, balance, and lift and drag. In the process, he finds the safest and most practical solution to a problem he had never before confronted. That is the essence of seamanship.

HURRICANE FRANCES

The wind was still howling. I felt by the shudder of the ship that the gusts were increasing. I slowly climbed the steps to *Westward*'s lab, located in her midships deckhouse, in order to have yet another look at the barometer. The needle stood at 999 millibars. It had fallen 2.5 mb in the last hour! Gently I tapped the glass and one of our students reminded me that this was not a recommended practice. I don't remember my exact response, but I do hope that I was civil. It was now nearly 0600 on Saturday, October 23. I had been glued to the barometer all night, checking it nearly every five minutes, or so it seemed. Peter, the third mate, must have thought I was trying to will the barometer back up, as I voiced my optimism at even the slightest hint of leveling.

The sun began to give the first hints of light to the east. The watch on deck was approaching the last hour of their four. They were now logging the wind as force 10 from the Northeast. The wind was still building! But it had also backed another point or so over the last hour. The backing wind was what I had been looking for. It gave me some hope that we had indeed succeeded in crossing the storm's track and were now in the "navigable semicircle." At 0600 there was a scheduled broadcast by Portsmouth Coast Guard of the offshore weather forecast. I knew they would be broadcasting the latest information from the National Hurricane Center in Miami. I took another look on deck before heading below to tune in the radio. I was hungry for an update on the hurricane.

Normally the report would give conditions and forecasts for the waters farther to the north first, and it would be up to 15 minutes before they were reporting the weather in our area. Hurricane warnings take precedence, however. The report started right in with Hurricane Frances, Advisory #4. This storm had developed fast! It was less than 18 hours since we had heard Advisory #1, at 1330 on the previous day. But what an 18 hours!

*Reproduced here by permission of Capt. Philip Sacks.

The ship I was sailing was *Westward*, a staysail schooner owned by Sea Education Association (SEA), a small educational institution located in Woods Hole, Massachusetts, which offers various ocean-focused programs. In addition to *Westward*'s crew, I was sailing with 24 college students participating in the six-week sea component of SEA's Sea Semester Program. We had departed Woods Hole nearly two weeks earlier. Our first landfall, the Caribbean Island of Martinique, was still two weeks away.

On the previous afternoon, Friday, we had been sailing a course of 130 degrees. *Westward*'s mainsail was set with a single reef, as well as the main staysail, fore staysail, and jib. The engine was also on in order to help us hold as close to the wind as possible. The wind we were experiencing at that time was force 4 from the ESE. The seas were 4–6 feet from the same direction. We had been monitoring reports of a developing gale to our southwest and we were attempting to distance ourselves as best we could from the stronger winds associated with the system. We had been through the edges of a storm the previous weekend, and the educational program on board was getting back on track. I didn't think another gale was what the people on board needed now. The weather reports were also describing another, larger storm well to our east that was drifting to the northwest. It was expected to dissipate. I was less concerned with this second gale, but I was hoping that we could slide between the two systems and avoid the gale force winds. Only that morning during our daily radio check-in with our office in Woods Hole I had jokingly posed the following riddle: "What happens when you are smack in the middle of two gales?" At the time I didn't really know the answer. We sure were to find out!

When we do our morning communications we usually also check in with SEA's other sailing vessel, the *Corwith Cramer*. The *Cramer* was approximately 200 miles to our northeast that morning. They were involved in a similar educational program of instruction in oceanography and nautical science. The *Cramer* had left Woods Hole the day before *Westward*. The captain on the *Cramer* for this trip was Mark Crutcher. Mark and I usually compare notes on the weather when we talk each morning. I was particularly interested in our chats about the weather the last few days because *Westward*'s weather-fax had stopped working several days before. Although we were still receiving voice forecasts, to my mind nothing beats a good weather map. The *Cramer* had a working fax and Mark had received a surface analysis that morning. He told me that the map showed a band of calm between the two gales and that they indeed were experiencing very light airs. They were traveling as we were under motor and sail, although because they were a bit farther to the east already they were now heading on a slightly more southerly course.

The winds we were getting were not the calms that Mark had described, and so I was a little unsure what to make of the information he had relayed concerning the weather map. What I did know was that we were experiencing a dramatic cloud show. Clouds of every type were in the sky—low clouds, mid-level clouds, and high clouds. The dark shadows and bright highlights produced by the sunlight made the scene even more spectacular. I had to admit that I didn't totally understand the story that the clouds were telling, but I did know that we were witnessing some unsettled weather. By the time I headed below for lunch, just after noon on Friday, I too was beginning to feel a little unsettled. I wasn't comfortable with such an active sky. I must admit that I had no premonition of what was yet to come. I did know, however, that shortly after lunch, at 1330, we could receive an updated weather report.

Our usual afternoon schedule aboard *Westward* includes a gathering of the students at 1400 for a review of the last 24 hours, followed by two classes—one in nautical science and one in oceanography. I sat down in the aft cabin to listen to the weather report before heading up to class.

The report started right in with the first advisory on a tropical storm that had just recently developed. The position they gave for it was two hours old and put the center at latitude 29.1° north, longitude 61.2° west. It didn't take me long to realize that this wasn't far from where we were, and that this was one to pay some serious attention to. In fact, *Westward*'s position at that time was 32°44′ N x 59°06′ W—less than 300 miles from the storm's center. This was where the adrenaline began to kick in and I carefully copied everything the report said about the storm and its predicted track for the next several days. One thing I have learned after many years of listening to radio weather reports is that one should just write down what is said, as accurately as possible, and then come back and process all the data afterward. This is exactly what I did. At 1100 the storm had maximum sustained winds of 35 knots with gusts to 45. The radius where winds of this strength were blowing was 30 miles in the northern semicircle and 60 miles to the south. The forecast was for the storm to intensify over the next 24 to 36 hours. Sustained winds of 45 knots with gusts to 55 were expected on Saturday morning building to steady 55 with gusts to 65 by Saturday evening. The forecast was for storm force winds out to a radius of 60 miles in all directions. The predicted storm track was for an advance to the North at 9 knots for the next 18 hours, and then to slowly begin its recurvature to the east. [See figure 14-2, at the end of the chapter, for a complete plot of the progress of both Frances and *Westward* during the period described.]

After I copied the entire report, I began to consider the situation. If the storm did take the predicted path, and we maintained our current course and speed, 130 degrees at 5 knots, we would have a closest point of approach (CPA) of approximately 120 miles. I knew this was taking *Westward* down the more dangerous side of the storm, but in consideration of the predicted track and development of the storm it was our best course of action. We continued on to the southeast, hoping that the forecasts were accurate and that the storm would pass far enough to our west to avoid the strongest winds near the eye.

Certainly one never wants to encounter storm force winds, but I was not yet overly concerned about winds to 45 with gusts to 50 knots. I have been through winds of that strength and stronger several times on *Westward* before. Only the previous week we had encountered winds to force 9 and seas to 20 feet. The crew and students were tested up to such conditions. I knew, however, that a tropical storm in that location might easily intensify and that its predicted northerly track could not be relied upon too heavily. I decided to excuse myself from the 1400 nautical science class I had been preparing to give and I asked Ellen, the chief scientist, to go ahead with her class in oceanography.

I went up on deck to discuss the situation with the mates. We decided to begin battening down immediately. We wanted to get the ship as ready as we could while we still had some daylight left. If the storm was to intensify and also perhaps veer more toward the east, we wanted—we needed—to be prepared. The mates began preparations on deck while I went below to catch the end of the oceanography lecture and to brief everyone on the situation.

I passed the information about the storm and its predicted track and development to the ship's company. My aim was to explain the possibilities and impress upon everyone the seriousness of the situation without causing undue alarm. The students and the rest of the staff took the news extremely well, and shortly many of the students were on deck helping to secure the ship. Most of the rest were getting things ready in other areas—the lab, the galley, the engine room. We all hoped that these precautions were not really going to be needed, but we felt much more comfortable getting ready.

On deck preparations were in full swing. We considered unbending many of the sails in order to stow them below, but we decided that we could secure them adequately in place. We slowed the engine down in order to decrease speed and ease the motion of the ship. Although the wind was still only about force 5, perhaps 6, the seas were now building to 8 feet or so. Out on the bowsprit the jib and jib topsail were double and then triple lashed. The *Westward* has a brailing course (a square sail that pulls into the mast like a curtain rather than bunting up to the yard as in traditional square riggers). The third mate and the steward went aloft and tightly spiralled a line around the sail and the mast.

Before departing Woods Hole we had put aboard a new spool of ¼-inch Manila line. We were thankful for that now because it is great stuff for getting very tight lashings. The rest of the daylight hours were spent securing everything that we thought had the remotest chance of moving. The name of the game in lashing is get it tight. If anything has even the slightest bit of play, the severe motion of the ship in a storm will work it free. The crew and the students did such a superior job of lashing that I can only remember a single item coming free later during the hurricane. That was *Westward*'s Avon rigid-bottomed inflatable rescue boat. It shifted in its gripes when a boarding wave came up over the bulwarks, and floated partially out of its cradle.

Additional safety life lines were rigged both port and starboard. In any severe weather the danger of someone going overboard is great, and the chances of being able to retrieve a person in the water nearly nonexistent. The safety lines run fore and aft with as few interruptions as possible. They allow a person to move around the deck if necessary without having to unclip the strap on their safety harness.

The sun was sinking in the west as we finished our preparations. At 1800 the wind was still SE force 5 to 6 with the largest seas about 10 feet. I knew that if they continued to build we would have a much harder time working to the southeast to avoid the storm. We felt the ship was ready. We had done what we could do for now. I gave the crew a hearty well done, and headed below to tune in to another weather update, glancing at the barometer as I passed. It stood at 1009 mb and was dropping slowly—at a rate of 1 mb in three hours.

I flopped down on the settee in my cabin anxiously awaiting fresh news. The broadcast came through loud and clear. The report gave the 1700 position for the eye, only one hour old, as 28.9° N, 61.5° W. We were still approximately 150 miles north and 100 miles east of the center. The good news was that the storm was moving 355 degrees true, just slightly to the west of north. This track was predicted to continue for the next 24 hours. We were still making some distance to the southeast so if the track held as predicted we could still clear the center by over 100 miles. The bad news was that the storm had intensified! Winds were now steady to 55 knots with gusts to 65. Predictions were for hurricane strength to be reached within the next 12 hours. Gusts to 80 knots were now expected for Saturday afternoon. The radius of winds up to 50 knots was only about 30 miles with winds to 34 knots expected 75 miles out from the center. Staying clear of the storm's center took on a greater sense of urgency. But for now our tactics seemed correct. We could continue heading south and east to dodge the brunt of the storm.

The forecasts from the National Hurricane Center include predicted positions given at 12-hour intervals for approximately two days as well as expected storm size and wind strength. I plotted out the hurricane's "predicted" path and our probable track in order to work out some CPA's. If the predictions were correct we could stay on the fringes of the storm. But it was not a time to rest easy. I knew that the northerly track was only a prediction—far from a certainty. My thoughts returned again to the *Corwith Cramer*. She was presently about 200 miles to our ENE. *Cramer* had taken it worse than *Westward* in the storm the week before. It now seemed that the score was about to even up. I was ready to swap places with them now. Out to the east seemed like a great place to be.

It was with that thought that I made a final check on deck while the watch was changing. The conditions were still about the same, but we decided to tuck the second reef in the mainsail. The wind was only force 5–6, but we needed to be prepared. It was a time to lessen the tension as best we could—on both the ship and the people. For now shortening sail was the best way to do this. On the other hand I knew that it was a mistake to sail *Westward* with too little sail. It is important to keep enough sail up to use the wind to dampen the roll set up by the sea. At the same time it was also crucial for us to continue making miles to the east, to windward. The mainsail would help keep her driving in to the wind. The second reef was the best compromise. Lessen the tension, but keep the motion reasonable while continuing on.

I thanked the off-going watch for a job well done and encouraged them to enjoy a good hot dinner and get some sleep. I headed below to do the same. I knew that if things got worse everyone on board would need all the strength available. If the hurricane did take a turn toward us, I didn't know if it would be safe to fire up the stove the next day. As I sat down to dinner I asked Gavin the steward to begin thinking about what we could eat the next day if it was too rough to be working in the galley. He started making plans. On deck the evening watch had struck the mainsail, tied in the second reef and reset it by 2000. The advice to bank some rest was just as important for me, so after dinner I lay down as well.

The hours until midnight passed without much change. I don't remember sleeping much but I did get some rest as I awaited the next weather report, due at 0000 hours. While I was waiting, I pulled out a copy of Bowditch to review the chapters on tropical cyclones. I had read these sections many times before but there didn't seem to be any harm in review. Besides, I wasn't falling asleep anyway. As I read, Bowditch reaffirmed my understanding of the "dangerous" versus the "navigable" sides of a hurricane. If an observer in the northern hemisphere stands at the eye of the hurricane and looks in the direction of the storm's track, the half of the storm that is located to the right of the track is considered the "dangerous semicircle" while the half of the storm that is to the left of the track is known as the "navigable semicircle." There are two primary reasons to avoid the dangerous side of the storm. First, on this side the winds experienced by a vessel are the sum of the cyclonic winds and the winds created by the storm's advance. In the navigable side these winds counteract each other. Therefore the wind a vessel feels on the navigable side of the storm is the speed of the cyclonic winds associated with the storm minus the speed of the storm's advance. This can make a considerable difference in the force of wind a ship experiences, particularly as the storm's speed of advance begins to accelerate. The second problem one encounters in the dangerous semicircle is that if you try to put the wind on your quarter you run directly toward the eye. To avoid the eye in the dangerous side of the storm a mariner must put the wind on the starboard bow of the vessel. As the wind and seas increase this can be at best damaging and perhaps impossible. In the navigable semicircle on the other hand, if you put the wind behind you, on your vessel's starboard quarter, you will be sailing away from the storm's track and the eye. Aboard *Westward* we currently were heading down the dangerous side of this storm. We had the wind on the port bow, but this tactic was only reasonable as long as we could skirt the edges of the storm and avoid the more intense winds near the center.

With these thoughts in mind, I anxiously tuned the radio in at midnight and began listening to and copying hurricane Frances Advisory #3. The 2300 position was given as 29.3° N, 60.4° W. The storm was now traveling 035 degrees at 5 knots. My heart jumped and my stomach tensed. I didn't have to hear the rest of the forecast to know what that meant. The hurricane was now coming right toward us! I took a deep breath to calm my nerves and I continued listening and copying the report. The news got even worse. The storm was now packing steady winds to 65 knots, gusting to 80. Hurricane force winds were now extending 50 miles from the center with gales reaching out 125 miles in the northern semicircle. The central pressure was now predicted to drop to 977mb and steady winds to 75 knots/gusts to 90 were expected.

My adrenaline started pumping again and I could feel my heart rate pick up as I stepped out to the chart table in order to plot the positions for the hurricane's newly predicted track. It didn't take a rocket scientist to know that the situation for us now looked a whole lot worse. Only by carefully plotting the storm's expected track and measuring courses and distances carefully could I be assured of making the best decision now as to our action.

After plotting the center position for the hurricane's eye for the next 36 hours, I swung arcs with a compass to represent the radii of extent for the winds of various strengths—gale to 125 miles, storm to 60 miles and hurricane to 50 miles. I then ran out *Westward*'s probable positions for the same period, assuming we tried to hold the southeasterly course we were currently steering. I knew that as the wind and seas continued to build it would be ever more difficult to hold the ship close on the wind, and that if we were forced to fall off and steer more to the south we would be spiraling directly for the eye. As I knew all along, this course ran us down the more "dangerous" side of the hurricane.

The new CPA plot showed we would be skirting within 50 miles of the eye in about 20 hours, and that was only if we could continue making some way to the east, which I felt was going to get much less certain as the storm strengthened and approached. I then plotted another CPA for the storm assuming we altered course now, and headed west, running with the wind on our starboard quarter. I saw that according to the current projections for the storm's track this could be a much better tactic. If we turned west and had the wind behind us we could probably make 8 to 10 knots. If we were able to make it across the storm's track, we would then be in the navigable semicircle. Then, with the wind on our starboard quarter, we would be distancing ourselves from the eye. The question was, could we make it in front of the eye with enough room to spare? My CPA plot showed that we could do it and clear the eye by 100 miles or so, perhaps feeling only gale force winds. But what if the forecast was incorrect? What if the storm accelerated? Or increased in strength and/or size?

These were some of the questions that were going through my head. I was facing one of the toughest decisions I have had to make as a captain. There were really only two choices, but which one should I make? Time was certainly of the essence, but I decided to try to get a little more information before making a decision. I used the radiotelephone to place a call to the National Hurricane Center. There was no answer at the number I tried. The tension was rising as I cursed under my breath. I knew that the center had to be open 24 hours when there was an active hurricane. I explained our situation to the High Seas Operator and she was able to find another number. She rang it and someone did answer. Relieved, I asked for information concerning the probability that the hurricane would follow the track currently predicted. Although the person on the phone could not quantify probabilities, he did confirm that they now saw steering winds aloft that should continue to push the system to the northeast. I thanked him as I signed off the radio.

We could either take the information provided by the hurricane center or ignore it. Did we have better information? I didn't think so. We were still experiencing only force 6 winds, but the barometer had started to fall a little more steeply. I consulted with Ellen Praeger, the chief scientist, and with John Hayward, the mate on watch. We discussed the possibilities. I made my decision. They agreed with the decision to change tactics and now run for the navigable side of the storm.

When we started to run before the wind, the mainsail would turn from a help to a hindrance. The sail area aft would add to the weather helm and try to turn *Westward* into the wind, making steering much more difficult. The watch struck the mainsail and secured it tightly as we had done to the other sails. I asked the mate to jibe over to the starboard tack. A compass heading of 295° would give us about 285° true. We would try to steer nearly perpendicular to the storm's track.

The time was 0135 on Saturday morning when we steadied up on our westerly course. I gave a short sigh for all the hard won easting we would be losing as we throttled up *Westward*'s 500-horsepower Cummins diesel to full ahead. We needed speed now. We would use both wind and diesel power. I felt we could make our best speed for avoidance with both the engine and our two small staysails. I knew that as the wind increased it would get ever more difficult to handle sail, therefore I felt the staysails were sufficient. *Westward*'s staysails are extremely strong. I felt confident that they could hold up to storm force winds. I didn't know how they might fare in winds any stronger. That was a question we might have to face. Now we needed the staysails to help steady the roll as we ran downwind. We oversheeted the staysails and ran an extra sheet to the clews. I was mindful that the *Cramer* had blown a main staysail to shreds in the previous storm when a sheet had parted during a jibe. I knew that running downwind at high speeds in building seas would open us up to the possibility of accidental jibes. I felt that a little less play in the sheets would considerably reduce the strain on the sails should this occur. The staysails also would function even better as roll dampeners slightly oversheeted. With the wind currently at force 7 and building they were still catching plenty of wind to drive the vessel. The fore staysail was certainly keeping the bow off the wind as we wanted.

Remembering the *Cramer*'s blown staysail caused my thoughts to drift 200 miles to the ENE, to think about the *Cramer* and her crew. I had been plotting the *Cramer*'s likely positions on the chart as well as our own. Their position no longer seemed definitely safer than ours, although it still seemed that they were far enough to the east to continue avoidance to the east side of the storm. I still would have traded positions with them.

As the hours of the early morning passed we noticed that the barometer was falling at a rate of over one millibar per hour. The wind was rising only gradually, but spectacular bolts of lightning lit up the otherwise pitch black sky. We were not yet feeling much rain, but the deep, rolling claps of thunder shook our bones and added to the ever-building tension. Reminding myself that conditions were not that bad yet, and that the watch had everything well in hand, I doffed my rain gear and headed below. I should continue to get some rest. I knew John wouldn't hesitate to get me if necessary.

As I lay in my bunk, I thought back to some of the joking we had been doing earlier in the day. While trying to keep things light I remarked that it was just our luck to be chased by a hurricane with a "woosy" name like Frances. I allowed that if we were to confront a storm I would have preferred a macho name like Butch or Duke. I am usually moderately superstitious at sea (as I suspect most sailors are) and I now regretted my jests. Perhaps we were in for our just rewards. With these thoughts, I fell off to sleep.

I woke a few hours later and noticed it was not quite dawn. I suited up in rain gear to check the situation on deck. Peter, the third mate, and his watch had relieved at 0300. He had reported to me the building conditions earlier and now I had a look for myself. The winds were force 8 to 9. I checked the log book and saw that the watch was estimating seas to 10 feet. In my judgement they were several feet larger. What really caught my attention was the wind direction. At midnight the watch had recorded wind from the SE. Shortly after we began running west, at 0200, the wind had backed to the east. East by north was logged between at 0300 and 0400. It was now 0430 and I felt the wind gusting from the ENE. I knew that it might have just been hopeful thinking as I was still extremely anxious about the storm's track. But a backing wind was exactly what we expected to feel if we were in fact crossing the track into the navigable half of the storm. The barometer was now falling nearly 2 mb per hour, but the backing wind lifted my spirits. I nervously, but optimistically, headed below to catch the 0600 weather broadcast.

The report began as Hurricane Frances Advisory #4. I was again struck by how quickly this storm had developed—we had been involved with our "friend" Frances for only 16 hours. The eye's position was given first: 30.0° N x 60.0° W at 0500—now tracking 030° true at 10 knots. I didn't need the chart to know what that meant. We had made it! We were in the navigable semicircle. I knew that we were far from in the clear—that the storm could at any time change its track again. But Frances had taken the expected track. We would now be able to distance ourselves from the storm by running with the wind on our starboard quarter. I felt a tremendous weight lift from my shoulders. On the other side of the cabin Ellen had also been listening to the report. Small smiles of relief grew on both our faces. I allowed myself the luxury of a minute's rest as I leaned back and let some tension drain away. I didn't sit long because I wanted to plot the details on the chart and pass the good news to the rest of the ship's crew. As we headed out to the chart table Ellen and I looked at each other and I believe shared a similar thought. *Cramer.* We knew our situation was still serious, but felt that for the first time since yesterday noon our prospects were looking up. We also realized that the crew on the *Cramer* were now in the very same position that we had been in on Friday afternoon. It looked as though they could still avoid the hurricane to the east, but it didn't look certain. At this point, I no longer wanted to trade places with them.

The wind was still building, but we faced it with much more confidence. The sun was rising to the east. The glow of daylight was an incredible relief. The intensity of a storm always seems much greater at night. The seas are also much more dangerous because the person on the helm can't see them coming. This makes it much more difficult to steer away from the larger seas that have a potential to poop the ship. At this time *Westward* was riding very well in spite of 12- to 15-foot seas.

Although our spirits were considerably lifted, I knew that the situation was still serious. Wendy, the chief mate, had been thrown out of her bunk by a deep roll of the ship early that morning. Luckily she was not seriously injured, but her bruised leg was stiffening. Noah, the engineer, went on deck to help with her watch. Through the morning the wind and seas continued to build. By 0800 we were logging winds of force 10, perhaps 11. At that point it is so difficult to know. The largest seas were 20 feet. They were rollers that looked somehow different from most other storm seas I have encountered. They appeared glassier, more smooth-surfaced. Perhaps this was due to the tops being blown off by the wind. I don't know what it was, but the seas were different—beautiful—and watching them was exhilarating. They were also still dangerous. The ship continued to ride well as we ran before the storm at better than 8 knots. Although I have seen *Westward* with much more water on deck, we were still occasionally being slapped on the side and boarded with considerable water. More than one wave brought several feet of green water on deck although it stayed mostly forward. The rescue boat was floated partially free by several waves, and it shifted in its cradle. The crew was able to get it back under control and no damage was done.

Steering was difficult but under control. I was very impressed that most of the students were handling the ship in those seas like old salts. We didn't ask anyone who was not comfortable to steer, but those who did take the helm were super. I don't remember being pooped once.

By 0800 I was sure—the barometer had reached its nadir. We were now distancing ourselves from the hurricane. I headed below to give a radio call to Mark on the *Cramer*.

By now, the electrical storm activity that we had seen during the night was greatly reduced, and so I was hopeful I would be able to get through. I called the *Cramer*. I heard a response. I was surprised to hear not Mark but Wallace Stark, SEA's marine superintendent, on the radio in Woods Hole. It was Saturday morning and so I hadn't expected to check in with the office until later in the day. Wallace had heard about the hurricane and came in early to stand by. Wallace is also one of the masters who sails *Westward* and *Cramer*. I knew he would understand what we were up against. I tried to let him know that I was confident about our situation. I explained that we were still in some pretty huge winds and seas, but that the ship and people were doing well, and that I expected the hurricane to be peaking for us shortly. In fact the winds and seas stayed at this strength and height through the morning without building any further. (After the storm I plotted *Westward*'s CPA with the center of the eye as having been about 120 miles at 1100 that morning.) I asked Wallace to assure the families of all on board that we were safe. We then broke our communication and stood by for the *Cramer*. Mark came up and reported to Wallace that they were also doing well. We were both working a frequency to give good propagation to Woods Hole, so I could not hear Mark very well.

Aboard *Westward* we were all relieved to know that the *Cramer* was also safe. Our own morale was now quite high but our concern began to shift from our own situation to theirs. The motion of the ship was still great enough that I reminded everyone to move around both on deck and below only as necessary. We didn't want an injury to complicate our situation. Everyone took this suggestion well and those below spent their morning reading, writing, talking and playing backgammon. The vessel rode extremely well. It was rough, but at the same time the comfort level and spirit of the people below was surprising. You might not have known that on deck our shipmates were grappling with a hurricane.

When I got back on the radio with Wallace, I informed him of our plans to continue running west with the wind on our starboard quarter. I let him know that we would be following the wind and we would turn more southerly as it continued to back. After Mark had completed his traffic with Woods Hole, he and I discussed the weather we each were experiencing. I told Mark of our wind, sea, and barometric readings of the previous 24 hours and he returned his observations. I let him know how at midnight it had become clear that we had to change tactics, and what we had done. I also told him of the

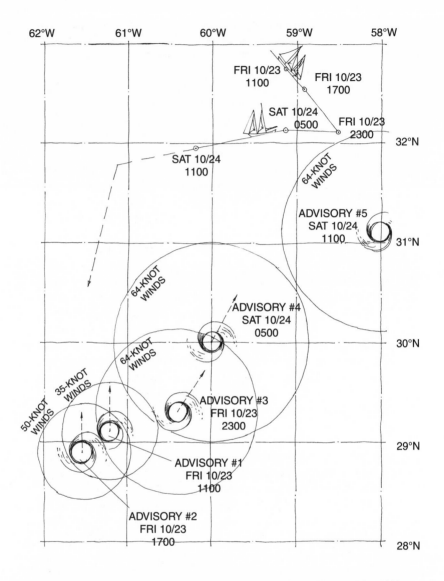

Fig. 14-2. Schooner Westward *and Hurricane Frances tracks for 10/23 and 10/24, 1992.*
Note the change in position from Advisory #1 to #2. This indicates a revision of the National
Hurricane Center's position estimates, not a reversal of the hurricane's track, and should
serve as a reminder to mariners that this information is to be taken as an estimate only.

electrical storms we had encountered during the night. We decided that both ships and Woods Hole would try to keep an open radio frequency throughout the day and check in every few hours. I wished Mark luck, as I think I had a very real understanding as to what the coming hours would be for him and all aboard the *Cramer*.

Further reading (see bibliography for details): Bowditch, *American Practical Navigator,* chap. 37; Kotsch, *Weather for the Mariner,* chap. 8; Kotsch and Henderson, *Heavy Weather Guide;* Lutgens and Tarbuck, *The Atmosphere,* chap. 11.

CHAPTER FIFTEEN

EMERGENCY HELICOPTER OPERATIONS

When sailors set out to sea these days, they do so with the knowledge that there is a very large, complex, and capable search and rescue network in place that has proven its ability to perform some extraordinary rescues far out to sea. What that sailor may not realize is just how complex, costly, risky, and limited that network is. What sailors must especially understand is that a helicopter evacuation from a sailing vessel is the helicopter pilot's worst nightmare. The fact remains that they do it, and do it with incredible skill. But the risk to themselves and the sailboat's crew is substantial. The more the sailor understands the process and the risks, the safer everyone will be.

The following article was written by Lt. Daniel Travers, a U.S. Coast Guard Search and Rescue helicopter pilot, who has flown many search and rescue missions. The section on the P1B salvage pump is included because that pump is the most frequently delivered piece of rescue equipment. Although it is delivered with very simple and complete instructions, the more a sailor knows about its operation in advance, the better.

Finally, there is a brief but important addendum on medical concerns in airlifting sick or injured patients by helicopter, a process known as MEDEVAC. This addendum is drawn from the *Operating Procedures Manual* for the National Guard Air Ambulance. These points should speak for themselves—not all patients should be airlifted by helicopter (when a choice exists). Some very significant effects are associated with helicopter air transport, and such transport could have tragic consequences if not carefully evaluated.

COAST GUARD SEARCH AND RESCUE FROM THE AIR
By Lt. Daniel J. Travers
U.S. Coast Guard Air Station Cape Cod

The United States Coast Guard Air Station Cape Cod helicopter and fixed wing jet aircrews perform an average of 382 search and rescue missions a year. During these search and rescue missions, the aircrews will deliver approximately 31 dewatering pumps to vessels in distress, conduct 50 medical evacuations (MEDEVAC), and assist or save over 150 people. This article will describe the search and rescue procedures that aircrews from Air Station Cape Cod follow and how sailors can better assist the aircrews in carrying out these rescue missions.

The best way to describe the procedures is through a fictitious search and rescue scenario. It is late at night and a vessel is sailing approximately 120 nautical miles southeast of Newport, Rhode Island, on the return trip from the annual Newport to Bermuda race. The strengthening winds are causing the seas to get more violent as a summer thunderstorm is fast approaching. With the worsening weather conditions, the sailors are in the process of dousing the sails. All of a sudden an unexpected rogue wave causes the boat to lurch resulting in an accidental jibe. A crewmember is knocked unconscious after being hit in the head by the shifting main boom. Quickly assessing the severity of the situation, the vessel's captain gets on the radio and puts out a call to the Coast Guard on 2182 KHz. A Coast Guard Station hears the call and responds. The Coast Guard Search and Rescue system has now been activated.

There are a few steps that occur before Air Station Cape Cod gets the call from the First Coast Guard District Rescue Coordination Center (located in Boston, Massachusetts) to launch a rescue aircraft. But once the launch request has been received and the Air Station duty officer has been briefed on the nature of the distress, the search and rescue alarm is sounded and the case begins.

Initially, the Air Station duty officer and pilots are concerned with getting as much pertinent information as possible, not only about the distress call, but also about the weather conditions at the distress scene and at their destination. While the pilots are gathering this information, the rest of the duty section is also abuzz as they feverishly work to ready the aircraft. In this scenario, the engineering mechanics know it is a MEDEVAC of a patient with head injuries from a sailing vessel 105 nautical miles south of Martha's Vineyard Island. Extra fuel will not be required, but additional medical equipment to assist with the patient's injuries will be loaded on the helicopter. A Falcon HU-25 jet aircraft will also be readied to act as an escort for the helicopter since the sailing vessel is 105 nautical miles offshore. Typically, anything greater than 100 nautical miles offshore will require a jet escort. This makes the rescue operation safer since the aircraft crews look out for each other and provide assistance if the other crew has problems and has to make an emergency landing in the water. With both aircraft ready, the aircrews will strap in, complete checklists to start the aircraft's engines, and depart Otis Air National Guard Base in the direction of the distress scene.

The HU-25 Guardian jet, built by Falcon Jet Corporation, can operate from sea level to an altitude of 42,000 feet at a maximum speed of 380 knots, fly 800 nautical miles offshore, remain on scene for 30 minutes, and return to base with a 20-minute fuel reserve. With this kind of speed and endurance, the jet will arrive on scene approximately 20 minutes after their takeoff from Otis Air National Guard Base.

While en route to the distress scene, the jet's crew will continuously try to establish communications with the sailing vessel to acquire an up-dated patient status, weather conditions, and to pass on their estimated time of arrival at the sailing vessel. Upon arrival on scene, the jet will establish itself at a safe altitude above the sailing vessel in a slow circling pattern. From this position, the jet's crew can overlook the helicopter during the hoist and can also act as a communications platform to coordinate all radio calls. The jet's altitude depends on the existing weather conditions and on the helicopter's altitude, which is usually less than 1,000 feet above the water. In any case, the jet will try to keep at least a 500-foot altitude separation from the helicopter.

The HH-60 Jayhawk medium range recovery helicopter, built by Sikorsky, has a maximum speed of 180 knots, can fly 300 nautical miles offshore, remain on scene for 45 minutes, and return to base with a 20-minute fuel reserve. Depending on weather conditions and winds, the helicopter will arrive on scene approximately 40 minutes after their takeoff from Otis Air National Guard Base.

While en route to the sailing vessel, the helicopter crew will receive continuous updates on the situation from the jet crew until the helicopter is able to establish communications with the sailing vessel. At this point, the helicopter crew will take over primary communications with the sailing vessel from the jet crew. The jet crew will continue to have primary communications with the Boston Rescue Coordination Center and Air Station Cape Cod. Once on scene, the helicopter will make a descending approach to the sailing vessel and will end up in a 50–100 foot hover downwind of the vessel. From this vantage point, the helicopter's crew can assess the situation to determine how they will conduct the hoist. Some of the considerations are: what location to hoist from on the sailing vessel, what rescue equipment to use, and whether a rescue swimmer will be lowered to the vessel to assist the crew with the rescue operation.

It is important to remember that each situation is entirely different, and as such, there is no cookbook solution for how the helicopter crew will conduct the hoist. Some hoists are straightforward, and others can be extremely complex. A sailing vessel at night in rough conditions is by far one of the more dangerous platforms to hoist from since it is extremely difficult to lower the rescue basket past the wildly swaying mast into the limited cabin area space. In these circumstances it is not uncommon to have the sailors put on survival suits, jump into the water, and hoist them from the water with the assistance of the helicopter's rescue swimmer. In any case, once the helicopter crew decides on a plan of action, they will give the vessel crew the following hoisting brief. (Note: A more specific brief will be given if the helicopter crew elects to hoist the sailors from the water. This brief will not be covered in this article since it is different for each situation.)

VESSEL RESCUE BRIEFING

1. Establish the desired course and speed if the vessel is able to proceed under way.

The course and speed will be 35–45 degrees to the right of the wind line at a speed of 5–8 knots under engine/motor power (not under sail), or during calm conditions, the vessel's heading will be whatever provides the most stable ride. The helicopter heading will be directly into the wind. This heading will provide the pilot with a better view of the vessel and the hoisting operation, and will also allow the helicopter to use less power since heading directly into the wind gives more lift to the helicopter. If the vessel cannot get under way, the rescue operation can still be completed, but it is more difficult since the vessel will be uncontrollable and thus at the whim of Mother Nature.

2. Establish what rescue equipment will be used, instruct the vessel's crew on how to handle it, and determine the location where the hoist will be conducted on the vessel.

The equipment used may include a rescue basket, a litter, a sling, a dewatering pump, or a polypropylene trail-line (or tag-line) with a five pound weight bag attached to one end to assist in delivery to the vessel. The basket is the primary rescue device since it is the easiest to use [see figure 15-1]. The litter is used for patients that are unable to sit in the basket or have an injury that requires them to lie flat [see figure 15-2]. The sling is used as another way to recover people from the water. It is usually used only when a Coast Guard rescue swimmer is in the water and has placed it on the person. The dewatering pump is lowered to assist vessels that are taking on water. Finally, a 105-foot trail-line, if used, is attached to the rescue device and is lowered first to allow the vessel's crew to assist in getting the rescue device on board their vessel. By attaching a trail-line to the rescue device, the helicopter does not have to hover directly over the vessel during the delivery, which makes the rescue operation safer. Once the trail-line is on board the vessel, the helicopter will back away a safe distance and start to lower the rescue device. As the rescue device is being lowered, the vessel's crew pull on the trail-line to bring the rescue device on board [see figure 15-3]. During the recovery when the patient is in the rescue device, the trail-line is used to keep the rescue device from swinging back and forth as it is hoisted to the helicopter. It is important to note that Coast Guard rescue equipment is specially stressed and rigged for aerial rescue operations and will be used to ensure the maximum safety of the survivor. The helicopter crew will not use any of the vessel's equipment except as a last resort. The helicopter crew will either give the vessel instructions on how to handle the rescue equipment or it will lower a Coast Guard

Fig. 15-1. *The HH-60 Jayhawk helicopter is shown lowering a rescue basket.*
Photograph courtesy U.S. Coast Guard.

rescue swimmer, who is a qualified Emergency Medical Technician (EMT),
from the helicopter to the vessel to stabilize the patient and assist during the
rescue operation.

3. Ensure the person to be hoisted and vessel's crew assisting with the
rescue operation are wearing flotation devices, and that the person to be
hoisted also has identification and any medications needed.

It is extremely important that all crew wear flotation devices during the
rescue operation since the helicopter produces a storm force downwash in
excess of 50 knots, and when coupled with bad weather, high seas and icy or
slippery decks, this downwash can easily knock a person down, or even
worse, overboard. Additionally, the helicopter pilot will ask that the person to
be hoisted be instructed to keep his/her hands inside the basket/litter and make
no effort to leave the basket/litter until inside the helicopter and told to do so
by the helicopter crew. If there is more than one person to be hoisted, the
people will be hoisted one at a time.

Fig. 15-2. *The rescue litter. Note the bright blaze of light from the reflective tape on the patient's shoulder. Photograph courtesy U.S. Coast Guard.*

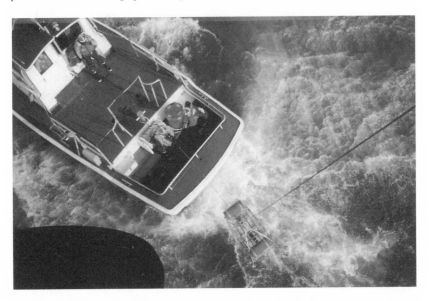

Fig. 15-3. *A rescue basket is lowered to a USCG vessel in a drill. The boat crew is hauling the basket to them using the tag-line. Note also that the surface of the water is whipped white by the downwash of the helicopter's rotors. This indicates a wind is being generated of at least storm force—this is no place to have any sails set. Photograph courtesy U.S. Coast Guard.*

4. Discharge static electricity prior to handling the rescue equipment.

Much like a child will shuffle feet across the carpet on a dry winter day and then touch an unsuspecting younger brother or sister's ear to shock them, the helicopter also builds up a static charge from the rotor blades moving through the air (any time of year), only this charge is a lot more powerful and can knock a person clear across the vessel's deck if it is not properly discharged. All that is required to discharge the static electricity is to allow the rescue device to touch the vessel, a wooden cane, or boatswain's hook before a person touches it.

5. Have the vessel's crew disconnect the hoist cable if the rescue device is to be moved from the hoisting area. Under no circumstances should the vessel's crew connect the hoist cable to any part of the vessel.

By connecting the hoist cable to the vessel, the helicopter is put in a very dangerous situation since it is now also connected to the vessel. It is very rare that the rescue equipment would ever have to be disconnected. In almost all of these situations, the Coast Guard rescue swimmer on board the helicopter will be lowered to assist the vessel during the rescue operation.

6. Instruct the vessel's crew to lower and/or stow all sails, secure rigging, move traveler and main boom as far to starboard as possible, and secure loose gear, hatches, etc., in the hoisting area and around the vessel.

Sails, loose rigging, and the main boom make it more difficult to complete a safe hoisting operation. The rescue equipment will have to be threaded down through this gear to reach the deck, thus potentially causing the device to become entangled. The reason for lowering/stowing the sails and for securing loose gear and hatches in the hoisting area is due to the storm force winds the helicopter creates when it is hovering above the vessel. As stated earlier, this downwash is in excess of 50 knots and in addition to knocking a person down, it can easily move loose gear and hatches around, thus causing more safety hazards for the vessel's crew.

7. Additional information to be passed as the situation dictates.

The helicopter crew will ask for the number of persons on board the vessel and will also tell the vessel the number of persons on board the helicopter. In the unlikely event the helicopter has an emergency and goes into the water, the vessel's crew will know how many persons to rescue from the helicopter. If the hoist is conducted at night, the vessel should light the pickup area as well as possible. It is important not to shine any lights on the helicopter since this can temporarily blind the pilot. If equipped with search lights, the vessel's crew should point them vertically to aid in locating the vessel before the Coast Guard aircraft arrive on scene and then turn them off when the aircraft do arrive on scene.

In this fictitious scenario, the Coast Guard jet was used as a communications platform and a helicopter escort. The HU-25 Guardian jet also has the capability of deploying dewatering pumps, survival rafts, and any other useful equipment or supplies that can be packaged in a plastic container and delivered via its aerial delivery system. The aerial delivery system utilizes a parachute and a trail-line packaged in a separate bag, a shock resistant and buoyant plastic container, a removable hatch in the bottom of the jet aircraft, and a harness assembly which holds the parachute bag and container over the open hatch until the pilot gives the signal to deploy. Once the signal is given, the crewman hits a release lever and the parachute bag and container drop from the jet through the open hatch. Within a few seconds, the parachute bag opens, thus allowing the parachute to fill. When the parachute bag opens, it also frees the trail-line which unravels as it continues its forward momentum toward the vessel. The goal of the aerial delivery system is to have the parachute safely float the container to the water as close as possible to the downwind side of the vessel, and to have the trail-line drape over the vessel so that the crew can pull the container to the ship. This aerial delivery system is extremely effective not only in time-sensitive situations, since the jet can get to the distressed vessel much quicker than the helicopter, but also in situations where the distressed vessel is too far from shore for the helicopter to safely assist.

Coast Guard Air Station Cape Cod uses its helicopters and jets to accomplish a variety of missions in the New England area, the most important of which is to aid persons and vessels in distress. The nature of distress can be a search for an overdue boat on a beautiful summer day or a medical evacuation of an injured crewmember off a vessel during a nor'easter snowstorm. Whatever the case, Air Station Cape Cod aircraft and aircrew will do their best to assist. Having sailors familiar with the procedures and preparations for a Coast Guard air rescue will help to make the operation both safe and successful.

The following instructions were designed to be kept in a vessel's cabin. These instructions give a quick reference list of preparations that can be made to the vessel to better assist Coast Guard Air Station Cape Cod aircrews during a rescue operation. Please copy them and keep a copy in the vessel's cabin.

VESSEL PREPARATIONS FOR A COAST GUARD
AERIAL RESCUE OPERATION

Prior to the arrival of Coast Guard rescue aircraft, the vessel's crew should:

1. Lower and/or stow all sails, secure rigging, move traveler and main boom as far to starboard as possible, and secure loose gear, hatches, etc., in the hoisting area and around the vessel.

2. Have all crewmen who will be out on deck assisting with the rescue operation put on flotation devices. If a person is to be hoisted to the helicopter, have him/her put on a flotation device and also bring identification and any medications.

3. Give one of the crewmen a wooden cane or boatswain's hook to discharge static electricity from the rescue equipment, or instruct him/her to allow the rescue equipment to touch the vessel's deck before handling it.

4. If equipped with search lights, point them vertically at night to aid the Coast Guard rescue aircraft in locating the vessel.

Once the Coast Guard rescue aircraft is on scene, the vessel's crew should:

5. Turn off vertical search lights after Coast Guard rescue aircraft have identified the vessel.

6. Light the pickup area at night as well as possible, but do not shine lights directly at the helicopter since this can temporarily blind the pilots.

7. Tell the Coast Guard rescue aircraft whether or not the vessel is capable of maintaining a speed of 5–8 knots under engine/motor power (not under sail).

8. Give instructions to vessel crew after receiving the hoisting instructions from the helicopter crew.

OPERATING THE COAST GUARD P1B SALVAGE PUMP

The United States Coast Guard Air Station Cape Cod helicopter and fixed wing jet aircrews perform an average of 382 search and rescue missions a year. During these search and rescue missions our aircrews will deliver approximately thirty-one salvage pumps to vessels in distress. In this article, the correct procedures for starting the CG-P1B salvage pump will be described.

The CG-P1B salvage pump is driven by a four stroke, three horsepower engine [see figure 15-4]. It is capable of running for three to four hours on a gallon of gas (six to eight hours total for the two gallons of gas provided), and will pump 120 gallons per minute of water overboard. Every thirty days, the pumps at Air Station Cape Cod are unpacked, assembled, and operated to ensure they are performing correctly. The pumps are then disassembled, placed in plastic garbage bags, and repacked in water resistant orange plastic containers.

When a pump is delivered to a vessel by an Air Station aircrew, it will be delivered in the orange plastic container. The first thing to do is remove the delivery strap that is wrapped around the container and set it aside. Next, remove the orange container lid by unsnapping the locking clips. The container lid is attached to the container by a nylon cord to ensure that the lid is not lost or discarded. This is important, because there is an extra suction hose gasket taped to the inside of the container lid. The first thing you will see inside the container is a set of instructions sealed in plastic. Attached to these instructions will be a flashlight to assist you if the pump is delivered at night. Remove the instructions and flashlight, and set them aside where you will be able to view them. The container will now contain two plastic bags, double bagged so that one is inside of the other. Open the outer plastic bag and you will see a yellow suction hose. Remove the suction hose and set it aside. Next, open the inner plastic bag and you will see the pump, discharge hose, and two one-gallon gas cans (one is a spare which also contains an extra starting cord).

Fig. 15-4. *The CG P1B salvage pump. The operator is priming the pump using the priming handle. The gas tank, fuel line, suction hose (pointing toward you), and the discharge hose (to the right) are visible here. Photograph courtesy U.S. Coast Guard.*

Remove the two gas cans. The only thing left in the container is the pump, and the discharge hose which is already attached to the pump. Remove the pump and attached discharge hose by twisting the pump as you raise it out of the container. The container is designed to be slightly bigger than the pump to ensure a snug fit, which prevents damage to the pump during delivery to your boat. By twisting the pump as you remove it, this helps break the seal that has developed between the pump and the container.

You should now have the following articles laid out on your deck: container lid with extra suction hose gasket, instructions and flashlight, suction hose, two gas cans, and the pump with attached discharge hose.

You are now ready to follow the attached instructions to operate your pump. We will go into the instructions in greater detail to explain more clearly what you are doing.

1. Before attaching the yellow suction hose, check the female end of the screw fitting to ensure that the rubber gasket is in place. If it is not, retrieve the extra gasket from the container lid and place it inside the female end of the screw fitting. This gasket is extremely important. Without it, the suction hose will not provide a good seal, and the pump will not remove water. Attach the yellow suction hose carefully as the female end contains plastic threads that could possibly be cross threaded

when it is attached to the aluminum (or gray plastic in some cases) male end on the pump.

2. Fully immerse the other end of the yellow suction hose into the bilge.

3. Unroll the blue discharge hose and place the red end of the hose overboard. Do not cut the hose at the red end even though it looks like there is no opening for water to pass through. The red end is designed this way to keep air and water from entering the discharge hose, thus keeping a good seal. The pressure of the discharge water will push the black rubber baffle out of the way when the hose is full, thus allowing the water to flow.

4. Attach one of the two gas tanks to the pump. Next attach the loose fuel line from the gas tank to the pump via the coupling nut. Ensure that you push the coupling nut on the whole way, or else you will not have a good seal and fuel will leak out.

5. Prime the pump with the priming handle until water fills the yellow suction hose. You will know the yellow suction hose is filled, and thus primed, when water discharges from the pump via the gray nozzle directly below the priming handle.

6. Even though the instruction card says to choke the pump, do not move the run/choke lever until after you have attempted two starts. The run/choke lever is set to the middle position by our mechanics when they pack the pumps. 95% of the time, the pump will start with the run/choke lever in this position. To start the pump, you need only pull the starter cord. If the pump does not start after two tries, place the run/choke lever to the choke position and attempt another start.

When the pump starts it sounds exactly like a lawn mower. Once the pump is running, move the run/choke lever to the run position and leave it there for as long as you need to run the pump. The only other thing you need to do is reprime the pump with the primer handle until water again discharges from the gray nozzle. This is a very important step that is not shown on the instruction card.

If you go through all the steps above, including choking the engine, and the pump still fails to start, ask for help from the Air Station aircrew. The aircrew has had training in use of the pump, and will be able to help you troubleshoot the problem. If need be, they will deliver another pump to your vessel.

In writing these articles, Lieutenant Travers relied on information from the following Coast Guard publications: *USCG HH-60J Aircraft Flight Manual*, A1-H60JA-NFM-000; *USCG HU-25 Aircraft Flight Manual*, C.G.T.O. 1U-25A-1; *USCG Air Operations Manual*, COMDTINST M3710.1C; *USCG Aviation Life Support Systems Manual*, COMDTINST M13520.1A.

MEDICAL CONCERNS

Most of us have a perception of the helicopter as a miracle machine that can show up when needed and deliver us to safety, should we get lost, sick, or injured. From the first part of this chapter we can see that the helicopter has some severe restrictions on its operations. Now we will learn that there are some severe restrictions on its suitability for medical transport as well. The following information is derived from the *Air Ambulance Standard Operating Procedures Manual* of the Army National Guard. These units provide air ambulance support in many rural areas across the country, though they are not normally used for offshore rescue work such as sailors would require. While these limitations are very real, and should be understood by all those involved, the major concern may well be that there is simply no other way to deal with the situation, and the choices are limited to risking the patient's life by leaving him at the scene, or risking his life while making a concerted effort to get him to safety.

The disadvantages of helicopter flight are several. First is the problem of hypoxia, a deficiency of oxygen reaching the tissues of the body. This results from flying at altitudes where the partial pressure of oxygen is reduced significantly. Whereas a healthy person can easily withstand flight at normal helicopter flight altitudes, if a patient is already suffering from compromised oxygenation, he could be put at risk. The solution to this is to fly very low, but that might not be possible in poor weather.

Second is the problem of noise. Helicopters are extremely noisy, making monitoring of a patient's cardiac sounds, or blood pressure, impossible without the use of a Doppler measuring system. The patient might also suffer directly from the sound level.

Third, there is substantial vibration. This could be extremely painful to a patient with any kind of acute fracture or other severe injury. It could be significant enough to destabilize the patient. (Curiously, and apparently inexplicably, MEDEVAC technicians have on occasion noticed the opposite effect. In a particular case involving a critically injured infant, they found that the longer they flew, the better the patient became. They guessed that this might be attributable to the vibration having a positive effect on the body, somewhat like a massage.)

Fourth, the level of care available aboard the helicopter is very limited. Supplies and equipment are minimal, and though the crew are EMT (emergency medical technician) certified, they too have limitations. The space aboard is very tight, lighting is poor, and conditions in general make in-flight care difficult at best. Added to this is the potential for airsickness, further complicating all the problems.

Fifth, any trapped gasses will expand with altitude, as the atmospheric pressure decreases. Gasses trapped in the abdomen or chest cavity due to traumatic accidents or illnesses, or facial fractures that penetrate the skull or around the eyes (facial injuries are particularly prone to the entrapment of air bubbles in and around the sinuses and the eyes), could expand to the point where they may seriously compromise the patient.

In general, a patient should be stabilized as much as possible and carefully evaluated before considering helicopter transport. Unfortunately that is not always possible, especially when one suffers a catastrophic accident at sea. In those cases, some of the above problems and risks can be mitigated by low-level flight. Also, if specific injuries or conditions can be communicated to the search and rescue coordinators before the helicopter is dispatched, special equipment—even personnel—may be loaded aboard the aircraft to cope with the problem.

Further reading (see bibliography for details): Maloney, *Chapman Piloting,* chap. 4.

CHAPTER SIXTEEN

SAILS, SPARS, AND RIGGING:
USE, MAINTENANCE, AND REPAIR

Maintenance of a sailing rig is one of the aspects of seamanship that is unique to a career under sail. The skills are steeped in tradition, yet have advanced with space-age technology. Square riggers are given new suits of Duradon sails, traditional vessels are resparred with carbon fiber masts, and 1920s vintage yachts are rerigged with Kevlar and Spectra rigging. While some of the newest materials are ill-suited to underway repairs (requiring special equipment), most of the gear we sail with can be readily maintained and repaired at sea with simple tools and know-how. The master or mate must be skilled in the art of marline-spike seamanship, in order to carry out or direct sail or rigging repairs at sea.

PROPERTIES OF SAILCLOTH

Before one can properly carry out repairs to a sail, one must understand at least the basics of sailcloth construction. This will allow the sailor to lay out the patches properly, utilize the repair material to the best advantage, and avoid creating a new stress concentration point in the repaired sail.

With any woven material, there are two sets of threads running at right angles to each other (fig. 16-1). On the loom, the threads running lengthwise are called the warp threads, and those running back and forth, from side to side, are called the weft, or fill, threads. Since it is not possible for these to lie perfectly flat, as they must run over and under each other, there will by necessity be some crimp in the threads.

The crimp can vary—normally the warp is held tightly and the weft gets most of the crimp, but the reverse can be accomplished if desired. Because of this crimp, the sail can be "stretched" in the direction of the crimp, as those crimped threads get straightened out under load. This is not truly stretch, but is actually called elongation, as the threads are merely straightening out. Since the individual fibers can actually stretch as well, there is a technical difference between stretch and elongation.

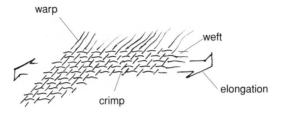

Fig. 16-1. *Warp, weft, and crimp.*

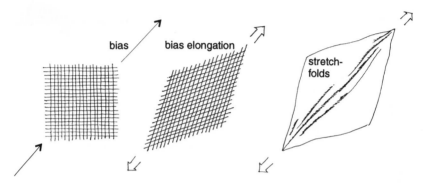

Fig. 16-2. *Bias, bias elongation, and stretch-folds.*

There is another problem inherent in cloth, which is bias elongation (fig. 16-2). The bias is the diagonal of the cloth, at a 45 degree angle to the warp and weft. When cloth is pulled in this direction it stretches considerably, and this is the major source of concern in selecting sailcloth. Bias elongation is best demonstrated by holding a square piece of mosquito screen by two opposite corners and pulling it along the bias. It will not only elongate substantially, but will also develop wrinkles, which run in the direction of the pull. These are called stretch-folds.

From the above we can learn that conventional cloth is least stable along the bias. Whether it will be more stable along the warp or the weft will depend on the relative size (normally referred to as weight) of the warp yarns versus the fill yarns, and the relative tensions of the two when woven. This knowledge will be important when planning the layout of a large patch for a repair, as it is advisable to duplicate as nearly as possible the stretch characteristics of the cloth being mended with the patch material being applied.

PROPERTIES OF VARIOUS SAILCLOTH MATERIALS

To understand the inherent properties of a cloth, one must look into its component parts—the yarns. Yarns are made up of a bundle of fibers, twisted together.

To make a length of yarn of good quality, you avoid using very short fibers. Choose the longest fibers obtainable, and twist them together tightly. The "glue" which holds the fibers together is just friction, and the longer the fibers the more friction there will be.

In nature, there are some plants whose stalks or flowers contain fairly long fibers, notably hemp, cotton, and flax. Of these, hemp is quite stretchy and coarse; cotton is quite fine, uniform, reasonably strong, and long enough to be effective. Linen fiber (from the stalk of the flax plant) is very strong, very fine, very uniform, and very long, up to 3 to 4 feet. For these reasons linen is well suited to sailmaking and was used extensively until the early part of the twentieth century. Cotton initially was the more expensive material in Europe, since it was a tropical plant, whereas flax was grown locally. But the invention of industrial spinning machinery, which was not suited to spinning linen, brought cotton production up and its price down to a point at which it became the more affordable material.

Unfortunately, all the natural fibers are biodegradable and therefore deteriorate after a time, especially in the damp conditions prevailing on a vessel. So it is imperative that sails of natural fibers be dried before storing and before furling, whenever possible. Most natural fiber sailcloths nowadays are treated with preservatives to lengthen their life span.

Synthetic fibers, being man-made, can come in virtually unlimited lengths. This creates a fiber that runs potentially the entire length of the yarn and is practically impervious to biodegradation. However, it is not impervious to ultraviolet degradation. The ultraviolet rays from the sun break down these fibers, and consequently sails of synthetic materials should be protected from sunlight by sail covers when not in use.

With the greater length of synthetic fiber and the ability to manipulate the substance of the fiber itself to achieve different characteristics of stretch, manufacturers of sailcloth have achieved some very high-quality products for sailmaking.

The most common and most generally suitable of the present sailcloths is polyester fiber (Dacron, the most familiar trade name, is Dupont's polyester sailcloth). This starts out as a soft, fuzzy cloth that is then run through various finishing processes for different purposes. It is pressed under pressure and heat to flatten out most of the crimp. It is resin-treated to help bond all the yarns together in the weave, thus preventing much of the slippage that causes bias elongation. The extent to which any of these finishing processes is applied will be determined by the intended purpose of the sailcloth.

A synthetic favorite among traditionalists is Duradon, whose manufacturer will not disclose its makeup. It appears to be an unfinished Dacron, perhaps with some other material blended in with it. This leaves a very soft texture, giving it the look and feel of cotton but with better resistance to rot. Its compromise is that it does not have the stability of finished Dacron.

There are more advanced materials as well, but their cost puts them out of the range of most commercial and pleasure vessels, being reserved for racing boats or those with large budgets and a desire for the extra edge afforded by them. The most prevalent of these are Kevlar, Mylar, and Spectra. These are used not alone but in layers sandwiched with traditional cloths, where they add strength (thereby reducing weight) and virtually eliminate stretch. Repair of these high-tech materials requires special techniques and equipment beyond the scope of this book, limiting our discussion to the more common and simpler Dacron, Duradon, and cotton cloths.

With a general understanding of sailcloth, we can look at some sail repair techniques. The most common damage requiring repairs will be tears. There are basically three choices for repairing a tear in a sail. It can be covered with a glued-on patch, sewn with a mending stitch, or rebuilt with a complete, sewn-in patch. Each of these methods has its applications, depending on the circumstances.

Gluing on a patch probably sounds like a cheater's way out, but if done properly the method has some distinct advantages over sewn patches, especially in an old sail which has become weakened and may not be able to withstand being punched full of holes, as with a sewn patch.

A proper sail needle is supposed to pass between the yarns or fibers of a sail without breaking them. The needle is triangular in cross section, with a very sharp point and rounded and smoothly polished edges. The point will pass between the fibers and spread them apart without breaking them. This will work well on healthy sailcloth, but on old material with substantially weakened fibers, it is inevitable that the needle will break some fibers as it passes through. A nice, neat row of stitches in an old sail will create a perforated line that will tear out easily, just like the edge of a postage stamp.

A glued patch will not have this problem. If not done properly, though, it will have other problems. A good glue for the purpose is Barge Cement, a rubber contact cement used by and available through shoemakers. It is strong, tenacious, and remains flexible, which is important. It is much more tenacious than the various sail tapes generally available. It has a further advantage over sail tape in that you can use it with whatever kind of patching material you wish. If you have a good stout sail, you can use a good stout patch. But if you have an old, rotten sail you will want to use a relatively lightweight patch.

Your choice of patch material is very important. The patch should stretch and flex as nearly identically with the sail itself as possible. To put a patch of Dacron sail tape over an older cotton sail will only invite a new tear, because the patch will not stretch in the same manner as the surrounding sail, causing it to break out. Furthermore, if you try to "beef up" a weak spot in an old sail by putting a patch on both sides of the sail, you will create a hard spot that will also behave differently from the surrounding material and it, too, will break out.

The above considerations apply equally to sewn patches and glued patches. If we choose to sew a patch onto an old sail, then we must avoid the perforation

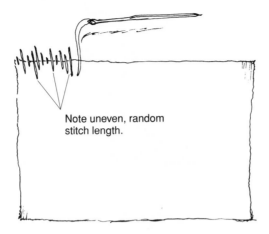

Note uneven, random
stitch length.

Fig. 16-3. *Sloppy stitches, used for weakened sailcloth.*

problem mentioned before by making the stitches sloppy. Make them long, loose, and random—not close, tight, and neatly aligned. Sloppy stitches will spread the strain over a wider area, rather than concentrating it in a single line (see figure 16-3). A glued patch will spread the strain over the greatest area, in the most uniform manner possible.

A small tear in a healthy sail can be mended effectively with a mending stitch such as the herringbone stitch. This is quick (a six-inch tear might take five minutes to mend), easy, and should hold indefinitely unless it is in a part of the sail where stress is especially concentrated. (See figure 16-4 for the method of sewing a herringbone stitch.) The purpose of the small cross-stitch that passes between the edges of the tear is to prevent the two edges from overriding one another, which would cause a pucker and a stress-concentration point.

The most thorough patch, essentially rebuilding the damaged portion of the sail, should only be applied to a sail in good condition. This involves cutting around the tear and folding the raw edges back to form a hem. A patch is then stitched over the entire area, and the hemmed tear is sewn to the patch as well (see figure 16-5). This is not appropriate for a weakened sail because it produces the same kind of hard spot in the sail as mentioned above, that will concentrate stress at that point, causing the patch eventually to break out.

REBUILDING A CLEW

Apprentice sailmakers often start out by building themselves a ditty bag—a small canvas bag to hold their tools. This is a good project to learn basic stitching and construction, and there are numerous designs available in many books on marlinespike seamanship. For a next step, the sailor should build a sample clew. This will be an eminently practical exercise that may turn out to

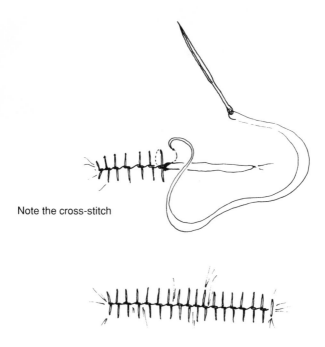

Note the cross-stitch

Fig. 16-4. *The herringbone stitch.*

have a real-life application in the near future. Once the sample clew has been built (assuming it is done well), carry it with you as part of your résumé. It will teach you a great deal and make an excellent prop for a job interview on any sailing vessel. (See figure 16-6 for a clew sampler.)

To rebuild a blown-out clew or to build a fine clew sampler, one must understand some of the stresses that develop around the corners of a sail. These stresses must be individually addressed, since as we saw before, the weave of any piece of fabric can support a strain without undue stretch only in the direction of its warp, and to a lesser extent, its weft. It cannot support these loads along its bias. Yet for headsails especially, and for all sails to a lesser extent, the load or strain is on the bias. The design and construction of the sail must make up for this weakness.

The best way to observe this strain is to pull on the corner of a tablecloth or handkerchief. Along the two sides, a strain will come on the edge or hem, whereas along the bias, the cloth will stretch and pucker in the stretch-folds we discussed before. The portion of the cloth that is stretching on the bias cannot take much strain, so inevitably the strain will be concentrated on the two edges. We can cope with this in two ways. First, we must build up these edges to handle the extra load. Second, we can add elongated patches, called tablings, which are cut lengthwise along their warp threads, and sew them to the sail in

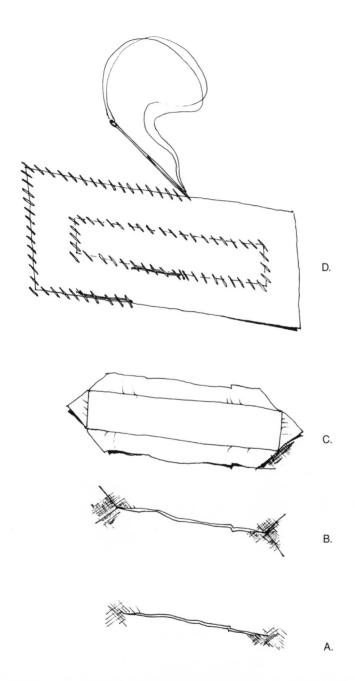

D.

C.

B.

A.

Fig. 16-5. *A hemmed patch, used only for a sail in good condition.* A. *The tear.* B. *Cuts made at each end of tear.* C. *Fold back the sides to form a hem.* D. *Sew around both the tear and the patch.*

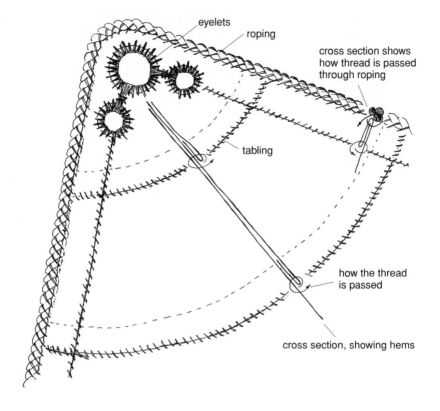

Fig. 16-6. *A clew sampler, showing eyelets, roping, and tablings.*

the direction of the bias of the sail's cloth. Tabling patches help distribute the stress to the body of the sail while simultaneously relieving the strain on the edges (the foot and leech) and help to hold the body of the sail in shape by preventing stretch-folds from developing. As with the smaller patches for tears, we are trying to distribute the strain over as much of the surface area of the sail as possible.

To get the whole clew, with its various patches and hems, to come out flat and neat, without any puckering or distortion, you will need to lay out the entire work very carefully, marking with light pencil lines every seam to be sewed. You will then need to follow these sewing lines very carefully as you work. To avoid letting one patch "creep" past the other as you sew them together, "strike-up marks" are made at about 6-inch intervals, perpendicular to and across the seam lines, as shown in figure 16-7. Pay close attention to these as you sew, and do not allow them to become even slightly separated, or you will end up with a pucker in the finished seam, which affects the ability of the tabling to distribute the load properly.

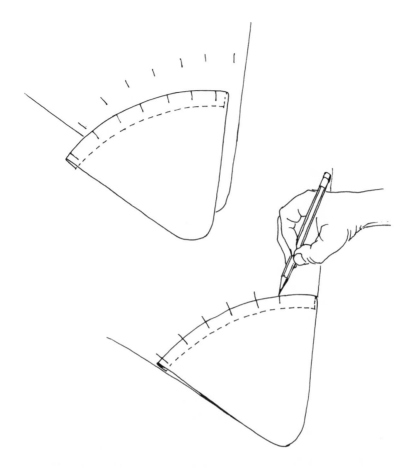

Fig. 16-7. *Strike-up marks.*

Now a sheet-attachment point must be provided in the form of a cringle, an eyelet, or a clew-iron. For this sampler a reinforced eyelet will be used. Again the strain must be distributed. A single, large eyelet would be unable to carry the strain developed there, but it can be backed up by two more eyelets to distribute that strain. Since the leech and foot have been built up, and some tabling added, you may be stitching through anywhere from six to fifteen layers of cloth here. After the large eyelet is sewn in, two smaller ones are sewn in behind and offset from it, to distribute the perforations in the cloth. The large one is then lashed to the smaller ones with a good deal of sail twine. These may be further backed up by sewing webbing or sailcloth straps through them. The stresses on the clew fitting will now be shared among all three eyelets and distributed more evenly to the sailcloth.

SEWING AN EYELET

Sewing a decent eyelet requires a certain fanaticism for neatness. As with the tablings, it is important to lay it out properly before you start and then follow your plan, or it will be distorted when you finish. Start with a brass ring. Without a ring, it will be difficult to get a good round shape, and it will certainly distort when it comes under load. Lay the ring on the cloth and draw a careful tracing around the inside and outside of the ring with a pencil. Now draw another circle outside these two, about the same distance out that the inside one is in. With a hole punch such as you get from an eyelet kit, or a sharp knife, cut out the inside hole, but make it slightly smaller than the inside circle. The sewing process will expand it (see figure 16-8).

Use a quadrupled length of waxed sail twine for sewing. With your pencil, mark off evenly spaced points around the middle and outer circles where you will put your stitches. They will alternate between the outer circle and the middle circle, in a sunburst pattern (again, to distribute the perforations in the cloth). Start sewing, burying the end of the twine under your first several stitches, and be gentle with those first stitches—do not pull them very tight. When you get around to the opposite side of the ring you will pull tight, and this will draw the ring up against the first stitches, pulling them tight. If you start with tight stitches they will pull the ring off center and it will be impossible to center it later.

Keep your stitches neat. Some people prefer to twist the four strands of sail twine up tight, while others let them remain untwisted, lying flat. Either way seems equally effective, although the flat version presents a lower profile on the surface of the cloth, which may be less prone to chafe.

When the stitching is completed, bury the end again under several stitches and cut off the excess twine. Now, if you have an eyelet kit with brass liners, set a brass liner into the inside of the finished eyelet. This will prevent the threads from chafing through on the inside bearing surface of the eyelet. Without a liner, you'll need to line it with leather for protection.

The finished clew, when done properly, is one of the most elegant pieces of work in sailmaking. When not done well, it will reveal your limitations in patience, skill, and attention to detail.

ROPING

In order to reinforce a sail's leech, foot, luff, or head, roping is sometimes required. This involves sewing a length of line (called a boltrope) to the edges of the sail. To do this you will sew each lay of the line to the edge of the sail, using quadrupled sail twine for strength. The trick here is to make the roping just a little tighter than the sailcloth, so that the rope carries just a little more of the strain than the cloth. If you overdo it, the cloth will pucker when slack, but if the roping is not tight enough, the cloth will take the strain instead of the rope.

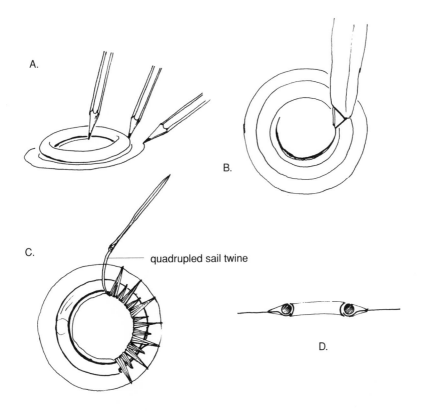

Fig. 16-8. *Sewing an eyelet.* A. *Marking the cloth.* B. *Cutting the cloth.* C. *Sewing the eyelet.* D. *Cross-section through the eyelet.*

The procedure to accomplish this is quite simple. When you get set up to sew the boltrope on, lay the cloth over your knees so that it curves down to the deck on each side of your lap. Now lay the roping just under the very edge of the cloth and keep it there while you sew. This puts it on the inside of the curve of the cloth and will cause the roping to come out slightly shorter than the cloth, so that when the sail gets pulled taut the roping will have a greater share of the tension (see figure 16-9). It makes sense, of course, to try a length and see how it goes. Different line stretches to different degrees, and you'll want to get a feel for the combination.

SPARS

The mate or master of a sailing vessel needs to have an appreciation of the stresses on the spars he is sailing with and the manner in which the designer

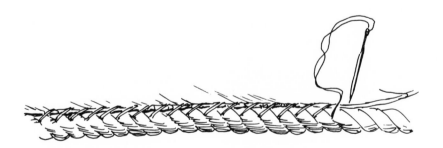

Fig. 16-9. *Roping*.

intended the spars to cope with those stresses. This will enable him to avoid putting loads on spars that may damage or destroy them, and will also allow him to fabricate a replacement or to repair a damaged spar in the event of an accident.

Spars were made of solid wood until the mid- to late-1800s, when some of the Tea Clippers began using hollow iron lower masts. Today, alloy spars are the norm for modern vessels but wooden spars are still commonplace aboard traditional vessels of all types. Spruce is the favored wood for most wooden spars, being the strongest wood for its weight generally available. In the past, white pine was used a great deal, especially on the U.S. East Coast, since it grew straight and tall to the immense sizes required for the big sailing ships of the day. Now, however, it is not easy to find pine trees of the size necessary to get a clear piece of solid wood for a large mast. Douglas fir, from the U.S. West Coast, was, and still is, also used. It is very strong, though heavy, and is still available in large sizes.

For the majority of traditional yachts, wooden spars are hollow, for reasons we will discuss shortly, but for the larger gaff-rigged or square-rigged vessels built for commercial purposes, solid wood spars are common, especially for the lower masts. Around the world various native woods are used as available.

The first hollow wooden spars were made around the mid-1800s but were not in common use until the 1900s. The advantage of a hollow spar over a solid one is that it is considerably stronger *for its weight*, and is much less likely to check and crack as it shrinks and swells with changes in moisture content. This is because the outer surface of a solid spar, being exposed to the air, dries and shrinks more than the inside. Also, wood normally shrinks and swells more tangentially than radially; that is, although the diameter of a spar doesn't change much in dimension, the surface of it does—frequently enough to cause the surface to crack or check.

Spars on a vessel are under two different kinds of loads. While booms and gaffs are beams, a mast is a column. Therefore, while booms and gaffs must withstand significant bending stresses, masts, properly stayed, remain primarily in compression. (This is not so with unstayed masts, which, being unsupported, must withstand terrific bending stresses.) To understand the stresses in booms and gaffs, we must understand how a beam resists a bending force.

To the beam shown in figure 16-10 a force is applied, and the beam is subjected to a bending stress. As it bends, the top of the beam is placed in compression, while the bottom of the beam is placed in tension. The area in the vicinity of the neutral axis, however, remains unchanged. Therefore, it is the top that must resist compression stress and the bottom that must resist tension stress, in order for the beam to resist bending. This is why steel I-beams look the way they do. The designers have put a maximum amount of material at the two surfaces that are doing the most to resist the stress and have removed almost all the material from the rest of the beam, where it is doing little or no good. The same is true for hollow spars. The designers leave the maximum

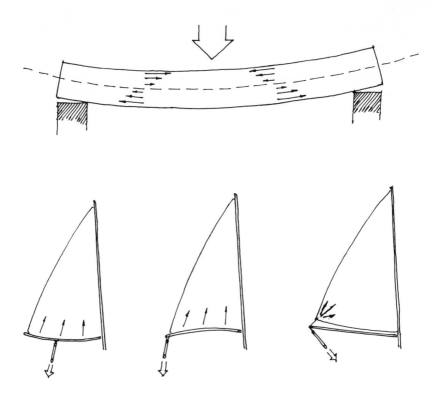

Fig. 16-10. *Bending stresses on a beam and on booms.*

amount of material at the outside surfaces and remove the "lazy" material from the center. An I-beam cannot be used for a spar because the spar may have to resist a load from almost any direction, so material is needed on all sides, not just two.

Because of the properties mentioned above, anything that weakens the top surface's ability to resist compression, or the bottom's ability to resist tension, will weaken the beam's ability to resist bending or breaking. For example, if mounting hardware which requires cutting or drilling into a boom or gaff, take care not to do so indiscriminately on the face that must handle the largest tension loads. Which face of a given spar will be in tension will vary depending on the particular arrangement of the spar and its gear (see figure 16-10). For example, a boom to which a sail is fastened will want to bend downwards (placing the bottom of the boom in tension) if the sheet is secured well in from the end of the spar. In this case the leech of the sail will be pulling the outboard end up, while the sheet pulls the middle part down. If, however, the sheet is secured at the very end of the spar, the sail will want to bend the middle of the boom upward, placing the top of the boom in tension. There is a third possibility—the loose-footed sail—where the sail is only attached at the tack and the clew, and not in between. If the sheet is secured at the end of the boom, and nothing else (such as a vang) is putting a strain in the midpoint of the boom, the boom will always remain in pure compression, and no bending forces will be developed. Other spars should be evaluated in a similar manner to determine what type of stress they are resisting.

Similarly, if a temporary repair to a cracked or broken boom is needed, reinforcement should be placed to resist a tension load on the bottom and a compression load on the top. Simply strapping a splinting arrangement around a cracked boom will not suffice, if the surfaces of splint and spar can slide by one another. The proper solution would be to screw, glue, or rivet a piece securely along the top face (for compression) and another along the bottom face (for tension). Pieces secured along the neutral axis will provide little support.

Masts, on the other hand, are columns, which if properly supported by their shrouds and stays remain primarily under compression (although the sail, since it is attached along the length of the mast, will put some bending load on the mast). Here the whole column is resisting the load, and a repair would be required only to hold the two broken pieces in column (a straight line). In that case a simple splinting arrangement of pieces strapped around the broken or cracked part would suffice—again assuming proper support from shrouds and stays.

Mounting hardware at any point on a mast should have little effect on the column, but avoid putting a sideways, or bending, load on the mast which may pull it out of column. An example of this would be the attachment of running backstays to any point other than where the existing stays and shrouds are attached. To do so would introduce a bending stress that the mast was not designed to accommodate.

With the advent of aluminum alloy and composite materials for spar-making, virtually all modern spars are now hollow, but they are more high-tech than that. They are very carefully engineered to pare down any excess material (and therefore weight) from wherever possible, relying on ultra-high-strength reinforcing in critical places. This might be as simple as using thicker aluminum in high-stress places, or as exotic as wrapping carbon fiber bands in helical coils around the length of the mast. In any event, the sailor should learn the structure of the spars so as not to defeat the technology by drilling through a key structural member to mount a piece of gear.

RIGGING

The stresses of the rig must be kept in balance, and each part of the rig is a significant part of a whole. The stress on the main sheet does not end with the shackle at the traveller. It continues past the shackle and through the screws or bolts of the traveller to the deck beam. It does not stop there either. It continues through the deck beams to everything the deck beams are connected to—the decking itself, the hanging and lodging knees, the hull planking or sheathing, the ceiling planking, the frames, the floors, and on down to the keel.

It is important to know that signs of strain can show up in any one or several of these places and should be traceable back to the initial load. When a deck leaks, it may be because the caulking is failing. But it may also be that the traveller is overstraining the decking because it was not properly through-bolted to a deck beam. The sailing load is not being properly distributed, and a stress concentration is developing in a section of the structure that is not capable of withstanding it. No single problem can be viewed in isolation, and it is the job of the mate and master to be cognizant of the interplay of stresses.

When a backstay parts and your heroic crew leaps into action, bringing a spare halyard back to a cleat and setting it up taught to relieve the strain on the mast, they have done the right thing. However, someone had better get below immediately and identify what that cleat is secured to, as it was certainly not put there to handle that particular strain. Perhaps it is strongly through-bolted to a deck beam, but more likely it was only screwed to the deck, since it may only have been intended to handle a horizontal load along the deck. In that case you should fairlead the halyard through something that will convert its near-vertical load to a horizontal one. But be certain the fairlead is sufficient to handle that kind of loading. Is it a turning block for a staysail sheet that is bolted to the coach roof? The block may look rugged, but it is not likely that the coach roof is stout enough for such a load. Remember that the load does not cease until it reaches the keel.

This is illustrated by a true story about the schooner *Bluenose II,* on which the crew decided the rig needed tightening. As they were sailing in a stiff breeze they took up some of the slack in the leeward shrouds. Then they tacked her and took up an equal amount on the other side. After evaluating their efforts they decided they needed to tighten her up a bit more, so they repeated the process. At some point someone noticed that the mast boot was folding up like an accordion—the mast was actually being driven down through the vessel. Afraid that they were driving the keel out from under her, they checked the bilges, but discovered instead that the mast step was being crushed. It was too soft for the job, but if it hadn't been, they might very easily have been opening up her plank seams. The moral is that all parts of a vessel are connected, and you must consider the effects of any stress on other parts of the structure or rig.

When any part of the rig fails, its load is instantly transferred to some other part of the rig. If, for example, a backstay fails, its load is transferred to the mast itself. The questions you must answer are, first, can the mast support the new load and, second, what other parts of the rig have now come under new stress? To illustrate this, assume your backstay has failed while on a run in good breeze and a fairly rough sea. Recall that the mast was designed to be primarily a compression member. Suddenly it is being asked to resist a bending moment that it was not designed for. It is probably not capable of supporting much of a load in this fashion, and some fast work will be required to relieve its bending load and put it back in compression.

Now look at what other parts of the rig lead aft. The shrouds lead somewhat aft, so they will be taking the bulk of the strain. The main sheet and the leech of the mainsail will be providing some support as well. Second, if you have a mizzen mast and a triatic stay between the tops of the two masts, that stay will be transmitting most of the load to the mizzen mast and its whole supporting rig.

The best first move is by no means a given but will depend on the circumstances. If you are on a run in a rough sea, heading up (with the intent of relieving the forward thrust on the mast) may be a poor reaction, as the vessel will begin pitching, causing shock loads, which are more severe than static loads. Another reflex action might be to strike sail, but this too might not be appropriate if in the course of dropping the sail it starts flogging. Also, as stated above, the sail and its sheet may be providing a substantial amount of support for the mast.

Therefore, the best first move might be to head up to a reach and sheet in, in order to get the strain off the aft end of the rig and put it on the headstay and shrouds. This maneuver would presumably also put your beam to the seas which would minimize pitching. It would induce rolling, but the rolling would be dampened by the sheeted-in main, and you still have the shrouds to handle that load. Furthermore, by sheeting in tight, the sheet and the leech of the sail can add their support.

Note that this requires a quick reaction and should take just seconds to accomplish. You have bought time to do what needs to be done, which may be to grab a spare halyard and lead it aft to a fairlead and winch, tension it, and thereby provide some aft-leading support for your rig. This move in turn will buy more time, allowing you to plan and execute a more permanent repair, such as getting a suitable piece of wire or low-stretch line aloft to a secure fitting at the masthead and to a strong connecting point at the deck in a manner that will allow you to tension it properly.

If a headstay parts, you must bear off quickly and head downwind to put the load on the shrouds and backstay. If a windward shroud parts, tack, putting it to leeward and relieving the strain. But beware of slacking your sheets to the point of luffing. A big sail luffing in a good breeze delivers punishing blows to a rig and may be just what the damaged rig cannot handle. Think about what heading will stabilize the vessel most, without putting undue strain on the defective part of the rig. Try to minimize both rolling and pitching. Since a sail full of wind is an excellent stabilizing device, consider setting more sail (on another mast perhaps) rather than reducing sail.

When you do get to the point of sending a good piece of wire aloft to replace the broken one, think about where it is going and what it will be doing. The mast must be put in compression, so the new piece must be secured at or near the same securing point as the shrouds and headstay. Attach it to the same fitting as the one the broken wire was connected to. If that is not feasible, choose the spot carefully. Do not secure a backstay around the spreaders, for example (a convenient place to secure to), if this location will induce a bending moment when coupled with the headstay at the masthead.

Choose your securing point on deck carefully. To avoid opening up a seam in your deck, do not overload a deck fitting that was never intended to carry that sort of load—whether in magnitude or direction. It may be necessary to provide extra support for the fitting to which the load is being delivered, and it is for this reason that standing rigging is not normally attached to the deck, but rather is generally run to chainplates which direct the load to the hull structure itself via the frames. Putting this kind of heavy vertical loading onto the deck, even via a deck beam, may overstress the deck structure and pull open a seam in the deck or at the hull-deck edge.

If you have to fashion a jury mast or spar, think of the kinds of loads these spars must handle. Masts are columns, primarily resisting compression. (The exception—the unstayed mast—would be very hard to repair at sea without resorting to stays and shrouds.) Therefore, to fashion a jury mast, what is needed is only an intact section of the mast itself, well stayed. Jury masts, for this reason, typically end up being stumpy versions of the original mast.

Booms and gaffs, however, must resist bending loads, and jury-rigged versions of these must be much more carefully put together. If you do not have a suitable piece of spar available to work with, you may instead resort to a loose-footed sail (remember this will put the boom in compression), or a scandalized sail having no gaff.

Further reading (see bibliography for details): Bassin, et al., *Statics and Strength of Materials;* Chapelle, *Yacht Designing and Planning,* chaps. 5–6 and appendix; Kinney, *Skene's Elements of Yacht Design,* chap. 17; Marino, *The Sailmaker's Apprentice.*

CHAPTER SEVENTEEN

RULES OF THE ROAD: SAIL VESSEL SPECIFICS

Before receiving a license to sail as mate or master of any U.S. Coast Guard inspected auxiliary sail vessel, a candidate will have to pass an extensive exam on the International Regulations for Prevention of Collisions at Sea, variously known as the COLREGS, the Rules of the Road, or just the rules. Furthermore, the candidate must get a 90-percent grade, or better, on this exam in order to pass. There is, therefore, no question that he or she will have studied the rules thoroughly, and the best text for that purpose is simply the rules book itself. There are sufficient books on the market that analyze and clarify the rules, but none of them focuses specifically on the considerations for sailors. That is the purpose of this chapter.

RIGHTS OF WAY

Too many sailors believe that vessels under sail always have the right of way over all other vessels. This is very wrong. In fact, in the hierarchy of who has the right of way over whom, sailing vessels are only one place up from the bottom of the list. Here is the list (from rule 18):

1. Vessels not under command.
2. Vessels restricted in their ability to maneuver.
3. Vessels constrained by their draft (only in international waters).
4. Vessels fishing.
5. Vessels sailing.
6. Power-driven vessels.

The rules require that a vessel give the right of way to any vessel in a category that is higher up the list. Thus, as we know, a power-driven vessel must give way to a sailing vessel (and all others). A sailing vessel, however, can only claim the right of way over a power-driven vessel and must give way to fishing vessels, vessels constrained by their draft, etc. In order for us to know what category another vessel is in, we must identify her lights, or day shapes, as specified in part C of the rules. There is one exception to the statement that a power-driven vessel must always give way to a sailing vessel, and that is if a sailing vessel is overtaking. Then the sailor must keep clear.

Beyond the rules, there is courtesy. If we are out for pleasure, with no particular destination or timetable in mind and we come upon another vessel on a schedule with her livelihood at stake, there is nothing to be gained by forcing the right of way issue. Since the rules apply only when "two vessels are approaching so as to involve risk of collision," they leave everyone the option of taking avoiding action early enough to prevent even reaching the point of such risk. It would be prudent and appropriate to call the vessel on the VHF and let her know of your willingness to alter course and allow her to continue on her way. But it is important to understand that if such contact is not made, or an agreement to depart from the rules is not reached, and you do reach the point where risk of collision can be considered to exist, all vessels are required to abide by the rules. Arbitrarily deciding to take action irrespective of the rules is a dangerous practice, since the maneuvering rules rely on one vessel taking avoiding action, while the other holds its course and speed.

SAILING VESSEL LIGHTS AND SHAPES

Rule 25 of the International and Inland Rules of the Road requires a sailing vessel under way at night (or in periods of restricted visibility) to exhibit sidelights and a sternlight. These are specific lights that meet the exact definitions given in rules 21 and 22. You should be very familiar with these definitions, which spell out the arc and range of visibility, color, and location. This required lighting imparts little visibility to a sailing vessel. From any given direction except dead ahead there will be just one light showing on your vessel, and two out of the three lights will be colored. These colored lights do not stand out nearly as well as white lights. Worse, these lights are often mounted low to the water, at least on smaller sailing vessels, and may, therefore, be obscured by your own bow wave or a genoa jib when you are heeled over, making your vessel virtually invisible from leeward. For this reason the rules allow a vessel of less than 20 meters in length to carry these three lights in a combination lantern at the masthead. In this way they are at least well up in the air, though they are not necessarily any brighter.

Another problem with the required running light configuration is that it does not always provide instant recognition. Most professional mariners are not sailors and, therefore, are not anticipating seeing sailing vessels. Since they are anticipating seeing other ships, they will be looking for a pattern of lights that normally includes two white masthead lights forming a range and one sidelight.

Seeing a single red or green light (and a dim one at that) is likely to be confusing, and this confusion is what must be prevented.

For just this reason, the rules also allow an additional set of special identity lights that positively identify a sailing vessel. These are two lights, a red one over a green one, shown at the masthead and visible all around the horizon. These are extremely valuable and, though optional, they should be installed on any sailing vessel doing any significant amount of night sailing. Even if someone on an approaching ship does not immediately recognize exactly what they signify, they are at least unusual enough to draw some attention. Those who do recognize the lights, even if they do not understand much about sailing, will realize that the vessel carrying them probably has the right of way.

USE OF VHF RADIO FOR COLLISION AVOIDANCE

The VHF radio was, like radar, the tool that everyone thought would put an end to collisions at sea. It was assumed that if ships could talk to each other, they could not possibly collide. Unfortunately it was not to be so simple, and there are plenty of cases to illustrate collisions that occurred despite radio communication between the ships.

For the VHF radio to be effective, the ships first must make contact. One must make the call, and the other must hear it and respond. For this to occur, the call must be on the right channel (frequency). This will be channel 16 at sea, and 16, 9, or 13 in most ports. Channel 13 is the channel that is set aside for ship-to-ship communication specifically with this kind of collision-avoidance traffic in mind. It is also wise to learn the channels that the local pilots and fishermen use in your area.

Assuming both ships are on the same radio channel, the caller then must clearly identify the vessel being called. The vessel being called may not even know there is someone else out there. The people on the bridge are probably fully engaged in the various details of conning their vessel, and the voice on the radio must get their attention. When you make such a call, you should identify the other vessel and your own as succinctly and unambiguously as possible. Too often a futile call is heard for a "starboard-side ship" over the radio. That, of course, means nothing to anyone except the caller. However, the opposite extreme is equally useless. "Ship bearing 227 degrees from me at 7.2 miles on course 078 degrees true, speed 14.8 knots" will probably get no response either. You have bombarded them with too much information, in too great detail, and since they do not know where you are, they cannot know, relative to you, where they are.

Your call should be complete, but as brief as completeness will allow. The information should be presented as it would appear from their bridge, not yours. Give your name, call sign, and identify the general area (note that if you are on channel 13, no call sign is required, but it is required on all other channels). Describe the ship if you can see it, give the bearing and distance from the ship to yours, then describe your own vessel and repeat your name. For example:

> This is the sailing vessel *Swan Five,* WAM-9652, 10 miles south of Monhegan Island, calling the blue-hulled, westbound containership. I am the white ketch approximately 4 miles off your starboard bow. This is *Swan Five,* over.

In this message, you have gotten their attention by naming the sailing area, but the ship you are calling will probably not remember your name. Once they are listening, they can see at a glance that there is a white sailboat about 4 miles on their starboard bow. They then get a second chance to write down your name when you repeat it at the end.

They will then call you back, and this may come as a surprise. This is where too many nonprofessionals lose their composure. They have geared up for the initial call, only to be startled by getting a response. Radio fright is at least as common as stage fright. Use your radio enough so it becomes just another telephone. Speak normally. It is good to say "over" at the end of a call so you do not break in on each other, but your intonation as you finish a call may suffice.

A word of caution here: Bear in mind that the wrong vessel may respond to your call. Try to establish with certainty that you are communicating with the right vessel. Ask for further identification, such as (if it is night), "would you mind flashing your masthead light off and on once so I can positively identify you?" or, "can you see my spotlight now?" It is better to have them flash at you, giving you no doubt about who has seen what, than for you to flash at them and wonder if they really saw you. Remarkably, it is not uncommon for two vessels to reach a passing agreement by radio, only to discover later that they were each talking to the wrong vessel. These situations have occasionally had tragic consequences.

Once communication has been established, if anything should go wrong later, (one of you loses your steering, or you get a sudden wind shift requiring a course change), you will be able to address the problem immediately. You will each know the other's name, location, and course and can get right to the point, rather than having to go through the rather long identification process when time is critical.

Note also that this process is by no means limited to big ships. You should be in the habit of communicating with vessel traffic of any consequence, if a meeting or passing arrangement is called for. The whole crew should become comfortable with radio usage. This is what the VHF should be used for.

DEALING WITH SHIPPING

As more sailors become comfortable with the use of the VHF radio and its protocols, they will improve relations between commercial shipping and the sailing industry. There are other ways for the sailor to improve these relations as well.

First, learn what you can about how ships operate, and do not dwell on the apocryphal stories about nonprofessional behavior aboard ships. Of course there is some of that, just as there is aboard sailing vessels. But for the most part the people who operate sailing vessels and merchant ships alike are trying to do their jobs well and would like others to do the same. Learn about the difficulties of handling a large ship. Understand that these ships are controllable, but they have different parameters within which they must work. Typically, the turning circle of an 800-foot ship will be between ½ and 1 mile. Its stopping distance will be a mile or more. (A tug with a large tow on a long hawser will need more room than that.) A ship of that size will have to commit to a plan of action before you may have even realized that any action would be required. You may be able to change your mind and turn around when a mere boat-length away, while they have been committed for the last mile or more. Generally, the master's standing orders on such large ships will require the mates to make their course change for collision avoidance at a distance of 3 to 6 miles from the threat vessel. Understand that when you begin to think you are getting too close, they may already be committed to their plan of action. If, however, you should find such a ship approaching to within a mile or two of you (in the open ocean) without having taken action, you can assume that it will be up to you to do so. You should already have been on the radio attempting to raise them, and perhaps have made other attempts to get their attention, such as flashing your spotlight on your sails if it is dark.

For these reasons traffic separation schemes have been devised for areas of heavy maritime activity. These smooth out traffic flow for large vessels so they can get through crowded areas safely. Small vessels should not operate in these traffic lanes unnecessarily. Paragraph (j) of rule 10 requires that "a vessel of less than 20 meters in length or a sailing vessel shall not impede the safe passage of a power-driven vessel following a traffic lane." "Shall not impede" is a potentially confusing phrase, however. This does not mean that the ship has the right of way. It means only that sailboats should not be there; but if they are, the normal rights-of-way still apply.

A similar rule (rule 9) applies in narrow channels, requiring sailing vessels, vessels less than 20 meters, and vessels crossing the channel not to impede the passage of a vessel that is confined to the channel. The sailor should appreciate the difficulties large vessels have with such factors as bank cushion and bank suction. In shallow water their hulls set up pressure areas that affect their maneuvering, as they "feel" the irregularities of the bottom. A high-pressure area is developed around their bow that tends to push them away from the bank at the channel edge, while a low-pressure area farther aft will pull them in back there. Similar problems develop between two large vessels when passing close by one another. This can be troublesome enough for them without having to worry about small vessels in the middle of the channel that have no particular need to be there. We are all entitled to go where we want, to some extent, but if we can extend the courtesy of giving large vessels sufficient maneuvering room, we will all be able to operate more safely. In many cases, a small sailing vessel is not truly confined by the channel limits, so it would be possible, and prudent, to leave the channel to allow a ship to pass. This is an important time to be using your VHF radio. Listen for a call, as they will want to know your intentions so they can plan theirs. Call a large vessel to tell them not to worry about you, that you will be well out of their way before they get to your location. The large vessel will be very pleased to hear from you.

Many busy harbors maintain a Vessel Traffic Service (VTS), an advisory service normally operated by the Coast Guard that keeps ships in touch with what others in their area are doing. You may not be required to participate (the requirement is usually based on tonnage), but you may find it useful, as they will tell you what traffic to expect on your way in or out of the harbor. The VTS will then keep other ships informed of your location and your route. They are there to assist everyone in making the harbor a safer place for vessels to operate. To learn if there is a VTS in a given area and what VHF channel they operate on, consult the *Sailing Directions* or *Coast Pilot* for the area.

Further reading (see bibliography for details): Cargal, *How to Avoid Collisions;* Maloney, *Chapman Piloting,* chaps. 6, 7, and 24; Smith, *Farwell's Rules of the Road;* United States Coast Guard, *Navigation Rules.*

CHAPTER EIGHTEEN

RULES AND REGULATIONS

The regulations that apply to vessels under U.S. law are found in the *Code of Federal Regulations* (the CFRs). These regulations are divided into general categories by subject area, and these areas are known as titles. Title 46 is Shipping, where the pertinent regulations for the vessels we are discussing are found. The titles are further divided into subchapters and parts. Subchapters are given letter designations and the parts are numbered. Parts are like numbered paragraphs. Subchapter R is titled Nautical Schools and contains the regulations governing sailing school vessels (SSVs) in part 169. Subchapter T is titled Small Passenger Vessels and contains the regulations for vessels under 100 gross tons carrying passengers for hire (often referred to as "T-boats") in parts 175 through 185. When referring to a particular item within the CFRs, it should be referenced by the title, part, and subpart numbering system. For instance, the opening paragraph of subchapter T is Authority, where the authority for these regulations is identified. This paragraph is referenced by the identification 46CFR 175.01. This takes us to title 46, part 175, subpart 01. Further incremental breakdowns by paragraph are common as well. These references will be utilized throughout this chapter.

The first consideration you should give to the regulations is to understand at what point a vessel falls under their purview. In a general sense, if you know someone is paying you or the owner a fee for riding on your vessel, you should read the part of both subchapter R and T entitled *Applications* very carefully and determine if you must comply. There are many ruses under which owners think they can get away with being paid for their expenses on a voyage without actually being considered as passenger vessels, but in most cases they are legally considered to be carrying passengers for hire, and the *captain* will be held responsible for compliance with these regulations.

There are many different certificates a vessel may be required to have (or may choose to have), and we will briefly identify these. You should make yourself aware of which ones your vessel carries and become familiar with the applicable parts of the regulations. Copies of these are found in appendix III. The most common certificate is the certificate of inspection, issued by the U.S. Coast Guard. We will look into this in more detail below, since most of the vessels described in this text will be carrying such a certificate.

If your vessel carries more than twelve passengers (or students), or cargo, on an international voyage, she will likely be required to have a SOLAS certificate. The acronym stands for the International Convention for the Safety of Life at Sea. This convention, under the authority of the International Maritime Organization, produced an international treaty setting down requirements for everything from lifesaving equipment to construction details for vessels operating internationally. Its purpose is to improve the safety record of vessels worldwide. The treaty was first signed in 1974 and has had several amendments. The regulations detailed therein have been incorporated into the CFRs, where appropriate, but can also be found as a body in a single volume entitled *SOLAS, Consolidated Edition.*

If your vessel is over 79 feet registered length, or over 150 gross registered tons, and is not a yacht, she will likely be required to have a load line certificate. These regulations are found in 46CFR part 42 (subchapter E). A load line is a mark on the side of a vessel's hull indicating the maximum safe draft to which she may be loaded. Also known as a Plimsoll mark after its originator, Mr. Samuel Plimsoll, these regulations were enacted to put a stop to the common practice of dangerously overloading ships in the mid 1870s. The certificate shows that the vessel has been surveyed by the classification society, for the purpose of determining what that safe maximum draft should be, and that they have indicated where that mark should be. A classification society is a regulatory body that may or may not be a government entity, but is a recognized authority for the inspection of vessels. In the United States, the American Bureau of Shipping (ABS) is the recognized classification society and is not a government agency. Other countries have similar societies, such as Lloyd's Register of London (LR), Bureau Veritas of France (BV), Nippon Kaiji Kyokai of Japan (NKK), Germanischer Lloyd's of Germany (GL), and Det Norsk Veritas of Norway (DNV), for example. These initials appear on the Plimsoll marks on the ship.

The American Bureau of Shipping also conducts its own hull and machinery inspections of vessels, separate from the Coast Guard. These inspections (for a new vessel) typically start with the inspection of the building materials before the vessel is even built. Standards are set for steel, aluminum, and fiberglass vessels, but no current rules exist for wooden vessels. A vessel holding a certificate from ABS is referred to as "in class." While classification of a vessel by ABS is strictly voluntary (not a legal requirement), it is essentially mandatory for large commercial vessels; it is unlikely that an owner could get insurance without it. Smaller sailing vessels are less likely to be classed, but the larger ones may well be. As with the Coast Guard inspections, periodic reinspections are required. The ABS standards can be found in the publication

Rules for Building and Classifying Steel (or aluminum, etc.) *Vessels*, published by ABS annually.

The Federal Communications Commission (FCC) requires a station license for any radio transmitting device installed aboard a commercial vessel. Note that this covers more than just radios—it includes radar and EPIRBs (emergency position-indicating radio beacons). These regulations are found in 46CFR.80 (subchapter D). A Radio Equipment Safety Certificate is also required. This is issued by the FCC after a safety inspection of the various radio installations aboard the vessel is performed. Third, the operator of the equipment must have an operating permit or license. The licensed operator may allow an unlicensed person to speak on the radio, but the licensed person must initiate the call, monitor the unlicensed person's use of the radio, and then conclude the call. The licensed operator assumes responsibility for the unlicensed person's use of the radio. Furthermore, the FCC requires that a log be kept of all radio traffic conducted at a particular station (vessel). The VHF radio log must contain the date and time of each radio call, the frequencies used, the nature of the call, and the operator's name. The FCC and/or the Coast Guard may, from time to time, visit a vessel and ask to inspect the radio installation, the various licenses and certificates, and/or the radio log. The operator may be fined for any exceptions noted.

Under the Telecommunications Act of 1996, recreational vessels that operate only in domestic waters, utilizing only VHF radio, radar, and an EPIRB, and that do not communicate with any foreign stations are not required to hold either a station license, a safety inspection certificate, or an operator permit.

Depending on your state's laws, you may have to carry a state registration for your vessel. In some states, this is not required if the vessel is inspected by the Coast Guard. In any case, a small boat, if it has a motor of any size, probably must be state registered.

THE CERTIFICATE OF INSPECTION

The legal document that your vessel must have on board if you are going to carry passengers, students, or cargo is the certificate of inspection, or COI. This is issued by the U.S. Coast Guard, must be posted and current, and its provisions must be complied with.

The following information/requirements will be found on the COI:

- Description of vessel.
- Identity and address of owner.
- Identity and address of operator.
- Type of certificate (SSV, subchapter T, etc.).
- Official number, tonnages, length, and date of build.

- Number and licenses of crew required (including master, mates, deckhands, engineers, etc.).
- Route permitted.
- Lifesaving equipment required.
- Requirements for special operations.
- Fire-fighting equipment/systems required.

You must make yourself completely familiar with all the requirements of the COI. If you are the master, you are personally responsible for compliance. Do not assume that just because the vessel was running before you got there everything is fine now. Every time a different inspector inspects a vessel, a different area will be examined, and a new inspector may find something wrong in an area that had never been scrutinized before. You must be the most thorough inspector of all.

USING THE REGULATIONS

There are essentially three different circumstances under which you may need to refer to the regulations, and they require different levels of familiarity. If you are involved with the design or construction of a new vessel, or with a major rebuild, you will need to have a thorough understanding of the applicable subchapters. If you are the mate or master during a periodic inspection for certification, you will need to have a secondary level of understanding. For day-to-day operations, you should understand at least the applicable parts.

Design/Construction

If you get involved in a construction or rebuilding project, you will need to become an expert on the regulations. You must read every word of every applicable subchapter, making extensive notes and clarifying the meaning and interpretation of every puzzling part. If you are the master, or plan to be, do not delegate this job to anyone else, because you will have to deal with any lingering problems after you are under way. The only way to be successful with the regulatory aspect of the job will be to involve the U. S. Coast Guard right from the earliest stages of concept design. The whole project should be discussed with them at the start and an open line of communication maintained with them throughout the project. Second, keep detailed records of every conversation, phone call, and letter. As the project proceeds, inspectors will be rotated on and off the job, and if you get an interpretation from one inspector that comes under question by another, you will want to be able to document the process by which the original interpretation was reached.

There will be other inspectors involved besides the Coast Guard. If your vessel is going to be classed by ABS, there will be another extensive set of regulations to learn and different inspectors to work with. Likewise, your insurance company might get involved with their own set of requirements and inspections, and if your vessel meets various criteria of size, purpose, or route, there will be load-line surveys needed, SOLAS regulations to meet, and FCC regulations and inspections to be dealt with. If for some reason the construction phase should progress without an appropriate inspection taking place, there may be monumental corrective measures required. These could be substantial enough to jeopardize the entire project. As master, you cannot assume that others are taking care of these things. You must make yourself aware of the process and see to it that all regulations are followed.

Where do you go to find this information? The *Code of Federal Regulations* is a government publication and should be found in any large library, in the legal or reference section. Ask also for the *Federal Register,* which is the monthly update of the CFRs. The *Federal Register* is also where you will find any Notices of Proposed Rulemaking, or NPRs. These are announcements that new regulations have been proposed; they include requests for public comment.

PERIODIC INSPECTIONS

Regulations for periodic inspections are found in 46 CFR 176 for Subchapter T vessels, or 46 CFR 169.200 for SSVs.

Most of the crew will be involved in the periodic inspection process. These inspections may involve the U. S. Coast Guard, the FCC, ABS, or an insurance surveyor. They need not be painful, though if they are it is usually not the fault of the inspector. This is an important, and often misunderstood, concept. The captain is in control of the inspection. She has all the regulations and schedules the inspection. Periodic inspections for most vessels are required either annually or every eighteen months, so there is plenty of time to prepare. There are several ways to help the inspection process go smoothly. First, study the regulations. Prepare a set of notes that condenses the regulations into a useable package of information that is specific to your vessel. In the process of making these notes you will learn most of what you need to know about the regulations.

The scheduling of the inspection is critical. Take whatever steps are necessary to allow enough time to prepare for the inspection, and leave sufficient time afterward to make any corrections the inspector requires of you. If the inspection is scheduled for one day between two trips, you may find yourself cancelling a trip if the inspector refuses to issue the new certificate. This is not the fault of the inspector; it is your fault for poor planning.

Third, make every effort to develop a good working relationship with the regional Coast Guard inspectors. If you make the effort to work with them, you will usually find they are very helpful and professional. But if you assume that they are there to make your life difficult, you will prove yourself right.

Finally, if you are the master, conduct the inspection yourself, with time enough before the real inspector is due to correct the deficiencies you find. Be your own toughest inspector. Prepare a written list of deficiencies and put a timetable on the corrections that will assure their completion in time for the actual inspection. If something cannot be rectified in time, call the Coast Guard and tell them what the problem is. Do not wait for them to come and find it. If it is only a matter of one or two items, they will probably come for the inspection anyway and may issue you your certificate with instructions to correct those deficiencies. For this the Coast Guard uses form number 835, known throughout the business as "an 835." As long as they feel the deficiency is not an immediate safety hazard they will issue you an 835 and allow you to continue to operate.

OPERATIONS

Operational regulations can be found in 46 CFR 185 for Subchapter T vessels and 46 CFR 169.800 for SSVs.

Operational regulations must be dealt with on a daily basis. They require such things as posting licenses, notifying the Coast Guard of any casualty, carrying proper charts and publications, posting station bills, wearing harnesses, holding emergency drills, etc. Requirements for specific logbook entries are also found in the operational regulations.

As a mate or master you must be thoroughly familiar with these aspects of the regulations. You must read the section thoroughly and again condense it into your own notes that you can carry with you aboard the vessel. Different vessels will have different ways of complying with these regulations, and perhaps even different interpretations of them. These may or may not be legitimate. If you are sailing on your license, your license is at stake, and it is therefore up to you to decide whether the practices being followed are appropriate and legal. The Coast Guard will be holding you accountable.

Further reading (see bibliography for details): *Code of Federal Regulations, Title 46;* American Bureau of Shipping, *Rules for Building and Classifying Steel Vessels;* International Maritime Organization, *SOLAS, Consolidated Edition.*

CHAPTER NINETEEN

VOYAGE PLANNING

ESTABLISHING GOALS

The first step in planning a voyage will be to establish the goals. Once you have a destination or objective in mind, you will begin to lay out the route and the schedule. In some cases the goal will be based on getting as far as you can in a given time period. If you have a geographic destination, you will need to determine how much time you need to get there. Or your goal may be to carry out a research project, wherever that may take you. In any case, you must define your goals and develop a timetable.

The first question is how far you can reasonably expect to travel in a day. Any estimate must be very conservative, if you hope to be under sail much of the time. If your vessel is capable of sustained sailing at speeds of 7 knots on a reach and 6 knots close-hauled, do not fool yourself by laying out a timetable based on a "conservative" 5 knots; you will end up under power most of the time. Remember that any time the wind is against you, you will be beating back and forth, gaining less than 4 miles toward your destination for every 6 miles you sail. (Your distance made good to windward when beating can be calculated by multiplying the distance run in one hour by the cosine of the angle off the wind. See figure 19-1.)

This is on a good day, without adverse currents or significant leeway. So, be more conservative than you can imagine having to be. This will allow you to do more sailing and enjoy the trip more. If you have a schedule to meet, then you must use the same conservative estimating process to establish your projected fuel consumption and planned refueling stops.

Also look at the prevailing winds and the general weather picture. A westerly run in the northeast trades will allow you to plan on more mileage per day than a run in northern waters, where the weather is more changeable. The best source of information, especially for longer passages, are the *Pilot Charts* published by the National Imagery and Mapping Agency (NIMA). These monthly charts give long-term averages for winds, currents, fog, gales, barometric pressure, sea and

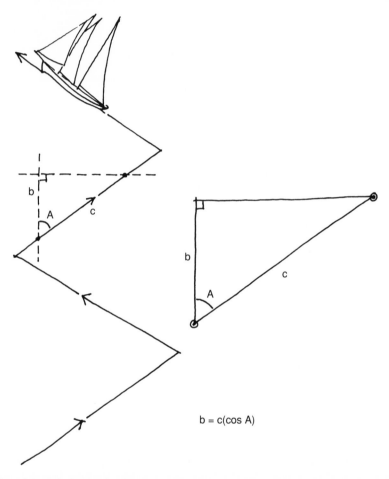

$$b = c(\cos A)$$

Fig. 19-1. *Calculating the distance made good to windward. A = angle off the wind; b = speed made good to windward; c = distance run on your course in one hour.*

air temperature, and much more. Other good information will be found in the *Coast Pilot* and *Sailing Directions* (published by NIMA in the United States—other countries have similar publications). Using these sources, you can predict, at least in statistical terms, what you can expect for headwinds, fair winds, foul and fair currents, fog, and gales. With this information you can add an appropriate number of hours, days, and gallons of fuel to your projected voyage plan.

Estimating time under power is difficult. Start with a worst-case scenario. Assume you will have to motor nonstop at a moderate rate of fuel consumption and see how far that can take you. Then make plans to refuel in case it should actually be necessary. If you are planning an ocean crossing and therefore cannot refuel, you may have to leave your arrival date open. You will then have to develop some guidelines for consuming fuel. For instance, you may find from a study of the *Pilot Charts* that it will make sense to burn some fuel right at the start in order to get past a foul current, or across a belt of calms or adverse winds, in order to get into more favorable sailing conditions. Or the opposite might be true, in which case you will plan to motor as little as possible for the first part of the trip in order to save fuel for predicted unfavorable conditions at the end. Failure to plan in this fashion could leave you hundreds of miles out with insufficient fuel remaining. Always keep enough fuel in reserve to cope with an emergency, such as being caught off a lee shore in a gale, which could easily happen on the last day of the voyage.

WATER

There is more than fuel to consider in calculating the endurance of a vessel on a long voyage. Fresh water will be a significant concern as well. At present, many vessels are being fitted with on-board water-makers, which are very useful—until they break down. Therefore, you should calculate your passage-making endurance based on the amount of fresh water you can store, not how much you can make, since if the unit breaks down, you will be relying on what is in your tanks. For that same reason, when you have a water-maker, run it frequently, always keeping your tanks topped up.

Daily water consumption will have to be estimated and, in the absence of previous experience, may be largely guesswork. Water consumption will change dramatically depending on circumstances. The best method of conserving water is to turn off all pressurized water systems. If all hands have to pump fresh water by hand, they will use only what they need. But if they can turn on a tap and let it run, a great deal will be wasted. For example, on one particular voyage, on a vessel with only hand-pumped water faucets and a saltwater supply for galley cleanup, sixteen people averaged about two gallons of fresh water per person per day without any particular attention to water conservation, on a northern voyage. This included all on-board water consumption. With pressurized water that figure could quadruple. Following a discussion on water conservation, the consumption was reduced to between one and one-and-one-half gallons per person per day. While this figure cannot be assumed to be accurate for any other vessel, or even for the same vessel in a different climate, it might prove useful as a general guide, and in any case, calls attention to the need for constant scrutiny.

CHARTS

Once the route is planned, charts must be ordered. Developing a list of charts for a major voyage is a time-consuming process, and at fourteen dollars apiece the expense involved will be one of the very substantial costs of the voyage. Charts are, however, just as important as fuel and food.

U.S. charts are published by two government agencies—the National Ocean Survey (NOS), which is a branch of the National Oceanic and Atmospheric Administration (NOAA); and the National Imagery and Mapping Agency (NIMA), which is a branch of the Department of Defense (DOD). The NOS produces charts for U.S. waters, while NIMA produces charts for the whole world. Both sets of charts are cataloged in a single set, published by NIMA, and the NOS produces its own catalogs as well. To determine what charts you will need, start with a small-scale, general chart (or several, if needed), and lay out the legs for the entire route. Transfer these legs to the chartlets in the chart catalog. In the catalog, mark (in pencil, since there will be changes) all the charts for the areas you will pass over or next to. You will need all of these. Then evaluate each leg and add charts for any good harbors along the way that you might conceivably need for a harbor of refuge or for repairs. For example, no one should attempt to cross the North Atlantic without complete charts for Bermuda and the Azores, even if there is no intention of going near either place. Unanticipated circumstances may very well require a call there for repairs, for resupply, or for medical assistance.

For coastal work, the chart kits that are commercially available can be a big help in holding your chart costs down. (These are spiral-bound, privately reproduced copies of the NOS charts.) For small vessels with small chart tables, kits may be all you need or want. But with an ample chart table, official charts are preferable. The mere fact that they are bigger makes them easier to use and more accurate. It is advisable, however, to carry a chart kit for backup. Then if a chart blows overboard, or a needed chart is missing, you will have a substitute. If you are working from the kits only, carry a duplicate kit.

Ordering the charts early will give you time to reorder the ones you discover you missed or that did not come; more importantly, it will give you time to get them corrected. Sailing with uncorrected charts is foolhardy and on an inspected vessel is illegal. Correcting charts is just as important as preparing all the other gear on the vessel.

Chart corrections for American charts are found in the *Weekly Notice to Mariners,* published and distributed by the National Imagery and Mapping Agency. This publication also includes corrections to the chart catalogs, *Coast Pilots, Sailing Directions, Light Lists,* and other publications, and provides broadcast warnings and miscellaneous marine information. In this computer age there is an excellent service available from NIMA that passes most of this information via electronic bulletin board (BBS) directly into your computer. If you have a satellite communication system, you can receive this information right on board your vessel. The notices in this form are actually easier to use, since they can provide all corrections to a given chart, rather than just those for the current week. The information can be accessed through the Navigation Information Network (NAVINFONET), which is provided as a service by NIMA (see end of bibliography for address).

Various publications should be ordered at the same time as the charts. All of these should be available at any well-stocked ship chandler. *Tide and Current Tables, Light Lists, Coast Pilots, Sailing Directions, Radio Aids,* and the *Nautical Almanac* all need to be ordered for the various areas you will be transiting, and they all must be corrected as well. Corrections for these publications are found in the *Notice to Mariners* and through NAVINFONET.

Ordering charts and publications is an important job, with no room for error. To find yourself at sea missing a chart for your next port is a very serious matter. Yet the ordering process is wide open to possible errors. Orders will contain long lists of numbers, with great potential for typographical errors and omissions. Therefore, this job should be given to someone who is meticulous by nature, and the work should be checked either by yourself or by someone else who is equally responsible. Part of the reason for starting early with the ordering process is to allow time to do this properly. Since the clerks at the chart supplier's shipping department also make mistakes, once the charts are on board check each one individually, circling the corresponding chart number on the appropriate page of the chart catalog. This provides a visual picture of which charts you actually have on board. If you and your navigator are careful at this stage, you should sail without any missing charts.

LEARN ABOUT YOUR DESTINATIONS

If heading for an area with which you are unfamiliar, learn everything you can about it before you sail. Following are some of the questions you will need to have answered: What sort of harbor is there? How do you get a berth there? What sort of weather can be expected at that time of year? Are there any particular problems in that port, such as ice, swells, local severe winds, criminals or terrorists, difficult police or harbor officials? Is bribery the accepted manner of doing business, or is this strictly illegal? (In some ports you will get in trouble if you do not grease the palms of the local officials. In others, you can get in serious trouble if you try to.) Are there particular landmarks that you will need to recognize for making the entrance? Where can you get fuel, water, showers, laundry, and groceries? Is there a ship chandler? Will you be required to take a pilot? Is there a VTS installation? How do you contact customs and immigration? Will you have to pay for your berth? What medical facilities are available? Is there a bank you will be able to use for the transfer of money or exchange of foreign currency? What is the currency exchange rate?

Most of this research can be done on the telephone. If you can find—and visit—someone familiar with a remote place on your route, much valuable information can be gathered in one afternoon of talking and looking over charts. To save time for both of you, brief yourself as thoroughly as possible beforehand. Bring a small-scale chart and make notes right on the chart.

If the port is a commercial seaport, there will be ship agents there. Good agents are worth a lot—and they cost a lot. They will know the customs of the country and can smooth out your official contacts. They will have a telephone you can use and will drive you to a bank or a doctor if needed. They pride themselves on being able to arrange for almost anything you need, whether it is as simple as groceries or as difficult as having a new anchor shipped in a hurry from another continent. If such an agent is not available, or is too costly, you might be able to get an introduction to a native who would be willing to help you with some of these things. Such friends deserve to be paid for their time, but if payment is not accepted, courtesy requires that your demands be kept to a minimum.

PLANNING SAFETY DRILLS AND PROCEDURES

If you do not already have standard safety drills and procedures established for your vessel, these should be included in the voyage plan. Work through various emergencies in your mind and then put down standardized plans on paper for the rest of the crew. Work out a plan for man overboard (under power and sail, night and day, good weather and bad), for fire, grounding, collision, flooding, medical emergencies including helicopter evacuation, and anything else that might come to mind.

Each of these emergency procedures should be discussed in detail with the crew before sailing. If yours is an inspected vessel, fire, emergency, and abandon-ship drills are required to be practiced on a weekly basis. Emergency procedures are also required to be posted on the vessel for all hands to read. The requirements are listed in the operations section of the applicable CFRs. Among other things, you are required to post a Station Bill, which assigns duties to each member of the crew and passengers in the event of an emergency. Put some thought into this. There is always the possibility that a key person (even yourself) may be incapacitated, and the others will have to respond to the emergency without that person's help. In some cases it makes more sense to assign fewer specific duties and instead assign people to respond as a group to various areas. They may be better able to cover for the one who is missing, and in general may be more flexible and better able to respond to variations in the "standard" emergency.

PLANNING FOR MEDICAL ARRANGEMENTS

While planning for emergencies, make your medical preparations carefully. Remember to plan for minor medical problems as well as for serious ones. On a boat, a minor medical problem such as a cut finger or a minor illness can easily become serious if not attended to properly. Since personal hygiene is often not up to the same standards as ashore, greater attention to small injuries is needed at sea. Infections of all kinds are of particular concern, as is dehydration. People can become dehydrated easily, especially if they are concerned about conserving water. Dehydration can be accelerated if someone is seasick, or if a person becomes ill with diarrhea, which can occur with foreign water supplies. The consequences can be quite serious if not attended to, and should not be taken lightly.

Often a master planning an offshore passage will know a doctor who can help prepare the medical kit and plan. This can be very useful but deserves a word of caution. If this doctor is willing to provide you with prescription medications to take with you, you must understand the implications of administering these. If you provide a crew member with prescription drugs that turn out to have a detrimental effect (an allergic reaction for instance), you will be responsible for the harm you cause. If you are not a doctor you do not have the training or the legal right to administer such medication.

The solution to this dilemma is to make arrangements that will permit you to be in communication with either a doctor or a medical service. In this manner you can receive medical advice at sea that will coach you through anything requiring more than first aid. There are subscription services available, such as Medical Advisory Systems, Inc. (see p. 301 for address) that provide this service to vessels for an annual fee. They have doctors on duty twenty-four hours a day and have satellite, telephone, fax, SSB (long-range) radio, and telex communication capability, enabling them to maintain direct contact with you regardless of your location. If this system is not right for you, at least make arrangements with a doctor you can call for advice. This will protect your "patients," and yourself.

RADIO CALL-IN PLAN

Whenever you take a vessel to sea, even on a coastwise trip, someone should always know where you are and when you are due at your next destination. For a passage of three or more days, daily calls should be arranged. In this age of instant global communications there is no excuse for being out of touch. When a serious emergency strikes and you and your crew are stranded in a life raft at sea, if no one knows you are missing no one will come looking for you, and your odds for rescue will fade rapidly.

To be effective, a radio call-in schedule must be taken very seriously by all parties involved. You must organize it, and you must see to it that it is followed. An effective plan should fit a schedule that is easy to maintain. Calling in every day is not excessive. Consider how long you would like to be floating in a raft before someone starts looking for you.

The person assigned to maintain the communications ashore will be taking on a significant responsibility and must be reliable. If your vessel has a home office this is not so difficult, but if you are asking a friend to do it, you must be sure that person will always be there at the agreed time. In establishing the fixed time for the daily call, it is usually best to accommodate the person on shore, since your time is more flexible. Don't forget to adjust your call-in time to allow for time zone changes as you travel.

Your daily call should give a recent position (this is the most important information and should always be the first information communicated, in case you get disconnected), the time of that position, and your anticipated course and speed (or route) for the next twenty-four hours.

Your contact ashore must be expecting you to call and must act if you do not. That person must have clear instructions spelling out what to do if you are not heard from. Since it is likely that you will have difficulty getting through occasionally, you do not want your contact to cry wolf, but you do want him to be concerned if your call is not received. The best compromise will vary with your route and your communication medium, but it would not be overly cautious to instruct him that if you are twelve hours overdue on your call, action must be taken. This would give you time to repair a broken antenna, wait for more favorable radio conditions, or contact a passing ship if your long-range communication system fails. (You may be able to call a nearby ship and ask the captain to make a collect call for you.)

If after the designated interval there has been no communication, your contact should alert the Coast Guard. The Coast Guard will want certain specific information, which your contact must have. This will include: name and description of vessel, including length, type, color, and rig; number of persons on board; type of communication equipment fitted; type of emergency equipment fitted; last position and time; and intended route. The Coast Guard will then try to establish radio contact. When they deem it appropriate, they will put out a general Pan-Pan message (urgent safety messages are preceded by the words Pan-Pan—pronounced "ponn-ponn"—repeated three times), giving all ships your last position and announcing that you are unreported. Any ship in your area receiving this message should then try to make contact with you.

If this fails to bring a response, the Coast Guard will decide at what point they feel a search is warranted. It is certainly preferable to start a search early, after these initial steps have been taken, rather than after you have been unreported for several days. A search involves significant risks under any circumstances, and the more difficult the search the more chances the Coast Guard may have to take. Chapter 15 on helicopter rescue operations goes into greater detail on this subject.

Your onshore contact will be reluctant to notify the Coast Guard when your call is overdue; it seems to be human nature to deny the possibility that there really might be a problem. Make certain that your contact person understands that he or she must make no assumptions and no exceptions. This, of course, puts the burden on you to be absolutely certain you call. There can be no excuse for failing to call on schedule. An alarm clock beside the radio makes an effective reminder.

LAST-MINUTE PREPARATIONS

In the final few days before sailing, there will be much to do. Jobs should be delegated as much as possible to distribute the work load evenly, and all should be followed up on to be sure they are getting done. There are some practices that will help to alleviate the last-minute crush.

If you are bound for a foreign port, plan to clear customs a day early. Your clearance is valid for forty-eight hours, so get that job out of the way. There can be unexpected delays in this process if, for example, it turns out that one of your crew is a foreign national without the proper papers. Clearing two days early is inadvisable, however, since any number of things could delay your planned sailing time, causing your clearance to expire.

Plan to sail a very short distance on the first day and anchor for the night. Anchor early enough to allow time for walk-through drills, organization of watch rotations, and general underway routines. Prior to sailing there is rarely enough time to do these important things, there will be many interruptions, and spectators are unwelcome during this important process. Also, since someone will probably have forgotten something important, this provides an opportunity to send for it.

If anchoring for the first night is not feasible, at least plan to depart during daylight, in the morning if possible. Daylight is needed to get remaining gear stowed, to conduct drills, and to get settled in before nightfall.

Sailing unprepared is an invitation to disaster, so stay flexible; delay sailing or change the route if necessary, in order to be fully prepared. You may get bad weather on the first night. A squall on the first night watch will be a severe test of your preparedness, and you should make all the above preparations with this in mind. Plan for the worst, and plan for it to happen early. If you succeed in this, you will be truly ready for sea.

Further reading (see bibliography for details): Cornell, *World Cruising Handbook* and *World Cruising Routes;* Hammick, *The Atlantic Crossing Guide,* part 1; Howard, *Offshore Cruising,* part 3; Rains and Miller, *Passage-making Handbook: A Guide for Delivery Skippers and Boat Owners.*

CHAPTER TWENTY

DELIVERIES

Deliveries are completely different from any other kind of sailing job. There is no program, and there are no passengers or students. There are few crew, and the vessel is probably new to you. You may know little of the condition of the vessel until you arrive aboard with your bags and your crew. Therefore, the most important part of a delivery will take place before you set sail. Find out all you can about the vessel before you head out to sea, or you may have some surprises in store for you.

BEFORE ACCEPTING THE JOB

To an inexperienced sailor, a first offer of a delivery job may sound like a paid vacation, but the experienced skipper knows better. It is serious work, and before accepting the job there is a long list of questions that will need answering. Let us say that you are asked to deliver a new, 40-foot, custom-built, fiberglass ketch from Miami, Florida, to St. Thomas in the U.S. Virgin Islands. Taking a new boat to sea presents many problems. Nothing about the boat has survived the test of time and trial. It is probable that something will fail; it may be major or minor. You will need to know who built the boat. If you do not know the yard, you will want to talk to someone who does, to determine its reputation. A new boat from a shoddy yard is a far cry from a new boat built by a yard with a first-rate reputation. The size and rig of the boat will indicate how many crew you will want. If she has roller-furling sails you may be able to sail with fewer hands, but only if the furling gear is of high quality. Otherwise you will worry about the sails coming unfurled in the middle of the night, in a blow. If she does not have a self-steering system, you will require one person at the helm at all times, so you must add to the crew accordingly. If she is of deep draft, your choice of harbors along the way—in the Bahamas—will be limited. This may mean more overnight sailing and consequently more crew. The boat in this example is ketch rigged, which is generally a handy rig for sailing shorthanded, but only if well designed. You will want to know who designed her. Have other boats of her design been well tested? Are you personally familiar with her type?

Next, find out about the owners. Are they experienced sailors who will have insisted on a well-built and well-equipped boat? Or are they first-time boat owners who bought their boat out of a builder's booth at a boat show? Have they had it built for passage-making, or do they intend to daysail it from the marina for cocktails? If the owners lack experience, it may be difficult to convince them of the importance of some of the equipment you feel will be necessary for the trip. Extra pumps, spare parts, and life rafts are things they will not need for their cocktail sails, but you *will* need for a 1,000-mile delivery trip. The owners may not have anticipated such a list and may not want to fund it. If so, you will need to weigh carefully your decision to take the job.

Call the yard and ask them about the boat and the owners. Call someone who knows the vessel or one like her. You may hear that she is a wonderful boat, or you may learn that she is very uncomfortable, and no one will get much sleep offshore. In this case you may want additional crew to share the extra burden. If you cannot find anyone who has sailed the boat (or one of her type), a chartering agency that has represented one like her may be able to help.

If the boat you are considering is not a new boat, there will be a good deal more information available, if you can find someone to give it to you. Questions you will want to ask are: Has she made a similar trip before? If not, has she ever been offshore before? Did she handle it well? Were any problems noted then? You will want to know what type of navigation equipment she has, what kind of engine, how much fuel and water capacity, safety equipment, charts, and onboard systems such as refrigeration, water-making, heating or air-conditioning, cooking, and generating. A previous skipper, crew member, or owner should be able to help with these questions.

The next step will be to rough out your timetable. The owner will probably give you a fairly specific time frame during which he wants the boat delivered, and you will have to determine if that is realistic. This information may also affect your decision on the number of crew to carry. If you have enough time to anchor at night, you may need less help than if you are running overnight. Most delivery skippers prefer to run overnight anyway, just to get the job done and get on to the next one. Overnight operations can be done with only two crew, but beware of overextending yourself and your helper. A tired crew invites an accident.

In order to establish the timetable you will need to refer to the chapter on voyage planning. Consult the *Pilot Charts, Coast Pilots,* and other material to determine what sort of weather to anticipate. You will probably be trying to make as much speed as possible, so plan on motorsailing most of the time, at least on the windward legs. Determine the boat's fuel capacity and fuel consumption and plan your refueling stops accordingly.

The information you have about the sailing abilities of the boat will be weighed against anticipated weather, and the resulting conclusion will influence your decision on number of crew. If you feel you can afford to wait out a gale, you can get by with minimal crew. If you feel you will need to push on in spite of all but the worst weather, you will want some extra hands. It is not uncommon for the delivery crew (including skipper) to be reduced to half-wages when waiting for weather, unless they can be productively employed on the vessel.

ESTIMATING THE FEE AND OTHER FINANCIAL ARRANGEMENTS

With as much of the above information assembled as possible, you can estimate the price for the job. There are different approaches to this. The owner may have offered you a fixed fee for the whole job, in which case you must figure out if it will be worth your while, given what you anticipate for expenses and time. Or, the owner may ask you to estimate the fee, perhaps in the manner of competitive bidding against other delivery skippers. Tally up the number and wages of crew, travel expenses, charts and publications, food and fuel costs, expenses for rental of extra equipment, and your own daily fee. Since most of this is going to be dependent on the number of days the trip will take, you may get the owner to agree to a cost per day instead of a flat fee for the whole trip. In order to sell this idea, you will have to convince the owner that you will in fact do your best to expedite the trip.

The timing of the payment for the trip will be different under different circumstances, but it is typical for the skipper to expect payment for any expenses up front. Payment for wages varies, but can range from receiving all up front to receiving all on completion; half in advance and half on completion; or a third in advance, a third at sailing time, and a third on completion. This should be settled so as to leave both parties satisfied that their interests are protected.

While discussing expenses with the owner, you must also discuss emergency expenses that might arise en route. If you have an equipment failure along the way, you will need some method of paying for the repairs, and they can be very costly. The owner might be willing to give you a credit card for the trip and, if so, check on the card's credit limit. Replacing a shaft, propeller, engine, or whatever could cost thousands of dollars, depending on the size of the boat. Getting the boat hauled for such work is in itself a major expense, aside from the cost of the actual repair. Many yards are not willing to send a bill for such work and will demand cash or equivalent payment on the spot.

You should also discuss the insurance coverage for the vessel. Make certain the owners are insured for the trip, as some policies restrict offshore sailing. It may be necessary to have yourself listed as a "named insured" on the policy, in which case you will probably have to send your sailing résumé to the insurance company. If you plan to do a lot of deliveries, you should consider getting your own liability insurance and, if you have a license, you should also look into getting license insurance. These policies will at least cover your legal expenses if you should be sued or if the Coast Guard decides to proceed against your license, after an accident.

CREW

Once a price and a contract have been settled upon, you will need to hire a crew. Do this very carefully. Again, you are not taking a vacation cruise, though it may sound like one to many potential crew members. Be certain that they understand the nature of the trip and are willing and able to do the job. Select people with some field of expertise that will supplement your own. Resourcefulness will be the most valuable attribute. Naturally, the more capable they are in terms of seamanship, the higher the wage they will probably expect, so you may not be able to afford the luxury of hiring top-notch sailors. But a non-sailor who really knows engines or electronics could be a great asset. Depending on the length of the trip a good cook is always a welcome companion. On short trips, however, you will probably do better to cook most of your food ahead of time and bring it, frozen, in a ready-to-heat state. Many boats now have microwave ovens, which are ideal for this purpose. You will probably eat better in this manner than if you depend on uncertain cooking facilities on a strange boat in rough weather.

Make certain that all your crew have proper identification. If the voyage is an international one, they will need passports and perhaps visas and innoculations or vaccinations. This may require some lead time, so start looking into this early.

If at all possible, hire people you know, or at least know indirectly. Not only will you have a better idea of their qualifications, but you will also be safer. Unfortunately, there have been incidents of drug traffickers or other criminals signing aboard for deliveries (or aboard yachts in general), with the intention of utilizing the vessel for illegal purposes. You and the rest of the crew could be in considerable danger as a result. The solution is to know as much as possible about the crew you hire. Inspect the boat before you sail, as well as the luggage of any crew you do not know personally. If you have any suspicions at all, check them out thoroughly before setting off.

ONCE ABOARD: SURVEYING THE VESSEL

Finally, after settling all of the issues described above, you will join the vessel. You must not allow yourself to be hurried at this critical point. You must conduct a thorough survey of the vessel before you sail, and you can fully expect to find things that need repair or replacement. The survey program and checklist included in appendix II was compiled by Capt. Hank Halstead, a manager of the Hinckley Company. Captain Halstead has many years of yacht delivery experience, including transatlantic and coastwise voyages. His list was prepared specifically for use when joining a vessel for a delivery job, although it could be employed on any vessel for any voyage. Captain Halstead emphasizes that you can have no faith in any piece of gear on the vessel if you have not touched it with your own hands and inspected it with your own eyes. You are trusting your life (and the lives of your crew) to this gear, and you cannot afford to be casual about the inspection. Using the checklist as a guide, inspect the entire vessel from the masthead to the through-hull fittings. The whole process can be done in a few hours, especially if the crew helps, and it may mean the difference between a successful delivery and tragedy. Captain Halstead stresses that once you leave the dock, the condition of the vessel in all respects is your responsibility. You cannot lay blame on the yard, the owner, or the previous captain for any gear, hull, machinery, or equipment failures that occur after you have made the decision to sail.

The checklist is written for a "blue-water," or offshore, passage. It might be scaled back a little for a shorter, coastwise run, or expanded in some places (particularly in the area of spare parts) for a transatlantic or transpacific passage. It is one person's idea (albeit someone with considerable experience in the business) of what should be done before a trip, and seamanship and good sense dictate that you should adapt it to fit your own experience and needs.

UNDER WAY

With the survey completed and all supplies and crew aboard, you should feel confident and ready for sea. Do not forget to file a call-in plan with someone before you sail. If you suffer any gear or equipment failures, analyze what went wrong and why you missed the weakness in your survey. You may want to add something to your checklist before the next job.

Further reading (see bibliography for details): Cornell, *World Cruising Handbook* and *World Cruising Routes;* Hammick, *The Atlantic Crossing Guide;* Rains and Miller, *Passagemaking Handbook: A Guide for Delivery Skippers and Boat Owners.*

CHAPTER TWENTY-ONE

ADMINISTRATION OF A SAILING VESSEL

Most people who choose a career in the sailing vessel business do so because they enjoy sailing. Typically they then invest a great deal of time, energy, and money in advancing themselves up the professional ladder with the goal of becoming the master of a vessel. They look up to the masters they sail with for examples of how to handle the boat well, how to get the most out of her sailing abilities, and how to make her look and perform her best. It is often not until they actually become a master themselves that they realize that a master spends most of her time being an administrator.

Typically, a master will find that getting the boat under way and handling her under sail and power are the most rewarding parts of the job, but the most substantial parts of it are done behind the desk and on the telephone. It is the master's job to keep track of money, keep crew positions staffed, fill the boat's schedule and berths, make arrangements for port visits, repairs, routine maintenance and inspections, and keep the home office or owners informed of all of the above. The ship's master is an administrator with a fairly complex job, equivalent to a middle-management executive in a company ashore. There will be occasions when you will wonder, while buried in paperwork, what you thought was so much fun about going sailing. However, many people discover that what they like so much about going to sea is always having new parts of the job to learn, and this is just one more. This is an opportunity to have a substantial impact on the operation of the vessel or organization.

MONEY

Usually, the first administrative responsibility that a captain confronts is dealing with the ship's finances. This may involve a small amount of petty cash in a bank bag, or it may involve large amounts of cash, credit cards, and multiple bank accounts; in all cases you must keep detailed and accurate accounts. This not difficult. It is essential to learn that there is no room for procrastination.

Money spent one morning must be recorded that morning. The ledger does not need to be complicated; one column for money in, one for money out will usually suffice. The owners may want things categorized, but even this does not have to be complicated if you start with the simplest possible categories and add more as needed. The simpler the system, the more likely you can keep it working.

To keep accounts accurate, balance them frequently. If you are on a multi-port voyage, balance the accounts after every port. While in port, balance daily while transactions are fresh in your mind. Work to the penny, not to the dollar; this makes mistakes easier to identify. A couple of accountant's tricks will help you: if your account is out of balance by $10.26, you can look for three things. Look for a missing receipt for $10.26, a double entry of $10.26, or an entry or receipt of $5.13 (half the amount). If you have added an entry that should have been subtracted or vice versa, it will show up as an error of twice the amount of the entry. The second trick is to notice if your error is divisible by nine. If it is, you have probably transposed two digits in an entry. If you enter 15.95 instead of 15.59, the error is 00.36, divisible by nine. If you enter 35.86 instead of 53.86, the error is 18.00, also divisible by nine. If you had been working to the nearest dollar, these would not be so obvious.

Accounting is a complicated subject, but a simple accounting system is easily mastered. Your company, or owner, may hold you personally responsible for the balance sheets, and may expect you to make up any differences out of your own pocket. A word of warning here: if you come out ahead on the balance, set that "extra" money aside and turn it in with the rest. The real accountant in the office will find out where it belongs and will come looking for it.

When you relieve the previous captain, require him to go over the accounting system and have both of you sign a receipt that details exactly how much cash you have received and the balance of any other accounts. If his accounting has been shoddy, let the home office or owner know, and discuss the best way to straighten it out. If you are receiving cash, count it by hand, down to the penny. Never just assume it is correct, no matter how many piles of bills you have to count.

Make people get receipts; be a stickler and warn that they get no reimbursement without a receipt. If a purchase is made from someone who does not give receipts, just have the vendor write the amount, date, and reason on a piece of paper and sign it.

OTHER RECORDS

There is more than money to keep track of. Vessels have many different certificates, documents, and registration papers that must be kept up to date. There should be a file for each of these, but you should start a record of all of them on a single page that identifies each required item, its date of issue, date of expiration, and any further requirements, such as intermediate inspections. This must be assembled in concise form and posted conspicuously in the office and on board the vessel, so everyone will be aware of it. It is very embarrassing, if not of worse consequence, to discover suddenly that your certificate of inspection, or some other certificate (or your own personal license), has expired.

Some of the documents to consider recording are (sample copies of these can be found in appendix III):

USCG certificate of inspection

SOLAS certificate

State registration

FCC ship station radiotelephone license

Oil pollution prevention certificate

Document (if a documented vessel)

Classification certificate (if classed by ABS or other)

Load line certificate

Stability letter

Furthermore, know the expiration dates of your mates' licenses (including their radar endorsement and FCC marine radiotelephone operator's permit). It is not uncommon for people to lose track of their own license expiration dates. This is one advantage of having all licenses posted on board.

SAILING TO FOREIGN PORTS: CLEARANCE AND ENTRY

If your vessel is bound for a foreign country, the paperwork will increase substantially. You will be dealing with the offices of the U.S. Customs, Immigration and Naturalization, and Department of Agriculture, as well as their foreign counterparts. Depending on the size of your vessel, the number of crew and passengers, and the kind of program you are running, you will have various requirements before sailing. The term for the process of getting official permission to depart from one country to any other is clearance; getting official permission to land in any country when arriving from another is called entry.

The process of clearance and entry may be as simple as making a single telephone or radio call, or it may involve going in person to the custom house, getting that paperwork certified, going to the immigration office and getting their part of the paperwork approved, and then returning with several inspectors for a search of the ship and a one-on-one identification of each person on board. This process can be time-consuming and tedious, but maintain a cooperative attitude throughout, as the officials are within their rights to refuse you entry, detain you, arrest you, or seize your ship if they find cause.

To assure a smooth entry or clearance process, have all your paperwork done in advance. To determine which forms to complete, call in advance. To determine who to call in a foreign country, if you are at home and in the preliminary planning stages of a trip, start by calling the U.S. Embassy in the country to which you are going. They can give you general information. You will save yourself time and irritation by speaking with the officials of both the country you are leaving and the one you are sailing to, as they have different requirements. Otherwise, you could find yourself arriving without the necessary papers. Once you are in a foreign country, to locate the proper authorities, you might start by calling the harbor master, the Coast Guard, or the customs department. Even the harbor pilots should be able to give you some general information on where to begin.

If you are on a yacht, you may be granted a "cruising permit," the process for which is simpler than that required of commercial vessels. If yours is a commercial vessel (most inspected vessels will be considered such), you will be expected to complete a formal clearance or entry process. In the United States this involves three government agencies—customs, immigration, and agriculture. Each of these has its own paperwork, user fees, and regulations, but it is not unusual to be able to accomplish all the steps in one visit to the customs house. Again, call before you go to be certain you have everything you need. Whatever you do, when arriving from a foreign port, do not allow anyone on or off your vessel until you have been granted your official entry. The fines for failure to observe this requirement are severe.

In general, you will need the following papers for clearance and entry:

> Crew list
>
> Ship's stores declaration
>
> General declaration
>
> Master's oath
>
> Crew's effects declaration

Make several copies (at least four) of the crew list, as different officials will want copies for various reasons. When leaving the United States, get one copy of the crew list "certified," even if they tell you it is not necessary. This simply involves having the immigration officer put his or her stamp on it (the customs officer can certify the crew list also). Keep it safe, and make no changes to it. You are required to produce the certified crew list at the first U.S. port after a foreign voyage. Unfortunately, some customs agents do not feel this formality is necessary and must be asked to complete it. If you sail without a certified list, you may have problems making entry at the end of the voyage if the agents at the entry port want to see one.

If you have any aliens (foreign nationals) on board, you will need to collect their passports and bring them with you to the customs house for both the clearance and entry process. It is worth calling ahead to find out if the immigration officials would like to see those people in person. At any rate, they must have their I-94 document—their official permission to be in the country—with their passport, and their visa must be current.

The quarantine inspector, from the Department of Agriculture, will be most concerned with what you might be bringing into the country. He or she will want to know if you have any plants, seeds, foodstuffs, or rodents that might be harboring any diseases that could infect the American ecosystem. Don't assume that just because you bought your vegetables or fruits at an upscale supermarket in a civilized country that you will be allowed to bring them in to the United States (or any other country, for that matter).

There are many other forms which you may be required to have. A de-rat certificate (issued by the U.S. Department of Public Health) certifies that your vessel is rat-free. (Without it, or if the quarantine inspector finds any signs of rat life, you may be required to have the vessel fumigated.) If you have had any significant repairs made to the vessel while overseas, these may (depending on the official's interpretation of your vessel's commercial status) have to be identified on a declaration of foreign repairs. The cost of these repairs may be subject to import duties, just as articles purchased abroad are. When making entry, you must have the crew fill out a crew's effects declaration, identifying articles (souvenirs, etc.) they purchased abroad and their value.

PORT NOTEBOOK

As you travel from port to port, you should develop a file of port information that stays with the boat. This information will be very useful in the future, for yourself or for the next captain. Include anything that was of interest to you, including prices of merchandise. Even though prices change, the old prices will serve to give some reference for the future. Include information on fuel, groceries, laundry, banks, chandlers, shipyards, machine shops, pilots, customs and immigration, showers, good restaurants, hotels, airline connections, port facilities, berthing arrangements, embassy, fresh water (availability and quality), and anything else you can think of. It should include a collection of business cards of people who were helpful. This will grow over time into an extremely valuable resource. When you leave the vessel, leave the notebook behind, but make a copy to take with you. It will be just as useful to you on your next vessel.

FUND-RAISING

Many sailing vessels, especially the schoolships, rely heavily on fund-raising. This is a profession all its own, but the captain and crew usually find themselves involved and should make every effort to be helpful. The crew members are (or should be) the best spokespersons for the vessel and her program. They know the most about it and have a vested interest in it. Sailors are often in love with their vessels. This is infectious, and it is a fund-raiser's dream. If your vessel depends on fund-raising, then your job, and those of all the crew, depend on it, and it is just as important as keeping the vessel painted. Part of your job will be to remember the key people and recognize them when you see them on the dock. Be prepared to invite them aboard, and show them what a good job the crew is doing. You will be worth your weight in gold, and the home office will know it.

CREW HIRING AND PERSONNEL MANAGEMENT

The first time you hire a crew member, you will probably learn a great deal about résumé writing. If you read many résumés, you will very quickly tire of the flowery ones, the padded ones, the scrawled ones, and the ones that look as if they were prepared by a New York marketing firm. (This will serve you well the next time you prepare your own.) True professionals with extensive credentials can easily represent themselves well in a one-page résumé, with a good, one-page cover letter attached.

When hiring your own crew, references will mean a lot, since there is more than credentials to evaluate. The nature of the business is such that people have to live and work together in a very small space with very little privacy, so personality will matter considerably more than for a candidate for an office job ashore. For this reason a person should never be hired without an interview and several recommendations.

The sailing business is still a fairly small and tightly knit community, so references can often be obtained from someone you know, or know of. This will help, but it brings up another point. Since you know how much you will depend on another person's recommendation, you must dispense your own recommendations carefully. If you give everyone you know a glowing recommendation (good recommendations are much easier to write than mediocre ones), you will spoil your opportunity to give truly deserving sailors good references later, as your credibility will be lost. Try to identify a few of the best sailors you have sailed with, at various levels of expertise, and use them as examples. Don't send everyone out with the highest recommendation. You must be more discriminating than that to be of service to the business.

Once your crew is on board, you will discover that a significant portion of your time will be spent in personnel management. This entails a complete spectrum of duties, from defining job descriptions to counseling distraught or troubled crew members. Again, there is a basic difference between shoreside employment, where personal matters can wait until after work, and shipboard employment, where such problems must be dealt with on the job, since your crew cannot go home after work. The mood of any one crew member can have a significant effect on the morale of the whole vessel, and since the morale of the vessel is ultimately the captain's responsibility, it may be necessary for you to take on some counseling work.

PROGRAM AND CURRICULUM PLANNING

You may have more or less involvement in the planning of the vessel's program, whatever it may be. If it is a charter vessel, the "program" will be the chartering plan. If it is a sailing school vessel, it will be the curriculum. If it is a yacht, it may be no more than the voyage plan. In any case, the more involved you are, the more respect you will earn from the owners of the vessel.

If you are very lucky, you may find yourself in an organization that wants you to develop the program for the vessel. This will give you the opportunity to test your creativity in developing a program that makes the best use of the vessel. If you choose to remain uninvolved in this aspect of the organization, you will be viewed as a simple "boat driver," and a temporary one at that.

Sailing vessel programs are often developed from the wrong end of a business planning process, and then success will depend on the personal creativity and energy of the captain. In a properly developed business plan, there is a goal, or a mission, that a company will be trying to fulfill. They will then develop the program, and when that is well on the way they will begin to look for a suitable means to fulfill the goal. In this business, however, the vessel is often the starting point, and the program is developed to make use of her. It is not unusual for a sailor to acquire a vessel she loves, and then try to come up with a program to support the boat. There are many very successful programs operating today that were formed this way, but the process is a tricky one. Those who embark on this kind of project should recognize this fact when they start. What it means more than anything is that the program should be flexible and a bit experimental at the outset. If financial problems develop, significant changes in the goals of the program may be necessary.

The captain should be an important part of the program design team. The captain probably knows more than anyone about what is possible on board the vessel. A good captain in today's commercial sailing fleet should be part educator, part businessperson, part fund-raiser and, above all, imaginative and creative. With these attributes, the captain will be a valuable asset to the owners, both in the planning process and throughout the life of the program.

An aspiring captain should be working on all of these skills, above and beyond the sailing skills that constitute what most people think of as the main part of the job. Sailing skills are the unique aspect of the captain's job, but they are not the major part. Administration may well take up the bulk of the captain's time, and administrative skills will very likely figure at least as strongly as sailing skills in the job application process.

Further reading (see bibliography for details): Cornell, *World Cruising Handbook;* Aragon, *Shipmaster's Handbook on Ship's Business.*

CHAPTER TWENTY-TWO

ORGANIZATIONS OPERATING SAILING VESSELS

There were, as of 1997, 506 active sail or auxiliary sail vessels inspected by the U.S. Coast Guard either under Subchapter T (passenger) or Subchapter R (sailing school vessel) regulations. There are a great many more uninspected sailing vessels, sailing as yachts, research vessels, or with fewer than six passengers. Each vessel has a slightly different program, or mission, and many have multiple programs. Each has its own needs and requirements, and the crew of a vessel must understand these in order to help carry them out satisfactorily. Therefore, it is important that a new crew member arriving aboard a vessel learn as much about the program and mission of the vessel or organization as about the rig and equipment of the vessel.

A person seeking a career in the sailing industry will probably soon develop a particular affection for a certain segment of the industry. Some people will find the yachting business enjoyable. Those who like to teach will probably focus on sail training or science education. Others enjoy the challenges of working with youth at risk. If one enjoys working with volunteers and the public, he will probably enjoy working on the "attractions" vessels.

When looking for a first job in the sailing business, you may not have a choice of, or a preference for, a particular type of program. You may take the first job offered in order to gain experience and begin to develop your résumé. Or you may seek out a job on a particular type of vessel, with a particular type of rig, or on a particular route. Job-seeking in sail is no different from the pathway into any other career in this respect. What is important is that you throw yourself into the program as well as the sailing of the ship. As in any career, your ideas of where you want to go and what you want to do will change as you gain experience. The broader your exposure to different vessels and programs, the broader your experience will be, and the better equipped you will be to make the right choice for your career. Also, with a varied background, you will be able to bring a greater variety of skills and techniques to every new job in the future. You will find yourself more marketable in the industry.

When you get to the point of looking for work in the business, you would be well-advised to join the American Sail Training Association (ASTA) and receive their directory (see the bibliography for their address). The directory is updated regularly and lists more than just sail training vessels. The directory includes, for each vessel, a photograph, a brief description of the vessel and its program, its certification, vessel particulars, and the address of the owners. You will also receive a periodical newsletter containing a "Billet Bank"—a listing of positions available in the business of commercial sailing. ASTA annual conferences draw quite a crowd from the business, providing interesting panels for discussion and opportunities for networking in this very closely knit community of sailing professionals.

PROGRAMS: PASSENGER VESSELS

The first question a job applicant should ask of a vessel operator is, "What is your mission for the vessel?" For a passenger vessel the answer is probably "to make a profit." This may sound mercenary, but it is simply business. If the boat is to survive, the business must thrive. Your concern as a crew member is to help the business make a profit.

To help the business make a profit, you must satisfy the customers. To satisfy the customers, you must make their stay on board as enjoyable as possible. You do that by keeping the ship (and yourself) clean and shipshape, you sail her well, and you cater to the passengers' wants and needs. Understand that you are in a service business and it is very intensive. You are not just selling something over a counter. You are living with the customers, day in and day out, on stage at every moment, and there is no room for a bad attitude. Most sailors love sailing, and most love their ship. That simple pleasure can be very infectious, and it will go a long way toward making the program work. But a ship is too small for abrasive personalities and bad moods, so stay upbeat. Some people are good at being upbeat, pleasant, energetic, and enjoyable for extended periods with strangers. Some simply are not and will probably soon decide to go into a different part of the business.

Do not be afraid to have fun, within limits that should be obvious to any professional. The passengers are there to have fun, and to an extent the more fun you are having the more they will have. This is where the passenger business rewards its workers. You work hard, but you should enjoy the job.

Do not be aloof and do not put yourself above the passengers. If they are spending their money on a sailing vacation, they would probably like to take part in the pleasant parts of sailing the vessel. Many of them will want to learn from you. If you make the effort you will find that each of them has something to offer in return. By making an effort to get to know them you will discover that they are much more than just tourists. Each has a field of interest or a profession and can be full of interesting information if you are curious enough to ask. If you learn from them, and they learn from you, you will make friends and happy customers; you will be a valuable asset to the vessel.

SAIL TRAINING

Sail training is an emerging business. The Sailing School Vessels Act was passed in the late 1980s, and since then there have been a surprising number of SSVs turning up. It can be a very exciting field, particularly for someone who enjoys teaching.

Teaching is the primary mission of a sailing school vessel. Not all will be focused on teaching sailing, however. The sailing vessel has turned out to be an excellent platform for teaching many things, from science and history to teamwork and management skills. Some vessels will change their program from trip to trip to take advantage of different markets, some will provide separate teachers for their programs, and some will expect their crew to teach. Whether you are teaching as part of the program or not, it will behoove you to learn the program and get as involved in it as possible.

In the case of SSVs, the student is the customer. Students are different from passengers because you will be making demands of them, and you will be requiring them to perform to a certain standard, which may make some unhappy. The concept of customer satisfaction is not as clear as it is with a passenger, who only has to be made happy. When the program is over the students should appreciate the knowledge they have gained. The student does have the right to expect you to know your subject, and you will find that answering difficult questions requires a tremendous amount of preparation. A teacher may spend four to six hours preparing a one-hour lecture and anticipating peripheral questions.

As part of the crew, you should become a part of the teaching environment, even if your job description does not include teaching. The more you contribute or participate, the more a part of the program you will become, and the more valuable you will be to the vessel. In this way the students will see that the academic curriculum is as much a part of the program as the sailing. Your participation will be supporting the mission of the vessel.

AMBASSADOR VESSELS

The ambassador vessel, a relatively new concept, is a vessel that represents a city or state, or even a country, in effect to advertise that place. This concept was undoubtedly hard to sell in the beginning, but the *Pride of Baltimore I* was so successful at it that other cities took notice, and now it seems that every waterfront town wants one. The ambassador vessel's mission is to carry the message that the vessel's home port is a good place to do business, visit, or live. It also provides a focal point for the area—something tangible that the residents can associate with and take pride in. The town fathers are marketing their town, using the sailing ship as a traveling platform to carry spokespersons and displays and to host receptions at which to court business people of all kinds.

In this kind of program the crew must also participate. They may not have students or passengers to mingle with and teach, although many of these vessels do mix the ambassadorial work with other programs, but they will still be expected to participate to some degree in the ship's mission, which involves talking with visitors about the ship and the city. "Open houses" are frequent, as are receptions and day-sails for guests. Many of these guests are high-level dignitaries and/or business people, who may be charmed by the saltiness of the crew but expect to be treated with a good deal of respect. (The word "schmoozing" comes to mind here.) The crew member either will be good at this or will soon be looking for another type of vessel to sail.

One of the attractive aspects of an ambassador vessel is that they usually sail with only a professional crew. It is a different kind of operation—sailing a large vessel without the crowded decks of a passenger or training vessel. You do not have extra hands to make light work, and you do more of the work (both the fun work and the serious work) yourself. For some people this is the ideal way to sail.

YOUTH-AT-RISK VESSELS

Several vessels now operate very successfully as educational vessels with the special mission of helping young people who have behavioral problems. Some programs take convicted criminals sent to them from within the court system, some take inner-city youths who are considered high-risk juveniles, but, in general, the mission is to provide an educational and character-building experience to teach responsibility, accountability, teamwork, self-reliance, and self-discipline.

Given the specialized nature of the program, specially trained instructors are usually sent along from the parent organization. The crew members certainly interact with the students, however, and are utilized to a greater or lesser degree in the program depending on the structure of the organization. This kind of program can be one of the most rewarding of all teaching experiences, though it can also have some very high-stress moments, given the potentially volatile nature of some of the youths.

MUSEUM OR ATTRACTION VESSELS

Most of the numerous maritime museums around the country have sailing vessels. Some of these never leave the pier, and others do. A vessel certified as an attractions vessel is entitled to charge admission for tours or programs that take place while the vessel is tied up to the dock, but may not charge in any way for programs that take place while under way. These vessels may still sail, but will do so with a professional or volunteer crew.

The mission of an attractions vessel is usually historical interpretation. If you enjoy history, enjoy living it, and enjoy showing it to others, this may be the program of your choice. There could be further educational opportunities for you in such a setting, either as a student or as a teacher.

In some cases, historical attractions vessels are maintained strictly in accordance with the techniques of the period they represent, while modern safety standards prevent operational vessels from being absolutely faithful to the old ways. For a vessel that does not leave the dock it may be feasible to hold more closely to historical accuracy, and on these vessels you will have an opportunity to learn traditional skills that those on SSVs or "T-boats" will not.

RESEARCH VESSELS

Oceanographic research and study is a field that fits well on board sailing vessels, especially as it combines nicely with sail training. There are several such programs operating around the United States and abroad.

If a vessel of limited size is certified solely as a research vessel (in which case she cannot combine her research mission with other missions), then she is exempted from inspection by the U.S. Coast Guard. Because the vessel is exempted from inspection, the mates and master are exempted from license requirements as well. If you are trying to acquire sea time, you may find that you can sail aboard one of these as a watchstander before you have a license.

If you sign on as a mate with a research vessel, as with other vessels, learn something about the mission. You are not expected to be a scientist, but the more you learn about the technical and academic aspect of oceanographic research the better you will be as a research vessel mate. The more you know about what kind of data are being collected and the methods of collecting, the better you will be able to handle the ship in a manner that makes these efforts successful. What is more, if you then go on to another vessel such as an SSV, you will have some valuable knowledge that you can add to their program. As it happens, you will learn some very important seamanship lessons when doing scientific station-keeping on a sailing vessel. You will heave-to frequently and learn to tow gear at very controlled speeds under sail. These techniques will be very valuable to you in the future on vessels of all kinds.

CONCLUSION

You should take one principle with you to any type of program: The more you take part—actively, not passively—in the vessel's program, the more you will get out of your time aboard, and the more you will contribute to the vessel, her program, and the others on board. You will not only enjoy the voyage more, but it will serve you well in your recommendations and, as noted before, in this business recommendations are extremely important.

Try many different programs and vessels. The breadth of your experience is just as important as the depth of your experience. Remember that a ship's master must above all be creative in terms of seamanship, administrative ability, program development, and operation. As a crew member at any level you should be working toward that goal. Role models are as important in this business as in any other, so be certain to learn all you can from every master, mate, engineer, teacher, scientist, and passenger you sail with. You can learn just as much from bad ones as you can from good ones—we often learn the most from mistakes. Do not assume when you have worked your way to a high degree of confidence on a certain vessel, and you transfer to another one, that you know everything. Each vessel is different; every ocean, lake, bay, and river is different; every captain is different; and every program is different. Sign aboard with your eyes and ears open. No matter what position you sign on for, you are there to learn as well as to work. With that attitude you will always be a welcome crew member.

Further reading (see bibliography for details): American Sail Training Association, *Directory of Sail Training Programs and Tall Ships.*

BALANCING A SAIL PLAN

So much of sailing has to do with the balance of your sail plan that it is helpful to be able to calculate the center of effort of your sail plan, or of different sail combinations, on paper before sailing. If you are having trouble getting your boat to do what you want it to do, perhaps you should calculate this information and establish whether you are working against an unbalanced sail configuration. Or, you may wish to order a new sail such as a storm trysail, in which case you should make certain that the size and shape you have drawn will balance with the rest of the sail plan.

What you will be calculating is actually the center of sail area—the approximate geometric center of the sail shape. This is technically different from the center of effort, which is the center of the aerodynamic forces. Locating the center of effort is a more complicated process, and it actually moves as you change the trim of your sail. Finding the center of sail area is close enough for estimating purposes, and is in fact all that most naval architects ever calculate.

MEASURING THE SAIL AREA

The area of a sail is found by dividing the sail shape into right triangles (see figure I-1), then finding the area of each right triangle by multiplying the length of either of its perpendicular sides by one-half the length of the other perpendicular side. The areas of all the right triangles are then added together to determine the area of the whole sail. The roach of a sail (the rounded part of the leech) need not be included unless it is extreme, in which case it may be estimated.

FINDING THE CENTER OF AREA FOR A SINGLE SAIL

The center of any triangle is found by drawing a line from each corner to the midpoint of its opposite side. When all three of these are drawn, they will

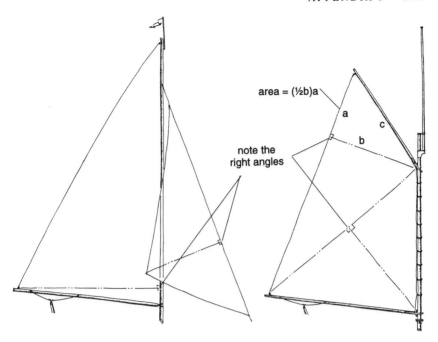

Fig. I-1. *Calculating the area of a sail—divide each sail into right triangles.*

intersect at one point, and this is the geometric center of the triangle (see figure I-2). Again, when applied to a sail, this does not take roach into account, but that is not a significant error for our purposes.

For a gaff sail, first draw lines connecting opposite corners of the sail. Label the corners A, B, C, and D, clockwise from the throat (see figure I-3). Where they intersect, label point E. You will then have connected A and C, and B and D. Now measure from A to E. Using this length, make a mark an equal distance up from C, along line AC. Label this point F. Now do the same along line DB, measuring the distance from B to E, and marking this distance down from point D. Label this point G. You now have a triangle, EFG, and can find the center of this triangle as you would any other. The center of this triangle is the geometric center of the gaff sail.

FINDING THE CENTER OF THE SAIL PLAN

Having found the areas and the center of areas for each sail in the sail plan, we must balance the areas of all the sails and find their combined center of area. This is again a geometry problem. On multisail plans, first find the center of two sails, then use the combined center and total sail area of those two as one, and find the center of that combination and a third sail, and so on, until all sails have been included.

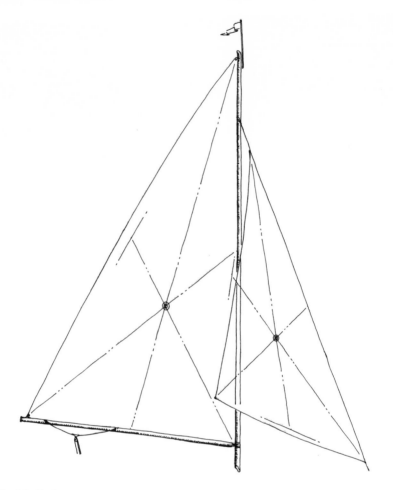

Fig. I-2. *Finding the center of area of a sail.*

Step 1. *Find the Combined Center of Two Sails*

Working with a ketch, first find the center of the main and fore staysail (see figure I-4.) Having found the area for each sail, and their respective centers, now draw a line connecting the two centers. Call this line AB. At A (center of area for the mainsail), draw a line perpendicular to AB, going up. Using any convenient scale measure a distance up this line equal to the area of the fore staysail. Label this point C. Now at point B draw a line perpendicular to AB but going down, and using the same scale measure a distance down that is equal to the area of the mainsail. Label this point D. Note that you are marking a line equal in length to the area of the opposite sail. Connect points C and D. Where line CD crosses line AB you have the center of combined sail area of these two sails.

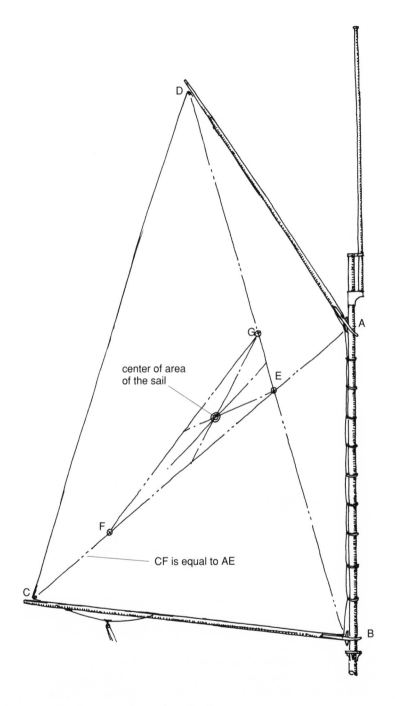

center of area
of the sail

CF is equal to AE

Fig. I-3. *Finding the center of area of a gaff sail.*

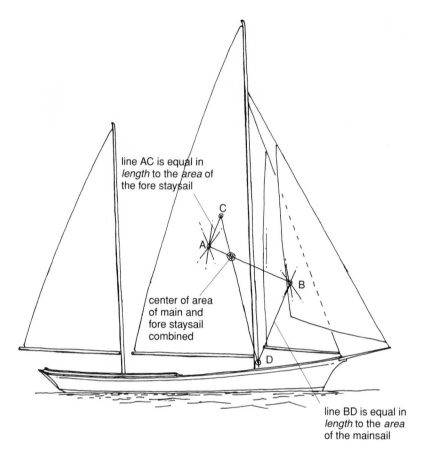

Fig. I-4. *Finding the combined center of area of two sails; in this case, the fore staysail and mainsail.*

Step 2. Find the Combined Center for a Third Sail

On our ketch, we will now add the mizzen. Employ the same process as in step 1, but now consider the mainsail and fore staysail as a single sail, using their combined center of sail area and their combined total sail area.

Connect the center of the mizzen (see figure I-5) with the combined center of the main and fore staysail, construct your perpendiculars, measure up and down a length equal to the area of the respective opposite sails or combinations thereof, and connect these points. Again, where they cross the initial line is the combined center.

This process can continue for as many sails as necessary, as long as you remember to keep combining the sail areas and use the combined centers.

Further reading (see bibliography for details): Marino, *The Sailmaker's Apprentice*, chap. 2.

Fig. I-5a. *Finding the combined center of area of the mainsail and fore staysail (combined), and the mizzen.*

Fig. I-5b. *Finding the combined center of area of the mainsail, fore staysail, and mizzen (combined), and the jib.*

BLUE-WATER CHECKLIST

This vessel survey procedure and checklist was compiled by Hank Halstead, of the Hinckley Company, specifically for the purpose of preparing for a delivery job, but it has applications aboard virtually any vessel under many circumstances. In its present (or a modified) form, it could be employed when joining any vessel, old or new, for the first time, to familiarize yourself with the vessel; preparing for a major voyage; or after a major shipyard period or extended layup, to establish the seaworthiness of the vessel.

PART I: PRE-VOYAGE SURVEY, VESSEL PREPARATION, AND SPARES

A. Hull Integrity

1. Overall construction: note weaknesses, leaks.
2. Through-hull fittings: note location of each, exercise valves, ensure double hose-clamps below waterline.
3. Stuffing-boxes (for propeller shaft and rudder stock): check for wear and leakage.
4. All seawater hoses: inspect for deterioration.
5. Hatches, ports, and deck fittings: check for leaks and secure; check for watertight integrity by spraying with water hose.
6. Storm ports (for all ports larger than two square feet): have stout covers made; use half-inch plexiglass or equivalent.
7. All heavy gear: stow and secure.
8. Inventory tools: if you decide to carry your own basic tool kit, design it to fit your needs.
9. Hull repair kit
   a. Underwater epoxy: one quart each of part a (epoxy) and part b (hardener).

    b. Appropriate patch material: depending on the type of hull—for a fiberglass hull, bring fiberglass cloth and epoxy, for a wood hull, bring plywood.

    c. Other sealants: silicone, bedding compound, structural adhesives. (There are several on the market—get one that will cure underwater, cure fairly quickly, and remain flexible.)

    d. Other fastenings: for a wood hull, galvanized drywall screws are good, but for a composite hull, you'll need self-tapping machine screws or similar.

    e. Duct tape.

B. Steering System

  1. Cable system

    a. Check wheel, sprocket, and chain.

    b. Tension and lubricate cables.

    c. Check all sheaves, pins, and points of attachment.

    d. Check rudder post, quadrant, and especially keyway (check connection of rudder stock to quadrant).

  2. Hydraulic system

    a. Fill reservoir.

    b. Check system for leaks.

    c. Check steering ram mounts, tiller arm, connections, and keyway.

  3. Test emergency steering system.

C. Engine and Drive Train

  1. Visual check

    a. Engine mounts, alignment, and shaft coupling.

    b. Oil leaks.

    c. All belts—condition and tension.

    d. Fluid levels.

    e. Electrical wires, connections, clamps, etc.

    f. Hoses (trace them out and check for corrosion)—especially exhaust hoses, gate valves, and vented loops.

  2. Running check

    a. Seawater exhaust for good flow.

    b. Exhaust smoke.

    c. Exhaust system leaks.

    d. Run under load, up to maximum operational rpm, and check for overheating.

3. Spares (as required for the duration of the voyage)

    a. Fluids and lubricants for at least one fluid change.

    b. Filters, complete set.

    c. Belts, complete set.

    d. Impeller and gasket.

4. Note fuel and water tank capacity and consumption rate. Budget power and charging time accordingly. Watch this closely—limit your power (fuel) usage more and more severely as the voyage progresses, so that you don't use up your fuel. Never arrive with empty tanks.

D. Spars and Rigging

1. Check all standing rigging (particularly end fittings) for cracking; check tangs for damage, check clevis and cotter pins. Tape as necessary to prevent chafe.

2. Check running rigging for chafe, wear, etc.

3. Check all winches, deck blocks, and sheaves for free operation and lubricate. When dismantling winches, keep an eye out for the small springs, such as pawl springs—don't let them get away.

4. Check gooseneck fitting (anodized ones are dangerous—double-check for cracks), mast partners, chocks, boot, and mast step (look for damage by electrolysis).

5. Inventory rigging spares and ditty bag (containing sail and rigging repair materials and tools).

6. Check for rigging cutters, pin punch, and a good hacksaw (be sure you have the right tool to cut through the type of rigging on the boat).

E. Plumbing (Essential Systems)

1. Bilge pumps

    a. Check operation and clean strainers.

    b. Inventory spares and rebuild kits for every pump aboard.

    c. Note possible alternative pumps and make provision for converting. (Main engine raw water intake pumps, head intake pumps, and sump pumps all make excellent emergency bilge pumps, usually requiring only the disconnection of the intake hose from the sea cock and plugging of the sea cock.)

2. Tankage: fuel and water

    a. Top off as required.

b. Check all deck fills and caps for watertight integrity.

c. Check all vents and overflows (insure they will not let salt water in to contaminate tanks).

d. Check system valves to isolate tankage as required (to prevent cross-contamination from one leaking tank to another).

3. Fresh-water pumps and plumbing

a. Check for leaks.

b. Inventory necessary spares.

c. Turn circuit breakers off for pressure pump when not in use (leave them off for prolonged offshore passages, to prevent pumping a tank dry if a valve is not closed tightly).

F. Electrical

1. Check alternators and voltage regulators for voltage output; also check belts, connections, etc.

2. Check batteries

a. Fluid level.

b. Terminals—clean any corrosion.

c. Battery boxes—secure against any possible movement.

3. Generators

a. Same visual/running inspection as main engine.

b. Output check.

c. Spares as necessary.

4. Essential lighting: check and repair as necessary

a. Navigation lights.

b. Compass light.

c. Steaming and signal lights.

d. Searchlights.

e. Night lighting below (red lights).

f. Flashlights.

g. Spares for each, including bulbs, sockets, wires, lenses, batteries, etc.

G. Deck Layout and Gear

1. Inventory and check man-overboard (M.O.B.) equipment

a. M.O.B. pole.

b. Life-rings.

    c. Strobe light with automatic turn-on feature.

    d. Drogue, sea dye, and heaving line.

    e. Smoke bombs.

    f. Lifesling, or other recovery system (if available, learn to use it).

2. Rig offshore lifelines (see chapter thirteen); locate secure points of attachment for harnesses in cockpit area.

3. Check lifelines and stanchions—make sure crew knows if they are inadequate.

4. Rig knives at standard locations, e.g., at steering station and mast.

5. Clear decks of all loose gear and secure all essentials.

6. Check radar reflector.

7. Check ground tackle. (Anchors and chain should be stowed away once you are offshore.)

PART II: CREW MANAGEMENT AND OPERATIONS

A. Watch System

Develop the watch system based on the number of crew aboard and the number of crew required for basic sail evolutions, such as sail changes and tacking. Distribute the skills and physical strength as evenly as possible.

B. Specific Responsibilities

1. Each crew member should be assigned a specific area of responsibility, from navigation and communications to mechanics, deck department, medical, safety, etc.

2. Each crew member should be assigned a position or responsibility for "all hands" calls during sail handling and emergencies (bow person, mast person, sheet person, helmsperson, etc.).

C. Personal Safety—check that each crew member is adequately outfitted with:

1. Foul weather gear, float coats, etc., so they will stay warm and preserve their strength.

2. Safety harnesses.

3. Personal strobe lights.

4. Life jackets (have crew try them on and keep them accessible).

D. Crew Drills—develop, teach, and practice:

1. Man overboard.

2. Abandon ship.

3. Storm—preparation and coping.

4. Fire.

5. Grounding.

E. Medical Supplies

1. The vessel should have a complete first aid kit, equipped to provide for all predictable injuries and to keep the victim comfortable for as long as the vessel is offshore. You must know how to use any gear you have.

2. Complete first aid manual or EMT textbook.

3. Crew members should be advised to bring all required prescriptions, medications, and supplies for their personal needs (such as diabetes or allergies).

4. Seasickness remedies, including Dramamine suppositories (necessary when a person can no longer hold anything down).

F. Food and Provisions

1. Make certain crew eats enough, and on a regular basis.

2. Provide plenty of food for around-the-clock meals.

3. Eat perishables first.

PART III: HEAVY WEATHER (see also chapter 13)

A. Storm Sails

1. Trysail or deep reef (note which is better for the given rig).

2. Heavy weather jib (a little bigger than a storm jib—used when still trying to make headway, before you heave-to).

3. Storm jib or staysail.

B. Sea Anchor or Drogue

C. Adequate Lines or Warps (for slowing the vessel when running before a storm)

D. Practice or Drill Appropriate Storm Techniques

1. Laying ahull.

2. Heaving-to.

3. Deploying warps or drogue.

4. Powering into the wind and sea.

PART IV: CHARTS AND NAVIGATION (see also chapter 18)

A. *Departure and Landfall Charts (with approaches and harbor details)*

B. *Small-scale Plotting Charts (departure to destination)*

C. *Universal Plotting Sheets*

D. *Emergency Landfall Charts*

E. *Light Lists, Sailing Directions, Coast Pilots, or Cruising Guides*

F. *Departure and Landfall Tide and Current Tables*

G. *For Celestial Navigation: sextant, almanac, tables, timepiece (twenty-dollar digital watch is sufficient)*

H. *Electronic Aids*

I. *VHF Radio*

J. *SSB Radio (for high seas weather, time tick)*

PART V: EMERGENCY GEAR

A. *Fire Extinguishers*

B. *EPIRBs*

C. *Handheld VHFs (in waterproof container)*

D. *SOLAS-approved Distress Signals (not less than six of each):*
   1. Red parachute flares.
   2. Red hand-held flares.
   3. Orange smoke signals.
   4. White hand-held flares (not for distress use, but useful for attracting attention).

E. Set of International Code Flags with H.O. #102—International Code of Signals. (When all your electronics are down, these will enable you to communicate.)

F. Set of Wooden, Tapered Plugs (to plug a broken through-hull fitting, etc.)

PART VI: ABANDON SHIP EQUIPMENT

A. Life Raft, High-Quality, with:

   1. Double floor and tubes.
   2. Canopy.
   3. Standard life-raft supplies.
   4. Extra food and all possible water.

B. "Ditch Kit" or "Grab-and-Go Bag." (Have this bag fully equipped and ready to go in the event of having to abandon ship.)

   1. Sea anchor and line.
   2. Stainless-steel knife.
   3. Bailer.
   4. Paddles.
   5. Raft repair kit and pump.
   6. Flashlight, batteries, and bulbs.
   7. Flare and smoke-signal kit.
   8. Seasickness pills and suppositories (critical for life in a raft).
   9. First aid kit.
   10. One plastic bag per person (to keep a few things dry).
   11. Fishing kit.
   12. Sponges.
   13. Signaling mirror.
   14. Survival information booklet.

Further reading (see bibliography for details): U.S. Sailing, *Recommendations for Offshore Sailing.*

APPENDIX III

PAPERS, DOCUMENTS, AND CERTIFICATES

CERTIFICATION DATE :	12JUN87

UNITED STATES OF AMERICA
DEPARTMENT OF TRANSPORTATION
UNITED STATES COAST GUARD

EXPIRATION DATE :	12JUN90

Certificate of Inspection

LAST HULL EXAM: 09MAY89 DRYDOCK

VESSEL NAME	OFFICIAL NUMBER	CALL SIGN	SERVICE
BOWDOIN	D221251	WF6145	SCHOOL SHIP
HOME PORT	HULL MATERIAL	HORSEPOWER	PROPULSION
BOSTON, MA	WOOD	190	AUXILIARY SAIL

PLACE BUILT	DATE BUILT	GROSS TONS	NET TONS	DWT	LENGTH
EAST BOOTHBAY, MAINE	01JAN86	66	15	66	75.700

OWNER	OPERATOR
MAINE MARITIME ACADEMY WATERFRONT BOX C-3 CASTINE, ME 04420	MAINE MARITIME ACADEMY WATERFRONT BOX C-3 CASTINE, ME 04420

THIS VESSEL MUST BE MANNED WITH THE FOLLOWING LICENSED AND UNLICENSED PERSONNEL, INCLUDED IN WHICH THERE MUST BE ____0 CERTIFICATED LIFEBOATMEN AND ____0 CERTIFICATED TANKERMAN.

_1_MASTER	____ MASTER & 1ST CLASS PILOT	____ ABLE SEAMEN	____ CHIEF ENGINEER	____ FIREMEN-WATERTENDERS
____CHIEFMATE	____ CLASS PILOT	____ ORDINARY SEAMEN	____ 1ST ASST. ENGINEER	____ OILERS
____2ND MATE	____ RADIO OFFICER(S)	_4_ DECKHANDS	____ 2ND ASST. ENGINEER	____
_1_ LIC._____MATES	____ OPERATOR(S)		____ ENG'RS.	____

IN ADDITION, THIS VESSEL MAY CARRY ____0 PASSENGERS, ____0 OTHER PERSONS IN CREW, ____0 PERSONS IN ADDITION TO CREW, AND INSTRUCTOR/STUDENT COMPLIMENT/11 . TOTAL PERSONS ALLOWED: ___17

ROUTE PERMITTED AND CONDITIONS OF OPERATION:

EXPOSED WATERS: AS A SAIL SCHOOL VESSEL.

* MASTER MUST HAVE OCEANS LICENSE WITH AUXILIARY SAIL ENDORSEMENT.

COASTWISE: BETWEEN EASTPORT, MAINE AND FALSE CAPE, VIRGINIA INCLUDING CHESAPEAKE BAY AND TRIBUTARIES, NOT MORE THAN TWENTY (20) MILES FROM A HARBOR OF SAFE REFUGE. THE VESSEL MAY CARRY PASSENGERS AND/OR SAIL SCHOOL STUDENTS/INSTRUCTORS. TOTAL PERSONS ON BOARD SHALL NOT EXCEED 49. THE MASTER MAY OPERATE ON COASTWISE VOYAGES ONLY WITH A NEAR COASTAL LICENSE, AUXILARY SAIL ENDORSEMENT.

WHEN VESSEL OPERATES LESS THAN 12 HOURS IN ANY 24 HOUR PERIOD, THE VESSEL'S CREW MAY BE REDUCED TO 1 MASTER AND 2 DECKHANDS AND THE INSTRUCTOR/STUDENT COMPLIMENT MAY THEN BE INCREASED TO 14 ON AN EXPOSED ROUTE.

WHEN OPERATING MORE THAN ONE (01) MILE FROM LAND NORTH OF LATITUDE 41 DEGREES 42 MINUTES NORTH, BETWEEN 1 NOVEMBER AND 1 APRIL, ONE-HUNDRED (100)

*** SEE NEXT PAGE FOR ADDITIONAL CERTIFICATE INFORMATION ***

WITH THIS INSPECTION HAVING BEEN COMPLETED AT CASTINE, MAINE CERTIFIED BY THE OFFICER IN CHARGE, MARINE INSPECTION, PORTLAND, MAINE WITH THE APPLICABLE VESSEL INSPECTION LAWS AND THE RULES AND REGULATIONS PRESCRIBED THEREUNDER. ON 12JUN87 THIS VESSEL IS , TO BE IN ALL RESPECTS IN CONFORMITY

PERIODIC REINSPECTIONS			THIS CERTIFICATE ISSUED BY:
DATE	ZONE	SIGNATURE	M. R. PERKINS, COMMANDER, USCG
			OFFICER IN CHARGE, MARINE INSPECTION
			PORTLAND, MAINE
			INSPECTION ZONE

DEPT. OF TRANSP., USCG, CG-841 (Rev. 3-85)
PREVIOUS EDITIONS ARE OBSOLETE

SN 7530-00-F01-0370

SAMPLE 1

DEPARTMENT OF TRANSPORTATION
UNITED STATES COAST GUARD

Certificate of Inspection

BOWDOIN   PAGE 2   CERTIFICATION DATE: 12JUN87

--- ROUTE PERMITTED AND CONDITIONS OF OPERATION, CONTINUED ---
PERCENT PRIMARY LIFESAVING EQUIPMENT IS REQUIRED.

WHEN VESSEL OPERATES ON OVERNIGHT TRIPS, THE MAXIMUM PASSENGERS ALLOWED IS
FIFTEEN (15).

WATCH PATROLMAN SERVICE SHALL BE PROVIDED BETWEEN THE HOURS OF 10PM & 6AM.

--- STABILITY ---
LETTER   APPROVAL DATE/ 19AUG88   OFFICE/ GMSC

--- LIFESAVING EQUIPMENT ---
NUMBER PERSONS   REQUIRED
TOTAL EQUIPMENT FOR   49   LIFE PRESERVERS(ADULT)...   49
  LIFEBOATS(TOTAL).......   LIFE PRESERVERS(CHILD)...   5
    LIFEBOATS(PORT)*.....   RING BUOYS(TOTAL)........   3
    LIFEBOATS(STARBD)*...   WITH LIGHTS*...........   1
    MOTOR LIFEBOATS*.....   WITH LINE ATTACHED*....   1
    LIFEBOATS W/RADIO*...   OTHER*................   0
  RESCUE BOATS/PLATFORMS.   1   IMMERSION SUITS.........   17
  INFLATABLE RAFTS.......   2   20 PORTABLE LIFEBOAT RADIOS.
  LIFE FLOATS/BUOYANT APP   1   8   EQUIPPED WITH EPIRB?.....   YES
  KBOATS (NOT REQUIRED)   (* INCLUDED IN TOTALS)

--- FIRE FIGHTING EQUIPMENT ---
TOTAL HOSE LENGTH/   100   NUMBER OF FIRE AXES/ 1   NUMBER OF FIRE PUMPS/ 1

FIXED EXTINGUISHING SYSTEMS
       SPACE PROTECTED   AGENT   CAPACITY
ENGINE ROOM   HALON   21
GALLEY   HALON   2
AFT LAZARETTE   HALON   14

FIRE EXTINGUISHERS - HAND PORTABLE AND SEMI-PORTABLE
       A-II   1 B-I   3 B-II   B-III
       B-IV   B-V   C-I   C-II

*** END ***

DEPT. OF TRANSP., USCG, CG-841 (Rev. 3-85)   SN 7530-00-FOI-0370
PREVIOUS EDITIONS ARE OBSOLETE

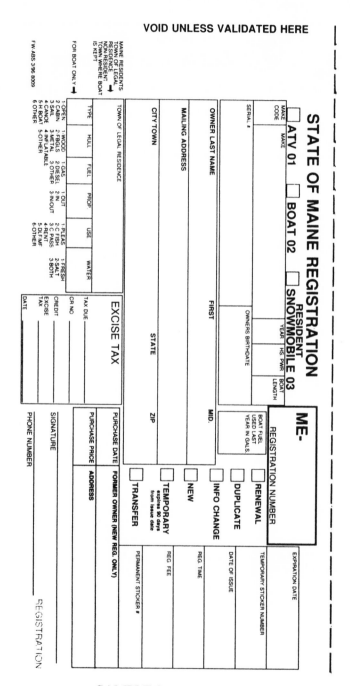

SAMPLE 2

1. This is your renewal application for the vehicle described on front. You may take this form to your local Recreational Vehicle Registration Agent or return to the address below with the appropriate fee to re-register this vehicle.

2. Boat excise tax must be paid by a resident to the tax collector of his town before renewing a boat registration. Prior to registering a motor boat which is located in Maine more than 75 days during a calendar year, a non-resident must pay an excise tax to the Maine town where the boat is moored, docked or located. If the boat is exempt from tax, a tax exemption form must be completed by the owner and submitted with registration application and registration fee.

3. No excise tax is due on a snowmobile or an all terrain vehicle.

4. Registration fees - make checks payable to Treasurer State of Maine

   BOAT - $ 4.00
   RESIDENT SNOWMOBILE - $ 20.00* Nonresident not eligible for this registration.
   ATV - $ 12.00

5. If an ATV plate is lost or stolen a replacement plate can be made for a fee of $2.50; replacement of a set of plates costs $5.00. Attach a separate request to your renewal form. Make a suitable temporary plate to display until your replacement plate is mailed.

6. Return address: Snowmobile Registration   Boat Registration   ATV Registration
                      41 State House Station   41 State House Station   41 State House Station
                      Augusta, Maine 04333   Augusta, Maine 04333   Augusta, Maine 04333

8011

OMB APPROVAL 2115-0056

PASSENGER SHIP SAFETY CERTIFICATE

This Certificate shall be supplemented by a Record of Equipment (Form P)

For: an International Voyage.

Issued under the provisions of the

INTERNATIONAL CONVENTION FOR THE SAFETY OF LIFE AT SEA, 1974, as amended

under the authority of the Government of

THE UNITED STATES OF AMERICA

by the UNITED STATES COAST GUARD

Particulars of Ship

― *SAMPLE* ―

Name of Ship	Distinctive Number or Letters	Port of Registry	Gross Tonnage

Sea areas in which ship is certified to operate (regulation IV/2)	IMO Number (Note 1)	Date on which keel was laid (Note 2)

THIS IS TO CERTIFY:

1. That the ship has been surveyed in accordance with the requirements of regulation I/7 of the Convention.

2. That the survey showed that:

2.1   the ship complied with the requirements of the Convention as regards;

2.1.1   the structure, main and auxiliary machinery, boilers and other pressure vessels;

2.1.2   the watertight subdivision arrangements and details;

Notes:
1. In accordance with resolution A.600(15): IMO Ship Identification Number Scheme, this information may be included voluntarily.
2. Date on which keel was laid or ship was at a similar stage of construction or, where applicable, date on which work for a conversion or an alteration or modification of a major character was commenced.

The Coast Guard estimates that the average burden for this report is 5 minutes. You may submit any comments concerning the accuracy of this burden estimate or any suggestions for reducing the burden to: Commandant (G-MVI), U.S. Coast Guard, Washington, DC 20593-0001 or Office of Management and Budget, Paperwork Reduction Project (2115-0056), Washington DC 20503.

SAMPLE 3a

PASSENGER SHIP SAFETY CERTIFICATE

2.1.3 the following subdivision load lines;

Subdivision loadlines assigned and marked on the ship's side at amidships (regulation II-1/13)	Freeboard	To apply when the spaces in which passengers are carried include the following alternative spaces.
C.1		
C.2		
C.3		

2.2   the ship complied with the requirements of the Convention as regards structural fire protection, fire safety systems and appliances and fire control plans;

2.3   the life-saving appliances and the equipment of the lifeboats, liferafts and rescue boats were provided in accordance with the requirements of the Convention;

2.4   the ship was provided with a line-throwing appliance and radio installations used in life-saving appliances in accordance with the requirements of the Convention;

2.5   the ship complied with the requirements of the Convention as regards radio installations;

2.6   the functioning of the radio installations used in life-saving appliances complied with the requirements of the Convention;

2.7   the ship complied with the requirements of the Convention as regards shipborne navigational equipment, means of embarkation for pilots and nautical publications;

2.8   the ship was provided with lights, shapes, means of making sound signals and distress signals, in accordance with the requirements of the Convention and the International Regulations for Preventing Collisions at Sea in force;

2.9   in all other respects the ship complied with the relevent requirements of the Convention.

3.   That an Exemption Certificate has been issued.

— SAMPLE —

This certificate is valid until: _____

Issued at: _____
Place of issue of certificate

_____   _____
Date of Issue   *Officer in Charge, Marine Inspection, U.S. Coast Guard*

RECORD OF EQUIPMENT FOR THE

PASSENGER SHIP SAFETY CERTIFICATE

(Form P)

This record shall be permanently attached to the
Passenger Ship Safety Certificate

RECORD OF EQUIPMENT FOR COMPLIANCE WITH THE

INTERNATIONAL CONVENTION FOR THE SAFETY OF LIFE AT SEA, 1974, as amended in 1988

— SAMPLE —

1. Particulars of Ship

Name of Ship	Distinctive Number or Letters	Number of Passengers for which certified	Minimum number of persons with required qualifications to operate the radio installations

2. Details of life-saving appliances:

		Port Side	Starboard Side
1.	Total number of persons for which life-saving appliances are provided:		
2.	Total number of lifeboats:		
2.1	Total number of person accommodated by them:		
2.2	Number of partially enclosed lifeboats (regulation III/42):		
2.3	Number of self-righting partially enclosed lifeboats (regulation III/43):		
2.4	Number of totally enclosed lifeboats (regulation III/44):		
2.5	Other lifeboats:		
2.5.1	Number :		
2.5.2	Type:		

DEPT. OF TRANSP., USCG, CG-968A (Rev. 6-93)   Page 1 of 3
PREVIOUS EDITIONS ARE OBSOLETE

SAMPLE 3b *(continued on following pages)*

RECORD OF EQUIPMENT FOR THE PASSENGER SHIP SAFETY CERTIFICATE

2. Details of life-saving appliances (continued)

3.	Number of motor lifeboats (included in the total lifeboats shown above):	_____
3.1	Number of lifeboats fitted with searchlights:	_____
4.	Number of rescue boats:	_____
4.1	Number of boats which are included in the total lifeboats shown above:	_____
5.	Liferafts:	_____
5.1	Those for which approved launching appliances are required:	_____
5.1.1	Number of liferafts:	_____
5.1.2	Number of persons accommodated by them:	_____
5.2	Those for which approved launching appliances are not required:	_____
5.2.1	Number of liferafts:	_____
5.2.2	Number of persons accommodated by them:	_____
6.	Buoyant apparatus:	_____
6.1	Number of apparatus:	_____
6.2	Number of persons capable of being supported:	_____
7.	Number of lifebuoys:	_____
8.	Number of lifejackets:	_____
9.	Immersion suits:	_____
9.1	Total number:	_____
9.2	Number of suits complying with the requirements for lifejackets:	_____
10.	Number of thermal protective aids (note 1):	_____
11.	Radio installations used in lifesaving appliances:	_____
11.1	Number of radar transponders:	_____
11.2	Number of two-way VHF radiotelephone apparatus:	_____

3. Details of radio facilities: ~ SAMPLE ~

Item	Actual Provision
1. Primary systems:	_____
1.1 VHF radio installation:	_____
1.1.1 DSC encoder:	_____
1.1.2 DSC watch receiver:	_____
1.1.3 Radiotelephony:	_____
1.2 MF radio installation:	_____
1.2.1 DSC encoder:	_____
1.2.2 DSC watch receiver:	_____
1.2.3 Radiotelephony:	_____
1.3 MF/HF radio installation:	_____
1.3.1 DSC encoder:	_____
1.3.2 DSC watch receiver:	_____
1.3.3 Radiotelephony:	_____
1.3.4 Direct-printing radiotelegraphy:	_____
1.4 INMARSAT ship earth station:	_____
2. Secondary means of alerting:	_____
3. Facilities for reception of maritime safety information:	_____
3.1 NAVTEX receiver:	_____
3.2 EGC receiver:	_____
3.3 HF direct printing radiotelegraph receiver:	_____
4. Satellite EPIRB:	_____
4.1 COSPAS-SARSAT:	_____
4.2 INMARSAT:	_____

Notes:

1. Excluding those required by regulations III/38.5.1.24 , III/41.8.31 and III/47.2.2.13.

DEPT. OF TRANSP., USCG, CG-968A (Rev. 6-93)   Page 2 of 3

SAMPLE 3b *(continued)*

**RECORD OF EQUIPMENT FOR THE
PASSENGER SHIP SAFETY CERTIFICATE**

3. Details of radio facilities (continued)

5. VHF EPIRB: ——————————————————
6. Ship's radar transponder: ——————————————
7. Radiotelephone distress frequency watch receiver on 2182kHz (note 1): ———
8. Device for generating the radiotelephone alarm signal on 2182kHz (note 2): —

4. **Methods used to insure availability of radio facilities (regulations IV/15.6 and 15.7)**

1. Duplication of equipment: ——————————————
2. Shore-based maintenance: ——————————————
3. At-sea maintenance capability: —————————————

5. **Ships constructed before 1 February 1995 which do not comply with all the applicable requirements of chapter IV of the Convention as amended in 1988 (note 2):**

	Requirements of regulations	Actual Provision
Hours of listening by operator:		
Number of operators:		
Whether auto alarm fitted:		
Whether main installation fitted:		
Whether reserve installation fitted:		
Whether main and reserve transmitters electrically separated or combined:		

6. **Ships constructed before 1 February 1992 which do not fully comply with the applicable requirements of chapter III of the Convention as amended in 1988 (note 3):**

	Actual Provision
Radiotelegraph installation for lifeboat:	
Portable radio apparatus for survival craft:	
Survival craft EPIRB (121.5 MHz and 243.0 MHz):	
Two-way radiotelephone apparatus:	

THIS IS TO CERTIFY that this Record is correct in all respects.

Issued at: ———————— *–SAMPLE* ————————
Place of issue of the Record

——————————— ——————————————————
Date of issue   *Office in Charge, Marine Inspection, U.S. Coast Guard*

Notes:

1. Unless another date is determined by the Maritime Safety Committee, this item need not be reproduced on the record attached to certificates issued after 1 February 1999.
2. This item need not be reproduced on the record attached to certificates issued after 1 February 1999.
3. This section need not be reproduced on the record attached to certificates issued after 1 February 1995.

DEPT. OF TRANSP., USCG, CG-968A (Rev. 6-93)   Page 3 of 3

OMB APPROVAL 2115-0056

EXEMPTION CERTIFICATE

Issued under the provisions of the

INTERNATIONAL CONVENTION FOR THE SAFETY OF LIFE AT SEA, 1974, as amended

under the authority of the Government of

THE UNITED STATES OF AMERICA

by the UNITED STATES COAST GUARD

— SAMPLE

Particulars of Ship

Name of Ship	Distinctive Number or Letters	Port of Registry

Gross Tonnage	IMO Number (Note 1)

THIS IS TO CERTIFY:

That this ship is , under the authority conferred by regulation _____

of the Convention, exempted from the requirements of: _____

_____

_____

_____

_____ of the Convention.

Notes:
1. In accordance with resolution A.600(15):IMO Ship Identification Number Scheme, this information may be included voluntarily.

The Coast Guard estimates that the average burden for this report is 5 minutes. You may submit any comments concerning the accuracy of this burden estimate or any suggestions for reducing the burden to: Commandant (G-MVI), U.S. Coast Guard, Washington, DC 20593-0001 or Office of Management and Budget, Paperwork Reduction Project (2115-0056), Washington DC 20503.

DEPT. OF TRANSP., USCG, CG-967 (Rev. 6-93)   Page 1 of 2
PREVIOUS EDITIONS ARE OBSOLETE

SAMPLE 3c

EXEMPTION CERTIFICATE

— SAMPLE —

Conditions, if any, on which the Exemption Certificate is granted:_____

_____

_____

_____

_____

_____

_____

Voyages, if any, for which the Exemption Certificate is granted: _____

_____

_____

_____

_____

_____

_____

This certificate is valid until _____

subject to the   Cargo Ship Safety Equipment Certificate,_____

to which this certificate is attached, remaining valid.

Issued at : _____

Place of issue of Certificate

_____   _____

Date of Issue   *Officer in Charge, Marine Inspection, U.S. Coast Guard*

INTERNATIONAL LOAD LINE CERTIFICATE (1966)

Issued under the provisions of the International Convention on Load Lines, 1966, under the authority of the Government of the

UNITED STATES OF AMERICA,

Commandant, U. S. Coast Guard,

by the American Bureau of Shipping

duly authorized for assigning purposes under the provisions of the Convention

8800163–3

Certificate No.

Name of Ship	Official number or Distinctive Letters	Port of Registry	Length (L) as defined in Article 2 (8); i. e., 46 CFR 42.13-15
CORWITH CRAMER	MS 2 RV	WOODS HOLE, MA	27.180 M

SUBDIVISION DRAFT

Freeboard assigned as:
* { A new ship
  { XXXXXHXXXXXX
* Delete whatever is inapplicable.

Type of Ship
* { XXXXXX"
  { XXXXXHXXX
  { XXXXXHXXXXXXXXXXXXXXXXXXXXX
  { Type "B" with increased freeboard

Freeboard from deck line TO CENTER OF RING & C1 1197 MM *Load Line*

Tropical	N/A	feet	N/A	inches (T)		N/A	inches above (S)
Summer	N/A	feet	N/A	inches (S)	N/A	Upper edge of line through center of ring
Winter	N/A	feet	N/A	inches (W)		N/A	inches below (S)
Winter North Atlantic	N/A	feet	N/A	inches (WNA)		N/A	inches below (S)

Note: Freeboards and load lines which are not applicable need not be entered on the certificate.

Allowance for fresh water for all freeboards   50 MM   XXXXX

Note: All measurements are to upper edge of the respective horizontal lines.

The upper edge of the deck line from which these freeboards are measured is

deck at side.

OPPOSITE TOP OF STEEL UPPER

THIS CERTIFICATE IS VALID ONLY SO LONG AS THE OPERATING RESTRICTIONS IN THE VESSEL'S STABILITY LETTER ISSUED BY THE USCG MARINE SAFETY CENTER DATED 11 SEPTEMBER 1991 ARE OBSERVED.

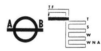

Date of initial or periodical survey   31 JANUARY 1993

THIS IS TO CERTIFY that this ship has been surveyed and that the freeboards have been assigned and load lines shown above have been marked in accordance with the International Convention on Load Lines, 1966.

This Certificate is valid until   31 JANUARY 1998   **, subject to annual surveys in accordance with Article 14 (1) (c) of the Convention, and endorsement thereof on the reverse side of the Certificate.

** At the expiration of this certificate, applicable reissuance should be obtained in accordance with the Load Line Regulations.

Issued at   HOUSTON, TEXAS.   9 FEBRUARY 1993

The undersigned declares that he is duly authorized by the said Government to issue this Certificate.

Survey Manager
ABS Americas

American Bureau of Shipping

SAMPLE 4

ANNUAL SURVEYS

THIS IS TO CERTIFY that at an annual survey required by Article 14(1)(c) of the Convention, this ship was found to comply with the relevant provisions of the Convention.

Place.. Date..

....Surveyor to the American Bureau of Shipping
       (Signature)

Place.. Date..

....Surveyor to the American Bureau of Shipping
       (Signature)

Place.. Date..

....Surveyor to the American Bureau of Shipping
       (Signature)

Place.. Date..

....Surveyor to the American Bureau of Shipping
       (Signature)

EXTENSION OF LOAD LINE CERTIFICATE

The provisions of the Convention being fully complied with by this ship, the validity of this Certificate is, in accordance with Article 19(2) of the Convention, extended until ....

Place .... Date..

....Surveyor to the American Bureau of Shipping
       (*Signature*)

Notes:

1. When a ship departs from a port situated on a river or inland waters, deeper loading shall be permitted corresponding to the weight of fuel and all other materials required for consumption between the point of departure and the sea.

2. When a ship is in fresh water of unit density the appropriate load line may be submerged by the amount of the fresh water allowance. Where the density is other than unity, an allowance shall be made proportional to the difference between 1.025 and the actual density.

3. It is the owner's responsibility to furnish the master with approved information and instructions for loading and ballasting this vessel to provide guidance as to stability of the vessel under varying conditions of service and to avoid unacceptable stresses in the vessel's structure, as defined in 46 CFR 42.09-1.

4. The Winter North Atlantic Load Line applies only to vessels of 328 ft. in length or less, which enter any part of the North Atlantic Ocean during the winter months as defined by the Load Line Regulations in 46 CFR 42.30-5 and 42.30-35. The periods during which the other seasonal load lines apply in different parts of the world are as stated in the Load Line Regulations of 46 CFR 42.30-5 to 42.30-30, inclusive.

5. This Load Line Certificate will be canceled by the Commandant, U. S. Coast Guard, if —
    (a) The annual surveys have not been carried out within three months either way of each anniversary date of the certificate.
    (b) The certificate is not endorsed to show that the ship has been surveyed as indicated in (a).
    (c) Material alterations have been made to the hull or superstructures such as would necessitate the assignment of an increased freeboard.
    (d) The fittings and appliances for the protection of the openings, guardrails, freeing ports, or the means of access to the crew's quarters have not been in as effective a condition as they were when the Certificate was issued.
    (e) The structural strength of the ship is lowered to such an extent that the ship is unsafe.

6. When this Certificate has expired or been canceled, it must be delivered to the Assigning Authority.

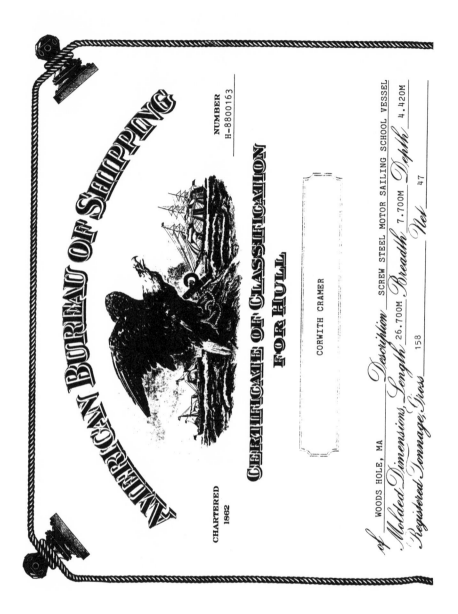

SAMPLE 5

Owner SEA EDUCATION ASSOCIATION, INC.

of WOODS HOLE, MA

Shipbuilder ASTILLEROS Y TALLERES CELAYA S.A.

VIZCAYA, SPAIN

Year of Build 1988   *Hull Number* 210

This is to Certify that the above Vessel has been surveyed in accordance with the Rules of this Bureau and entered in the Record with the Class ✠ A1 ⓔ.

New York, 7 JUNE 19 88

W. Grim
ASSISTANT VICE PRESIDENT

C. M. George
ASSISTANT SECRETARY

NOTE: *This certificate evidences compliance with one or more of the Rules, Guides, standards or other criteria of American Bureau of Shipping and is issued solely for the use of the Bureau, its committees, its clients or other authorized entities. The classification certificate is a representation only that the vessel, structure, item of material, equipment or machinery or any other item covered by this certificate has met one or more of the Rules of American Bureau of Shipping. The certificate is governed by the terms and conditions on the reverse side hereof, and governed by the Rules and standards of American Bureau of Shipping who shall remain the sole judge thereof.*

AMERICAN BANK NOTE COMPANY.

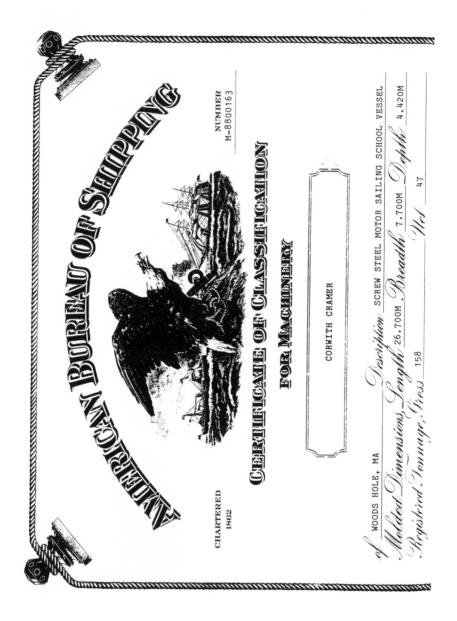

SAMPLE 6

Owner SEA EDUCATION ASSOCIATION, INC.

WOODS HOLE, MA

Shipbuilder ASTILLEROS Y TALLERES CELAYA S.A.

VIZCAYA, SPAIN

Engine Builder CUMMINS ENGINE CO., INC.

SEYMOUR, IN

Engine Year of Build 1988   *Hull Number* 210

This is to Certify that the Machinery of the above Vessel has been surveyed in accordance with the Rules of this Bureau and entered in the Record with the Class ✱ AMS

New York, 7 JUNE 19 88

W. Flynn
ASSISTANT VICE PRESIDENT

C.M. Harp
ASSISTANT SECRETARY

NOTE: *This certificate evidences compliance with one or more of the Rules, Guides, standards or other criteria of American Bureau of Shipping and is issued solely for the use of the Bureau, its committees, its clients or other authorized entities. The classification certificate is a representation only that the vessel, structure, item of material, equipment or machinery or any other item covered by this certificate has met one or more of the Rules of American Bureau of Shipping.* **The certificate** *is governed* **by the terms and conditions on the reverse side hereof,** *and governed by the Rules and standards of American Bureau of Shipping who shall remain the sole judge thereof.*

AMERICAN BANK NOTE COMPANY.

SHIP/AIRCRAFT RADIO STATION LICENSE

FEDERAL COMMUNICATIONS COMMISSION
WASHINGTON, D.C. 20554

	AIRCRAFT	FAA NUMBER OR FCC CONTROL NUMBER	NUMBER AIRCRAFT IN FLEET	EFFECTIVE DATE		EXPIRATION DATE

| X | SHIP | NAME OF SHIP *BOWDOIN | | OFFICIAL NUMBER ..221251 | RADIO CALL SIGN WF6145 | SELECTIVE CALLING NO. |

EFFECTIVE DATE 04-03-86	EXPIRATION DATE 04-03-91	ENDORSEMENT DATES

FREQUENCIES AND CONDITIONS

```
RADIOTELEPHONE      4000-23,000 KHZ     156-158 MHZ
RADAR               9300-9500 MHZ
EPIRB               121.5 MHZ           243 MHZ
```

THIS LICENSE SUBJECT TO FURTHER
CONDITIONS SET FORTH ON THE REVERSE SIDE

NOT TRANSFERABLE

(Must be posted aboard aircraft or ship)

FCC/559
November 1984

```
SCHOONER BOWDOIN
POB 1117
ROCKLAND                    ME
04841
```

SAMPLE 7

UNITED STATES OF AMERICA

FEDERAL COMMUNICATIONS COMMISSION

COMMUNICATIONS ACT SAFETY RADIOTELEPHONY CERTIFICATE

NAME OF VESSEL	OFFICIAL NUMBER	RADIO CALL SIGN	PORT OF REGISTRY	GROSS TONNAGE
BOWDOIN	221251	WF-6145	Boston, MA	66

The Government of the United States of America certifies that the radiotelephone installation on board the above-described vessel complies with all relevant provisions of Part III of Title III of the Communications Act, the rules of the Commission made pursuant thereto, the terms of the station license, and successfully completes an operational test at the time this certificate is issued.

Notwithstanding the above, it is unlawful for any vessel of the United States, transporting more than six passengers for hire, to be navigated in the open sea or any tidewater within the jurisdiction of the United States adjacent or contiguous to the open sea, unless the vessel is equipped with an efficient radiotelephone installation in <u>operating condition.</u>

Type of radiotelephone installations on board this vessel: ☑ VHF ☐ MF

When a VHF station only is provided, this certificate is valid only while the vessel is within communication range of a public coast station or U.S. Coast Guard station operating in the band 156 to 162 MHz which maintains an efficient watch for reception on 156.8 MHz at all times while the vessel is navigated, and the vessel is never more than 20 nautical miles from a 156.8 MHz receiving location of such station.

This Certificate will remain in force until May 15th, 1991

Issued at Boston, MA on the 15th day of May 1986

Validated:

ISSUING OFFICER

FEDERAL
COMMUNICATIONS
COMMISSION

FCC Form 824
January 1985

SAMPLE 8

CG-835
(Rev. 3-68)

DEPARTMENT OF TRANSPORTATION
UNITED STATES COAST GUARD

Office of Officer in Charge,
Marine Inspection Port ____ *Portland* ____ Date *30 MAY 91*

To *Mr. Chase* S.S. *M.V. Bowdoin* G.T. *66*

You are directed to inform the above officer when the following requirements have been corrected.

1. *At NEXT Drydocking install Automatic NON-return valves on all OVBD Discharge Pipes penetrating the sideshell as required by 46CFR 56.50-95*

2. *Prior to 30 JUNE 1991 provide onboard Fire nozzles that meet the requirements of 46CFR 181.15-5*

Marine Inspector.

Acknowledged *GAChase*   Time *1145*   Date *5/30/91*

SAMPLE 9

OMB APPROVAL 2115–0526

INTERNATIONAL OIL POLLUTION PREVENTION CERTIFICATE

(*Note*: This Certificate shall be supplemented by a Record of Construction and Equipment)

Issued under the provisions of the

INTERNATIONAL CONVENTION FOR THE PREVENTION OF POLLUTION FROM SHIPS, 1973

as modified by the Protocol of 1978, relating thereto,
(hereinafter referred to as "the Convention")
under the authority of the Government of

THE UNITED STATES OF AMERICA

by the UNITED STATES COAST GUARD

Name of Ship	Distinctive Numbers or Letters	Port of Registry	Gross Tonnage

Type of ship:

☐ Oil Tanker (*Form B Supplement attached*)*

☐ Ship other than an oil tanker with cargo tanks coming under regulation 2(2) of Annex I of the Convention (*Form B Supplement attached*)*

☐ Ship other than any of the above (*Form A Supplement attached*)*

THIS IS TO CERTIFY:

1. That the ship has been surveyed in accordance with the requirements of regulation 4 of Annex I of the Convention ; and
2. That the survey shows that the structure, equipment, systems, fittings, arrangement and material of the ship and the condition thereof are in all respects satisfactory and that the ship complies with the applicable requirements of Annex I of the Convention.

This certificate is valid until: _____

subject to surveys in accordance with regulation 4 of Annex I of the Convention.

Issued at: _____
Place of issue of certificate

_____   _____
Date of issue   *Officer in Charge, Marine Inspection, U.S. Coast Guard*

* Delete as appropriate

The Coast Guard estimates that the average burden for this report is 20 minutes. You may submit any comments concerning the accuracy of this burden estimate or any suggestions for reducing the burden to: Commandant (G–MVI), U.S. Coast Guard, Washington, DC 20593–0001 or Office of Management and Budget, Paperwork Reduction Project (2115–0526), Washington DC 20503.

DEPT. OF TRANSP., USCG, CG–5352 (Rev. 6–93)
PREVIOUS EDITIONS ARE OBSOLETE

Page 1 of 2

SAMPLE 10

INTERNATIONAL OIL POLLUTION PREVENTION CERTIFICATE

ENDORSEMENT FOR ANNUAL AND INTERMEDIATE SURVEYS

THIS IS TO CERTIFY that at a survey required by regulation 4 of Annex I of the Convention the ship was found to comply with the relevant provisions of the Convention.

Annual survey:	Signed: _____
	Place: _____
	Date: _____

Annual */Intermediate* survey:	Signed: _____
	Place: _____
	Date: _____

Annual */Intermediate* survey:	Signed: _____
	Place: _____
	Date: _____

Annual survey:	Signed: _____
	Place: _____
	Date: _____

*   Delete as appropriate

DEPARTMENT OF TRANSPORTATION U.S. COAST GUARD CG-1270 (REV. 5-82)	CERTIFICATE OF DOCUMENTATION	OMB APPROVED 2115-0110
1. VESSEL NAME B O W D O I N	14. PROPULSION Yes	15. HULL MATERIAL Wood
2. OFFICIAL NUMBER 2 2 1 2 5 1	3. TONNAGE GROSS 66 NET 15 L. 75.7' B. 20.2' D. 9.4'	16. TRADE ENDORSEMENTS. DO NOT INSERT ANY TRADES FROM WHICH VESSEL IS RESTRICTED. SEE BLOCK 8.
4. HOME PORT Boston, Mass.	THIS VESSEL IS PRESENTLY DOCUMENTED FOR: COASTWISE	THIS VESSEL IS PRESENTLY DOCUMENTED FOR:
5. BUILD: PLACE(S) East Boothbay, Maine	YEAR 1921	
6. OWNER Schooner Bowdoin Association, Inc.	3/11/85 ~K J Brodie DATE SIGNATURE K. J. BRODIE	DATE SIGNATURE
7. OWNER'S ADDRESS 15 Limerock Street Rockland, ME 04841	THIS VESSEL IS PRESENTLY DOCUMENTED FOR:	THIS VESSEL IS PRESENTLY DOCUMENTED FOR:
8. RESTRICTIONS NONE		
9. ENTITLEMENTS NONE	DATE SIGNATURE	DATE SIGNATURE
10. PORT OF ISSUANCE Boston, Mass.	11. DATE OF ISSUANCE 11 March 1985 CG-1280A (REV. 8-97)	THIS VESSEL IS PRESENTLY DOCUMENTED FOR:

SAMPLE 11

EXPIRES LAST DAY OF

APR 1989

221251

12. SIGNATURE & SEAL,

K. J. BRODIE
By direction

DATE

SIGNATURE

*INDICATES CHANGE IN ITEM. NATURE OF WHICH IS REFLECTED ON REVERSE OF DOCUMENT.

PREFERRED MORTGAGE ENDORSEMENTS

MORTGAGE ENDORSEMENT

MORTGAGE AMENDMENTS

INSTRUMENT

PM ____, INST. ____

MORTGAGOR

INSTRUMENT

PM ____, INST. 571

MORTGAGOR

Schooner Bowdoin Association, Inc.

1. INSTRUMENT AMENDED

PM ____, INST. ____

CHANGE

DATE AND TIME OF ENDORSEMENT

MORTGAGEE

Key Bank of Central Maine

MORTGAGEE

SIGNATURE AND SEAL

AMOUNT
$150,000.00

MATURITY DATE
05 Jul 2004

DATE AND TIME OF ENDORSEMENT
31 Oct 85
12:35 p.m.

AMOUNT

MATURITY DATE

DATE AND TIME OF ENDORSEMENT

PORT

2. INSTRUMENT AMENDED

PM ____, INST. ____

CHANGE

DATE AND TIME OF ENDORSEMENT

SEPARATE DISCHARGE (IF ANY)

SEPARATE DISCHARGE (IF ANY)

SIGNATURE AND SEAL
Anthony T. Giantonio

PORT
Boston, Mass.

SIGNATURE AND SEAL

PORT

SATISFACTION

SATISFIED BY PM ____

INST. ____, FILED AT

DATE OF ENTRY

SATISFACTION

SATISFIED BY PM ____

INST. ____, FILED AT

DATE OF ENTRY

SIGNATURE AND SEAL

PORT

3. INSTRUMENT AMENDED

PM ____, INST. ____

CHANGE

DATE AND TIME OF ENDORSEMENT

SIGNATURE AND SEAL

PORT

SIGNATURE & SEAL

U.S. Department
of Transportation

**United States
Coast Guard**

Commander
Third Coast Guard
District (mmt)

Governors Island
New York, NY   10004
(212) 668-7063

16710/BOWDOIN
Ser H50452
June 20, 1985

Licensed Operator, Schooner BOWDOIN, O.N. 221251
c/o Schooner Bowdoin Association, Inc.
P.O. Box 1117
Rockland, Maine 04841

Subj: SCHOONER BOWDOIN, O.N. 221251;   STABILITY LETTER

Dear Sir:

A stability test witnessed by the U.S. Coast Guard was performed on the
BOWDOIN, O.N. 221251 at Boston, Mass. on May 17, 1985. On the basis of this
test, stability calculations have been performed. Results indicate that the
BOWDOIN as presently outfitted and equipped, subject to the restrictions
specified below, has satisfactory stability to meet the requirements of 46 CFR
171.035 for the carriage of 49 persons (passengers, students and crew) on a
partially protected route under all reasonable operating conditions.

Since passenger capacity and route are based upon other criteria, as well as,
stability, and may be further limited thereby, you are cautioned that:

THE NUMBER OF PASSENGERS TO BE CARRIED AND THE ROUTE SHALL BE AS SPECIFIED
ON THE CERTIFICATE OF INSPECTION.

The following restrictions apply:

1. The sails which may be carried shall be limited to the mainsail,
foresail, fore staysail, and jib as shown on the "SAIL PLAN" bearing U.S.
Coast Guard approval stamp dated April 25, 1985.

2. At no time shall the vessel be operated at a mean keel draft in excess
of 10 feet 2 inches, which corresponds to a freeboard (from the top of the
deck) at side amidship of 3 feet 4 inches.

3. The bilges of all compartments shall be kept pumped to minimum content
at all times.

4. No weight shall be added or removed from this vessel without the prior
written consent of the Officer in Charge, Marine Inspection in whose zone the
vessel is certificated.

It shall be the licensed operator's responsibility to maintain the vessel in a
satisfactory stability condition at all times.

This stability letter shall be posted under glass or other acceptable
transparent material in a conspicuous location in the aft cabin.

Sincerely,

T. C. GREENE
Commander, U. S. Coast Guard
Chief, Merchant Marine Technical Branch
By direction of the District Commander

Copy to: MSO Boston, Mass.
         COMDT(G-MTH)

SAMPLE 12

WHSE. NO. 0861

TREASURY DEPARTMENT
UNITED STATES CUSTOMS SERVICE

UNITED STATES DEPARTMENT OF JUSTICE
Immigration and Naturalization Service

PASSENGER LIST

CREW LIST
(Cross out one)

(Oath to be taken on Customs Form 1300)

Form Approved
OMB No. 43-R0516

Sheet No.

Class *(First, Cabin, Tourist, or Other)*

CARRIER *(Nationality, name, and official number of carrier)*

Date of arrival/departure *(Cross out one)*

Port of arrival/departure *(Cross out one)*

Last foreign port before arrival in United States *(Place and Country)*

(Date departed)

If departing, show first port at and date on which carrier arrived in United States on this trip. | If departing, show first foreign port after departure from United States.

(1) NAME IN FULL		(2) Date of Birth Nationality and passport number	(3) CREW		(4) Crew *(departing U.S. Flag vessels only)* USCG Z or C.D.B. number and name and address of next of kin	(5) This column for use Government officials only *(except when carrying certain passengers. See Instructions)*
Family name	Given name and middle initial		Position	Where shipped or engaged		

Total Number
1-418 (Rev. 7-1-74) Y

Agent _____

SAMPLE 13 *(continued on following pages)*

INSTRUCTIONS

ALL NAMES AND OTHER DATA INSCRIBED ON THIS FORM MUST BE IN THE ENGLISH LANGUAGE

PASSENGERS

Incoming.—Complete columns (1) and (2), and (5) when required below. Deliver one complete alphabetical list, regardless of nationality, to United States Public Health Service, United States Immigration Service, and two such lists to United States Customs Bureau on arrival at first port in the United States. If insufficient space in column (2), information may extend into column (3).

In column (5) show opposite a passenger's name the compartment or space occupied if that passenger is not allotted space for his or her exclusive use in the proportion of at least 36 clear superficial feet (steerage); the sex and the married or single status of each passenger in such case; and the age of each passenger of 8 years or under. In addition, the age of each deceased passenger and the cause of death shall be shown, regardless of class.

Departing.—Complete columns (1) and (2). Deliver one complete list to the United States Immigration Service at the last port of departure—to which is attached the Arrival/Departure Card (Form I-94) given to each nonimmigrant alien when he last arrived in the United States; otherwise, prepare and attach a new Form I-94.

CREW

Incoming.—Complete columns (1), (2) and (3). Deliver one complete alphabetical list to United States Public Health Service, United States Immigration Service, and two such lists to the United States Customs Bureau on arrival at the first port in the United States.

Where a crewman is a returning resident alien, show his alien registration receipt card number in column (2) in lieu of passport number.

Departing.—Submit a single copy of this form to the Immigration office at the port from which the vessel is to depart directly to a foreign port or place, executed in accordance with the following instructions. Complete all items in the heading of the form and place the following endorsement on the first line of the form: "Arrival Crewlist, Form I-418, filed at *(Show U.S. port of arrival)*." A Form I-418 which does not bear this endorsement will not be accepted.

Notification of Changes in Crew.—(1) Under a heading "Added Crewmen," list the names of nonresident alien crewmen who were not members of the crew and manifested on Form I-418 as such when the vessel last arrived in the United States, and attach for each added crewman his Form I-95 or Form I-94 given to him when he last arrived in the United States; otherwise, prepare and attach a new Form I-95. (2) Under a heading "Separated Crewmen," list the names of all alien crewmen who arrived in the United States on the vessel as members of the crew on the occasion of the vessel's last arrival in the United States but who for any reason are not departing with the vessel, and for each such separated crewman, show his nationality, passport number, specific port and date of separation, and the reasons for failure to depart. (3) If there are no added and/or separated alien crewmen upon departure, endorse the form "No changes in nonresident alien crew upon departure."

The list required under (1) and (2) may be incorporated in a single Form I-418, if space permits.

United States Flag Vessels Only.—Complete column (1), (2), (3) and (4). Deliver two complete crew lists to United States Customs Bureau at the last port of departure. The customs officer will certify one copy of this crew list in the space provided below and that copy shall be presented to the United States Customs Bureau at the first port of arrival in the United States and on the return voyage. Show birthplace in column (2) in lieu of passport number.

CREW LIST VISA APPLICATION

Submit form in duplicate to a United States consular officer. For each alien crewman not in possession of a valid individual visa or Immigration and Naturalization Service Form I-151, note columns (4) and (5) of the duplicate copy as follows: column (4) insert his date, city and country of birth, column (5) insert place of issuance and the authority issuing passport held by such crewman. Same information is required at port of entry when applying for waiver of visa.

Execute the following oath before a Customs Officer as to all arriving passengers on all vessels. The oath is to be executed before a Customs Officer as to all departing crew on United States Flag Vessels, and before an Immigration Officer or other officer authorized to administer oaths as to all departing passengers on all vessels.

SAMPLE 13 *(continued)*

I certify that Customs baggage declaration requirements have been made known to incoming passengers; that any required Customs baggage declarations have been or will simultaneously herewith be filed as required by law and regulation with the proper Customs officer; and that the responsibilities devolving upon this vessel in connection therewith, if any, have been or will be discharged as required by law or regulation before the proper Customs officer. I further certify that there are no steerage passengers on board this vessel (46 U.S.C. 151-163).

Signature of Master

Show in box below number of United States citizens and alien passengers embarked or to be debarked separately at each foreign port involved. If passenger list consists of more than one page, summarize on last page only. Separate summary should be prepared for each class when manifested separately.

Foreign Port of { Embarkation (Cross out one) Debarkation	Number of passengers	
	U.S.C.	Aliens
Total		

CERTIFICATION OF COPY OF CREW LIST OF UNITED STATES FLAG VESSEL

I certify that this is a true copy of the original crew list of the above-named American vessel, which original crew list is on file in this office.

Given under my hand and seal of office at the customhouse at

_____ on _____

_____ Customs Officer.

DEPARTMENT OF THE TREASURY UNITED STATES CUSTOMS SERVICE	SHIP'S STORES DECLARATION ☐ Arrival ☐ Departure	Form Approved O.M.B. No. 48– RO486 Page No.

1. Name of ship		2. Port of arrival/departure	3. Date of arrival/departure

4. Nationality of ship	5. Port arrived from/Port of destination

6. Number of persons on board	7. Period of stay	8. Place of storage*

9. Name of article	10. Quantity	11. For Official Use
DECK		
Ammunition, 38 cal.	. . . . Rds.	
Revolver, 38 cal.	. . . . Ea.	
Rope, Fiber	. . . . Ft.	
Rope, Wire	. . . . Ft.	
. . . .	. . . .	
. . . .	. . . .	
. . . .	. . . .	
ENGINE		
Diesel Oil	. . . . .Gals.	
Fuel Oil	. . . . .Bbls.	
Fresh Water	. . . . .Tons	
Lube Oil	. . . . .Gals.	
. . . .	. . . .	
STEWARD		
Cereal & Paste	. . . . Lbs.	
Coffee	. . . . Lbs.	
Dairy	. . . . Lbs.	
Eggs	. . . . .Doz.	
Fish *Frozen - Fresh & Salt*	. . . . Lbs.	
Fruit *Fresh - Dried & Canned*	. . . . Lbs.	
Meat *Fresh - Canned & Salt*	. . . . Lbs.	
Poultry	. . . . Lbs.	
Vegetables *Fresh - Frozen & Canned*	. . . . Lbs.	
Sugar	. . . . Lbs.	
. . . .	. . . .	
. . . .	. . . .	
. . . .	. . . .	
GENERAL		
Detergents & Soap	. . . . Lbs.	
Grease	. . . . Lbs.	
Kerosene & Solvent	. . . . .Gals.	
Paint	. . . . .Gals.	
Paint, Additives	. . . . .Gals.	
. . . .	. . . .	
. . . .	. . . .	
BONDED		
Beer , ...	. . . . . . Cases	
Cigarettes	. . . . .Ctns.	
Cigars	. . . . Ea.	
Gin	. . . . Btls.	
Liquers	. . . . Btls.	
Tobacco	. . . . Lbs.	
Whiskey	. . . . Btls.	
Wine	. . . . Btls.	
NARCOTICS		
Codeine Sulfate. . . . . .gr.	. . . . . . .Tablet	
Morphine Sulfate. . . . . .gr.	. . . . . . .Tubex	
Paragoric	. . . . . . .Pints	
Phenobarbital. . . . . .gr.	. . . . . . .Tablet	
. . . .	. . . .	
. . . .	. . . .	

Also such broken and sundry stores as linen, crockery, silver, spare parts, tools, instrument hospital supplies and slop chest stores as required by law and/or necessary for the safe and efficient navigation and operation of the vessel.

12. Date and signature by master, authorized agent or officer

Not required by the United States.

CUSTOMS FORM 1303 (3-20-75)

SAMPLE 14

DEPARTMENT OF THE TREASURY
UNITED STATES CUSTOMS SERVICE
Part 4, C.R.

GENERAL DECLARATION
☐ Arrival   ☐ Departure

Form Approved
O.M.B. No. 48—RO489

1. Name and description of ship	2. Port of arrival/departure	3. Date-time of arrival/departure
4. Nationality of ship	5. Name of master	6. Port arrived from/Port of destination
7. Certificate of registry (Port; date; number)	8. Name and address of ship's agent
9. Gross register tons	10. Net register tons	
11. Position of the ship in the port (berth or station)	

12. Brief particulars of voyage (previous and subsequent ports of call; underline where remaining cargo will be discharged)

13. Brief description of the cargo

14. Number of crew (include master)	15. Number of passengers	16. Remarks

Attached documents
(indicate number of copies)

17. Cargo Declaration	18. Ship's Stores Declaration
19. Crew List	20. Passenger List
22. Crew's Effects Declaration	23. Maritime Declaration of Health*

21. Date and signature by master, authorized agent or officer**

This space for U.S. Customs use only

*Only on arrival.
**Only the Master, Licensed Deck Officer, or Purser may sign; documents attached as shown in items 17–22 need not be signed.
This form may be printed by private parties provided it conforms to the official form in size (except that it may be up to 14 inches in length), wording, arrangement, style, size of type, and quality and color of paper. (Section 4.99 C.R.) For sale by district directors of Customs.

GPO 964-543

(Previous editions may be used)

Customs Form 1301 (3-9-78)

SAMPLE 15

SAMPLE 16

DEPARTMENT OF THE TREASURY
UNITED STATES CUSTOMS SERVICE

Form Approved
O.M.B. No. 1515-0060

MASTER'S OATH OF VESSEL IN FOREIGN TRADE

19 CFR 4.7, 4.8, 4.9, 4.20, 4.61,
4.63, 4.75, 4.81, 4.85, 4.87

☐ ENTRANCE   ☐ CLEARANCE

1. NATIONALITY, NAME & TYPE OF VESSEL	2. VESSEL BUILT AT	3. MANIFEST NO.
		4. NAME OF DISTRICT AND PORT
5. NAME AND ADDRESS OF OWNER	6. NAME AND ADDRESS OF OPERATOR	7. TIME AND DATE OF ARRIVAL
		8. MAXIMUM DRAFT ON ARRIVAL/DEPARTURE

MASTER'S CERTIFICATE ON PRELIMINARY ENTRY

I certify that the within manifest contains a just, true, and full account of all the cargo, and other items, including passengers and their baggage, required by law to be manifested.

_____ Master's Signature

I certify this manifest was this day produced to me as the _____ manifest. If produced as copy, I certify I have examined and compared it with the original and find it agrees therewith.
(Original/Duplicate)

_____   _____
Date, Time, Preliminary Entry   Customs Officer's Signature

MASTER'S OATH OF FORMAL ENTRY/CLEARANCE

On Entry: (a) I swear that the statements contained in any manifest (including any passenger or stores list) presented on entry or on arrival at domestic ports in a coastwise movement (or, if a foreign vessel, in any declaration made on such arrival that the vessel is in ballast only) are true. (b) I do solemnly swear that I have to the best of my knowledge and belief delivered to the appropriate post office every letter and every bag, packet, or parcel of letters on board the said vessel during her last voyage, or in my possession or under my power or control, except where waybilled for discharge at other ports in the United States at which the said vessel is scheduled to call and which the Postmaster General has not determined will be unreasonably delayed by remaining on board the said vessel for delivery at such ports. (c) I solemnly swear that the ownership of this vessel, except as may be otherwise stated on this form, is as indicated in any register, or document in lieu thereof, produced on entry.[1] (d) I swear that no part of the vessel has been sold or transferred since the granting of the register, except as may be otherwise stated on this form, and that no foreign subject or citizen has, to the best of my knowledge and belief, any share, by way of trust, confidence, or otherwise, in the vessel.[1] (e) If the vessel is documented to engage in trade on the northern, northeastern, and northwestern frontiers of the United States, I swear that any articles purchased in a foreign country for the use of the vessel and designated "sea stores" are for the exclusive use of the vessel and are not intended for sale, transfer, or private use.

On Clearance: (a) If clearing for a foreign port, I do solemnly, sincerely, and truly swear that the manifest of the cargo on board the vessel, now delivered by me to the District Director of Customs, and subscribed with my name, contains, according to the best of my knowledge and belief, a full, just, and true account of all the goods, wares, or merchandise now actually laden on board the said vessel, and of the value thereof; and if any other goods, wares, or merchandise shall be laden or put on board the vessel previous to her sailing from this port, I will immediately report the same to the said District Director. I do also swear that I verily believe the duties on all foreign merchandise therein specified have been paid or secured, according to law, and that no part thereof is intended to be relanded within the United States, and that if by distress or other unavoidable accident it shall become necessary to reland the same, I will forthwith make a just and true report thereof to the District Director of the district wherein such distress or accident may happen. So help me God. (b) I swear that the statements contained in any manifest presented on departure from domestic ports in a coastwise movement (or, if a foreign vessel, in any declaration made in such a movement) that there has been no lading on board the vessel are true. (c) I swear that I do not have under my care or control and will not receive or transport any letter that has not been regularly received from a United States post office or does not relate to the cargo of the vessel. 18 U.S.C. 1699; 19 U.S.C. 282, 1431, 1434 & 1435; 39 U.S.C. 902(b); 46 U.S.C. 42, 91, 94, 313 & 314.

9. NAME OF MASTER OR AUTHORIZED OFFICER	10. SIGNATURE OF MASTER, LICENSED DECK OFFICER OR PURSER

CUSTOMS USE ONLY

11. LOAD LINE EXPIRES	12. TONNAGE MARK ☐ NONE ☐ SUBMERGED ☐ NOT SUBMERGED
13. SOLAS CERTIFICATES EXPIRES	14. PASSENGERS ALLOWED PER COAST GUARD CERTIFICATE	15. NO. PASSENGERS DISEMBARKING/EMBARKING
16. CERT. FIN. RESP. NO. (Oil Pollution)	17. CERT. FIN. RESP. (Passenger Death/Injury)	18. CERT. FIN. RESP. (Passenger Transportation Indemnification)

19. PURPOSE (Entrance)	20. PURPOSE (Clearance)
☐ D (Discharge foreign cargo) ☐ X (Export cargo aboard on arrival) ☐ L (Lade cargo for export) ☐ F (Foreign cargo to be retained on board) ☐ N (No cargo transactions) ☐ Y (Military cargo for discharge)	☐ D (Discharge foreign cargo) ☐ X (Export cargo aboard on arrival) ☐ L (Lade cargo for export) ☐ F (Foreign cargo retained on board) ☐ N (No cargo transactions) ☐ Y (Military cargo laden)

21. TONNAGE YEAR BEGINS[2]	22. NO. AND RATE OF PAYMENTS[2]	23. AMOUNT[2]	24. CERTIFICATE NO.[2]
25. FIRST PAYMENT AT[3]	26. DATE[3]	27. LAST PAYMENT AT[3]	28. DATE[3]
29. FEE CERTIFICATE NO.	30. TOTAL FEES	31. TIME AND DATE ENTERED	32. TIME AND DATE CLEARED

33. SIGNATURE AND TITLE OF OFFICER RECEIVING ENTRY/CLEARANCE

FOOTNOTES: 1. Applicable to American vessel arriving direct from a foreign port.
2. Arrival only.
3. To be filled in only if no tonnage duty is collected because five payments have been made during the tonnage year at the rate applicable to the current entry of the vessel.

The Paperwork Reduction Act of 1980 says we must tell you why we are collecting this information, how we will use it, and whether you have to give it to us. We ask for the information to carry out the Customs Service laws of the United States. This form is used by the master of a vessel to attest to the truthfulness of the forms, certificates, and manifest on board and which must be presented to Customs. This form is also used by Customs to verify the various certificates and numbers and expiration dates same. It is mandatory and to your benefit.

This form may be printed by private parties provided the supply printed conforms to the official form in size, wording, arrangement, and quality and color of paper. For sale by District Directors of Customs.

Customs Form 1300 (082085)

SAMPLE 17

DEPARTMENT OF THE TREASURY
UNITED STATES CUSTOMS SERVICE

CREW MEMBER'S DECLARATION

Customs Form
5129 (9-22-76)

4.7, 4.7a, 4.81, 6.7, 6.9, 148.61-67, C.R.

Form Approved
O.M.B. No. 48-R0495

1. CREWMEMBER'S ARTICLE NO.

Nr ▬ 11456388

2. CARRIER *(Vessel Flag, Name)*

3. PORT OF ARRIVAL

4. CREWMEMBER'S NAME

5. RANK

6. DATE OF ARRIVAL

7. ADDRESS

List all articles obtained abroad and prices paid, or fair value if not purchased. Include serial number with all articles subject to registration such as cameras, radios, etc. List articles to remain on board separately from those articles to be landed in the United States. List separately articles intended for sale, barter, exchange, or carried by you as an accommodation for someone else. See additional instructions and information on reverse.

I. To be Filled in by Crewmember		II. For Customs Officer's Use			
QUANTITY AND DESCRIPTION OF GOODS	COST, OR VALUE OF GIFTS, ETC.	TARIFF DESCRIPTION	VALUE	RATE	DUTY

I certify that the above statement is a just, true and complete account of all articles of foreign origin for which written declaration and entry are required when landed in the United States (defined on reverse side) and I also certify that this statement is a just, true, and complete declaration of all such articles which I am landing in the United States.

TOTAL⟩

8. CUSTOMS OFFICER ACCEPTING ENTRY

9. SIGNATURE OF CREWMEMBER

10. DATE

- -

RECEIPT FOR DUTY AND RELEASE SLIP
To be filled in by Crewmember

PORT

CREWMEMBER'S ARTICLE NO.

NAME

CARRIER

Nr ▬ 11456388

REPEAT LIST OF ARTICLES TO BE LANDED *(Include serial numbers when appropriate.)*

For Customs Officer's Use

DATE	DUTY
	$

Articles listed at left have been examined and passed.

PIECES OF BAGGAGE RELEASED:

of Customs

The customs officer accepting the declaration and entry shall draw lines through unused spaces on receipt with ink or indelible pencil.

NOTICE: Liquidation of amount of duties and taxes, if any, due on this entry is effective on date of payment of this amount (Section 159.10, C.R.). For importer's right to protest or Government's right to redetermine this amount, see section 514 Tariff Act of 1930 as amended.

M-52

SAMPLE 18

DEPARTMENT OF THE TREASURY
UNITED STATES CUSTOMS SERVICE
CREW'S EFFECTS DECLARATION
19 CFR 4.7a (b) (d)

Form Approved
O.M.B. No. 1515-0001

Page No

1. Name of ship	2. Articles acquired abroad by officers and members of the crew (except those exclusively for use on voyage or cleared through Customs authorities)	
3. Nationality of ship		

4. No.	5. Family name, given names	6. Rank or rating					7. No. of crewmember's declaration of articles intended to be landed (if none, show "None" opposite name)

9. Date and signature by master, authorized agent or officer

This form may be printed by private parties provided the supply printed conforms to the official form in size, wording, arrangement, and quality and color of paper. For sale by District Directors of Customs.

CUSTOMS FORM 1304 (10-26-81)

SAMPLE 19

Customs Form 1378
TREASURY DEPARTMENT
4.60, 4.61, 4.74, 4.83, 4.86, 4.87, 4.89,
C.R.
April 1960

The United States of America

TREASURY DEPARTMENT
BUREAU OF CUSTOMS

CLEARANCE OF VESSEL TO A FOREIGN PORT

District of ....

Port of ....

These are to certify all whom it doth concern:

That ....

Master or Commander of the ....

burden .... Tons, or thereabouts, mounted with ....

Guns, navigated with .... Men, ...

.... built, and bound for ....

....

....

....

....

with passengers and having on board ....

....

....

MERCHANDISE AND STORES,

hath here entered and cleared his said vessel, according to law.

Given under our hands and seals, at the Customhouse of ....

...., this .... day of ....

one thousand nine hundred ...., and in the ....

year of the Independence of the United States of America.

....
Deputy Collector of Customs.

SAMPLE 20

BIBLIOGRAPHY

BOOKS

American Bureau of Shipping. *Rules for Building and Classifying Steel Vessels.* New York: American Bureau of Shipping. (Updated annually.)

American Sail Training Association. *Directory of Sail Training Programs and Tall Ships.* Newport, R.I.: American Sail Training Association, 1996.

Aragon, James R. *Shipmaster's Handbook on Ship's Business.* Centreville, Md.: Cornell Maritime Press, 1988.

Bassin, Milton G., et al. *Statics and Strength of Materials.* New York: McGraw-Hill, 1988.

Bishop, Joseph M. *A Mariner's Guide to Radiofacsimile Weather Charts.* Westborough, Mass.: Alden Electronics, 1988.

Bowditch, Nathaniel. *American Practical Navigator.* Washington D.C.: Defense Mapping Agency Hydrographic/Topographic Center, 1995.

Caracena, Fernando, et al. *Microbursts—A Handbook for Visual Identification.* Washington D.C.: National Oceanic and Atmospheric Administration, National Severe Storms Laboratory, U.S. Government Printing Office, 1990.

Cargal, Michael. *How to Avoid Collisions.* New York: Sheridan House, 1991.

Chapelle, Howard I. *Yacht Designing and Planning.* New York: W. W. Norton, 1971.

Chase, Carl A. *Introduction to Nautical Science.* New York: W. W. Norton, 1991.

Code of Federal Regulations. Title 46, Subchapters R (Sailing School Vessels) and T (Small Passenger Vessels). Washington D.C.: U.S. Government Printing Office. (Check for most current edition.)

Coles, K. Adlard, and Peter Bruce. *Heavy Weather Sailing.* New York: John De Graff, Inc., 1992.

Cornell, Jimmy. *World Cruising Handbook.* Camden, Me.: International Marine Publishing Company, 1994.

Cornell, Jimmy. *World Cruising Routes.* Camden, Me.: International Marine Publishing Company, 1995.

de Kerchove, René. *International Maritime Dictionary.* New York: Van Nostrand Reinhold Co., 1961.

English, Henry, & Associates. *Trim For Speed.* Videocassette. Milford, Conn.: North Sails Group, 1990.

Fujita, Theodore. *The Downburst.* Chicago: University of Chicago Press, 1985.

Glénans Sea Center. *The New Glénans Sailing Manual.* Boston: Sail Books, 1978.

Hamlin, Cyrus. *Preliminary Design of Boats and Ships.* Centreville, Md.: Cornell Maritime Press, 1989.

Hammick, Anne. *The Atlantic Crossing Guide.* Camden, Me.: International Marine Publishing Company, 1994.

Harland, John. *Seamanship in the Age of Sail.* Annapolis, Md.: Naval Institute Press, 1992.

Herreshoff, L. Francis. *The Common Sense of Yacht Design.* vol. 1. New York: Caravan–Maritime Books, 1974.

Houghton, David, and Fred Sanders. *Weather at Sea.* Camden, Me.: International Marine Publishing Company, 1988.

Howard, Jim. *Offshore Cruising.* New York: Sheridan House, 1994.

International Maritime Organization. *SOLAS, Consolidated Edition.* London: International Maritime Organization, 1992.

Kinney, Francis S. *Skene's Elements of Yacht Design.* New York: Dodd, Mead & Co., 1973.

Knox-Johnston, Robin. *Seamanship.* New York: W. W. Norton & Co., 1986.

Kotsch, William J. *Weather for the Mariner.* Annapolis, Md.: Naval Institute Press, 1983.

Kotsch, William J., and Richard Henderson. *Heavy Weather Guide.* Annapolis, Md.: Naval Institute Press, 1984.

LaDage, John, and Lee Van Gemert. *Stability and Trim for the Ship's Officer.* 3d ed. Centreville, Md.: Cornell Maritime Press, 1983.

Lutgens, Frederick K., and Edward J. Tarbuck. *The Atmosphere.* N.J.: Prentice-Hall, Inc., 1995.

Maloney, Elbert S. *Chapman Piloting.* New York: Hearst Marine Books, 1994.

Marchaj, C.A. *Sailing Theory and Practice.* New York: Dodd, Mead, and Co., 1982.

Marino, Emiliano. *The Sailmaker's Apprentice.* Camden, Me.: International Marine Publishing Company, 1994.

Maritime Training Advisory Board. *Marine Fire Prevention, Fire Fighting, and Fire Safety.* Washington, D.C.: U.S. Government Printing Office.

National Imagery and Mapping Agency Hydrographic/Topographic Center. *Sailing Directions.* Washington, D.C.: NIMAHTC. (Updated annually.)

National Ocean Service. *United States Coast Pilot.* Washington, D.C.: National Oceanic and Atmospheric Administration. (Updated annually.)

Phillips-Birt, Douglass. *Sailing Yacht Design.* Camden, Me.: International Marine Publishing Company, 1971.

Priebe, Paul D. *Modern Commercial Sailing Ship Fundamentals.* Centreville, Md.: Cornell Maritime Press, 1986.

Rains, John, and Patricia Miller. *Passagemaking Handbook: A Guide for Delivery Skippers and Boat Owners.* Camden, Me.: Seven Seas Press, 1989.

Ross, Wallace. *Sail Power.* New York: Alfred A. Knopf, 1984.

Schult, Joachim. *The Sailing Dictionary.* New York: Sheridan House, 1992.

Smith, Richard A. *Farwell's Rules of the Road.* Annapolis, Md.: Naval Institute Press, 1994.

Underhill, Harold. *Sailing Ship Rigs and Rigging.* Glasgow: Brown, Son, and Ferguson, 1969.

United States Coast Guard. *Eagle Seamanship.* Annapolis, Md.: Naval Institute Press, 1990.

United States Coast Guard. *Navigation Rules.* Washington D.C.: U.S. Government Printing Office, 1983.

U.S. Sailing. *Recommendations for Offshore Sailing.* Newport, R.I.: U.S. Sailing Association, 1995.

Van Dorn, William G. *Oceanography and Seamanship.* Centreville, Md.: Cornell Maritime Press, 1993.

Willoughby, R. M. *Square Rig Seamanship.* London: Nautical Institute, 1989.

ADDITIONAL INFORMATION

NAVINFONET
   e-mail: navinfonet@nima.mil
   Telephone: 301-227-3296
To subscribe to *Weekly Notice to Mariners:*
   Telephone: 800-826-0342
   Contact local U.S. Coast Guard offices for *Local Notice to Mariners.*
Medical Advisory Systems, Inc.
   8050 Southern Maryland Blvd.
   Owings, Md. 20736
   Telephone: 301-855-8070
American Sail Training Association
   P.O. Box 1459
   Newport, R.I. 02840
   Telephone: 401-846-1775
To obtain poster *Microbursts: A Spotter's Guide:*
   National Severe Storms Laboratory
   NOAA
   1313 Halley Circle
   Norman, Okla. 73069

INDEX

ISBN 0-87033-493-X